BEE PEOPLE
AND THE
BUGS THEY LOVE

Frank Mortimer

CITADEL PRESS
Kensington Publishing Corp.
www.kensingtonbooks.com

CITADEL PRESS BOOKS are published by

Kensington Publishing Corp.
119 West 40th Street
New York, NY 10018

PUBLISHER'S NOTE
This book is based on the author's beekeeping experiences spanning an eleven-year period. The events described are real and all of the bee facts are accurate. Other than family members and a few close friends, however, names and identifying details have been changed. Some characters are composites and certain characters are wholly reimagined, and such composite and reimagined characters are not intended to have any resemblance to actual persons, living or dead.

The author has made diligent efforts to include Internet addresses that are accurate at the time of publication; however, neither the author nor the publisher is responsible for inaccurate or incomplete addresses, or for changes occurring after the book was printed and published. Moreover, the publisher and the author have no control over any such third-party Internet sites or the content contained thereon, and are not responsible for any such content.

All Kensington titles, imprints, and distributed lines are available at special quantity discounts for bulk purchases for sales promotions, premiums, fund-raising, educational, or institutional use. Special book excerpts or customized printings can also be created to fit specific needs. For details, write or phone the office of the Kensington sales manager: Kensington Publishing Corp., 119 West 40th Street, New York, NY 10018, attn: Sales Department; phone 1-800-221-2647.

CITADEL PRESS and the Citadel logo are Reg. U.S. Pat. & TM Off.

ISBN-13: 978-0-8065-4083-2
ISBN-10: 0-8065-4083-4

First Citadel hardcover printing: April 2021

10 9 8 7 6 5 4 3 2 1

Library of Congress Control Number: 2019951387

Printed in the United States of America

Electronic edition:

ISBN-13: 978-0-8065-4085-6 (e-book)
ISBN-10: 0-8065-4085-0 (e-book)

*This book is dedicated
to my wife, Sofie,
and to A. C. "Dr. P." Pellegrino,*

*The two people who have always believed in me
and repeatedly said, "Write your bee book!"*

CONTENTS

CHAPTER 1

How I Started in Beekeeping

PEOPLE OFTEN ASK ME how I got in to beekeeping, and while I wish there was some grand elaborate reason why I wanted to be a beekeeper, the truth is that for as long as I can remember I have felt a connection to bees.

I was lucky, when I was a kid there were bees everywhere I looked. Beekeeping is divided into two time periods, Pre-V and Post-V. These abbreviations stand for *Before* Varroa and *After* Varroa, and in later chapters there will be more about *Varroa destructor* and how these non-native parasitic mites are destroying the world's honeybee population. I grew up in Pre-V, which meant there were a lot more bees flying around than there are today, so growing up outside of St. Louis, I got to see a lot of bees. I would always pause to watch honeybees going from clover to clover in the grass. I was amazed at how much purpose they always seemed to have and how little they cared that I, or anyone, was close by watching them work. I also liked to walk around barefoot, which meant that occasionally I stepped on, and was thereby stung by these remarkable creatures at least a few times every summer. But the freedom of walking barefoot across the lawns and open fields outweighed the occasional little sting.

My fascination with bees persisted from my childhood summers through adulthood. Whenever I'd see a program about bees on TV, or read about bees or beekeeping, my desire to be a beekeeper was further fueled. For business, I would sometimes visit the University of Northern Iowa, and in their biology building's lobby they had a working observation hive. The hive was made of Plexiglas, and you could watch the bees inside, busily at work. Whenever I was on campus, I always found a reason to visit the biology department and spend some time in the lobby, just watching the bees at work. Then, on my trip home, I would think about the bees and create elaborate plans to have my own hives. No matter how excited I was to start, however, there always seemed to be a reason to defer my dream. Either I was traveling too much for work, or I didn't think I had the "right" backyard for bees, or the people in my life thought I was crazy and persuaded me to let someone else be the beekeeper.

During the bee-less years of my life, I always felt like something was missing, a void that I needed to fill. I dreamed of having a passion for something that would make me feel like my life was meaningful and could define who I was. At work, I'd see people getting pumped about digging into an Excel spreadsheet or jazzed over critiquing the latest round of reports, but for me, becoming the Inter-Office Memo Master of Manhattan was not how I wanted to be remembered. I'd see how full of life other people would be when they talked about their interests, hobbies, or the sports that they played, and yet none of those things appealed to me. I tried more traditional hobbies like wine tasting, golf, comic books, and art collecting, but I never felt comfortable or like I belonged in any of these worlds.

Years later, I saw an upcoming event in the calendar section of my local weekly free newspaper: Backyard Beekeeping. Someone would be talking about honeybees and beekeeping at the local library around the corner from my house. Bees were becoming a hot topic. There were a lot of stories in the news about the declining honeybee population and Colony Collapse Disorder (CCD). This mystery disorder was devastating the world's honeybee population. It was awful, but at least the media attention made people aware that bees were in trouble and called attention to the vital role they play in our environment.

When I arrived at the library for the bee talk, I was struck by how many people were also there for the lecture. Up until this moment, I had not encountered anyone who was interested in beekeeping, and now I was sitting in a room full of bee people. The speaker touched on all aspects of keeping bees, the issues of honeybee health, the different parts of a hive, but mostly he overwhelmed the room with his love and passion for beekeeping. The two life-changing pieces of information I took from his lecture were recommendations for a few good books on beginning beekeeping, and that there was a local beekeeping club in my area. Living in northeast New Jersey, the most densely populated part of the most densely populated state in the United States, I was a bit stunned to learn that there was a local club of actual beekeepers in my area, and that there were actually

enough beekeepers in northeast New Jersey to create and pop-
ulate a beekeeping club.

At work the next morning, I was still thinking about the lecture from the night before, so I hopped on Google to find out
more about this local beekeeping club. As it turned out, the
president of the club lived just a few towns over from me. Somewhat impulsively, I sent him an email, asking for more
information about the club and beekeeping in general. I had
never known anyone who kept bees, and even though I liked
the idea of keeping bees, I had never actually been around a
working hive, so a little part of me was still unsure if it was the
right venture for me. I just wanted to gather some information,
no big deal, and I figured I would get a form response or possibly
a recommendation for other resources. Instead, I had an imme-
diate reply along with the offer for me to come over to his
house and see his hives. Wow! This was perfect; I could go over
to his house, spend time around his hives, and get a feeling for
what it would be like to have bees in my own backyard. Within
a half hour of sending my first email, we had exchanged half a
dozen messages and he invited me to stop by his place around
lunchtime to check out his bees. I explained that I worked in
Manhattan so we'd have to find another time, but he was determined, and now apparently on a mission to introduce me to his
bees. He suggested—almost demanded—that I come by tonight,
after work. He would meet me at the train station, take us back
to his place, and then he'd drive me home after we had looked
at his bees. All I could say was, yes.

The workday couldn't end soon enough, and all I could
think about was what it was going to be like to finally be around
bees. As the train finally pulled into my station, my heart began
to beat a little faster, as I thought, "This is it." I wasn't sure what

to expect when I stepped off the train, until a seemingly normal middle-aged, heavyset, balding man standing next to an older model SUV asked, "Are you Frank?" And before I could do more than nod, he blurted out, "My name is Charlie Badgero, but everyone calls me the Badger. I'm not mean or nothing, but I do L-O-V-E honey! Guess I'm a Honey Badger. No, really, I got the name back when I was a kid, and it stuck. I guess a nickname is like honey, once it's on you, it sticks!"

I wasn't sure what I was expecting, but the Badger sure was a character. He enjoyed hearing himself talk, and with a hint of a nervous smile, he put on a show with stories and well-rehearsed one-liners. I jumped into his SUV and we drove back to his house. We stopped on a busy street in front of an average-size house partially hidden by overgrown trees and bushes. We waded through tall grass into what I assume was his front yard and he pointed and said, "There are my hives." I was amazed that his hives were right there, and while they were out of view thanks to all the trees and bushes, they were still only twenty-five feet away from a heavily traveled sidewalk! When I turned my gaze toward his three hives, I could see a lot of little dots filling the air. I realized they were his bees zooming into and out of their hives.

As I stood about ten feet away from my first real beehive, I expected the Badger to start telling me what to expect as he brought out bee suits and other bee gadgets for our journey into the hives. Instead, all he said to me was, "Let's go."

THE LONGER I AM AROUND beekeepers, the more I see that beekeeping attracts all sorts of personalities, all of whom approach beekeeping and their hives differently. There are the Surgeons, who don full head-to-toe bee suits and approach their hives the same way a surgeon walks into the operating room—fully protected and prepared to operate with precision. On the other extreme, there is the Cowboy. The cowboy is someone who doesn't wear any type of veil, usually has forgotten to bring his smoker, and just jumps in without any real plan and improvises along the way. The Badger was definitely a cowboy. He was wearing a button-up, short-sleeved shirt, cargo pants, and a baseball cap with the local volunteer fire department's insignia on it. Unprotected and empty-handed, he walked over to the hives, and so I followed. Sitting on top of one of the hives was a mini crowbar, or as I would come to learn, a hive tool. He grabbed the hive tool and used it to pop open the top cover. You could hear a slight snap, or pop, as he unsealed the cover from the rest of the hive. After the roof—or in beekeeping terms, the outer cover—was removed, he repeated the process again with the inner cover that was now exposed.

Once the inner cover was removed, I was face-to-face with the inside of a real beehive. Not knowing what to expect, I took my cue from the Badger who remained calm and leaned in for a closer look. I was taken aback that the bees weren't concerned that the top of their house was now missing. Instead, the bees kept moving around like they had more important things to do than worry about where their roof went. As I peered down into the hive, I could see there were ten wooden slats, each evenly spaced about three-eighths of an inch apart. And peering out of all the spaces on either side of those slats were thousands and thousands of bee eyes all looking at me. All I could do was stare back. I was amazed at the orderliness of it all. Row after row filled with bee heads, all looking up to see what was going on. I was also in awe of the calm around me and the gentleness of the bees. Let's face it, for most of us, our collective knowledge of bees has come from old Bugs Bunny cartoons and bad 1970s beexploitation movies. Part of me expected the bees to start buzzing into a cloud and form into a big fist to sock me on the chin. Instead, the bees calmly stood in formation looking to see why their roof was suddenly missing.

The Badger turned his cap around and put his face toward the hive. He looked at me, and by the slight smile on his face I could tell he was showing off, the same way a cowboy might jump on a wild horse without a saddle, and testing me to see if I would "jump on" and follow along. Not knowing any better and eager to learn, I leaned over the hive to get a better look. The Badger used his hive tool as a pointer and was talking to me about the different parts of the hive. But I was so focused on the bees that most of what he said was drowned out by the gentle buzzing. After about five minutes, he closed up the hive. No stings, no giant bee fists forming in the air, just bees going about their normal bee business.

I felt good about my first baby step toward becoming a real beekeeper. In my mind, I still needed to spend more time around hives. I thought I'd ask the Badger if any beekeepers wanted an assistant, or at least if any of them would mind if I helped out, or just stood around and watched as they worked their hives. I figured that I'd spend the summer being around other people's bees and then maybe next summer, I would be ready for my own hives. I soon found out that the Badger had other ideas.

We walked to his front porch and he handed me a bee supply catalog. I had no idea that bee supply catalogs existed. I guess I should have known; I have never seen a bee supply store at the mall or anywhere else, so it made sense that there are specialty companies that make and supply you with everything you require for your beekeeping needs. Then the Badger handed me a pen, and he started pointing to what I should order. He said, "Everything you'll need—except for the bees—are in this one catalog."

BEE NERD ALERT: Ask several beekeepers where they buy their bee supplies. Most will prefer one company to another, but very few will rely on only one supplier, and neither should you.

After I finished circling about a dozen different things, I heard the Badger say, "And expedite the shipping. I'll have some bees I can give you in about two weeks, sometime around Memorial Day weekend."

Those words changed my life, and I am still thankful the Badger said them, because it was at that moment I realized I was either jumping in or running away.

I chose to become a beekeeper.

Two weeks. I had two weeks to figure out what this catalog of stuff was, which things I needed to get, and have it all shipped to me before my bees arrived. I also had two weeks to negotiate with my wife that keeping bees was a good idea and that I really needed to buy all this bee stuff. We had been drifting apart for years, and our relationship was more like that of roommates than husband and wife, so I focused on how beekeeping would get me off the couch and outside, thereby giving her more time for herself. I also explained how beekeeping was something that I planned on doing with our son Miles, so he, too, would be outside more, giving her the solitude she craved.

The Badger told me to order a beginner's kit, because it had everything I would need. In hindsight, I would have been better off if I had ordered the components I wanted separately.

BEE NERD ALERT: Try to order your components individually, that way you will be certain that you are ordering what you want, not what the company has packaged together to sell you.

Beginner kits contain everything needed to construct a hive, the boxes, the frames, the base, and the covers. It's the beekeeper's equivalent of IKEA furniture; you just open the box and put all the pieces together. In addition to the beginner kit, or what's known as the "woodenware," I also ordered a smoker, a hive tool, gloves, and a veil. As instructed, I also paid for the expedited shipping to make sure everything arrived on time.

Four days later, two giant boxes were delivered to my house. Each box was large enough to house a baby hippopotamus, and also large enough to hold everything I needed to start keeping bees—including my very first hive. When my wife saw two huge boxes blocking the garage, she shot me the stink eye. But before any words were exchanged, Miles excitedly said he wanted to use them to build a fort, so I didn't have to explain— yet again—why keeping bees was a good idea.

The modern hive, or Langstroth hive, I ordered was originally developed in 1851, by Lorenzo Langstroth while he was a schoolteacher in Philadelphia. Langstroth discovered that bees naturally left three-eighth-inch gaps between the comb they built. He realized that if he built his hive utilizing this "bee space," then he would be able to remove the honeycomb without damaging it, or destroying the hive.

The concept of movable comb revolutionized beekeeping, as it meant two very important things for the beekeeper. First, it now made it possible for the beekeeper to take out each frame of comb to inspect it. This meant that for the first time, a beekeeper could go comb by comb, or frame by frame, and actually see his bees, especially the queen, and make sure the queen was doing what she was supposed to be doing. Second, it meant that the beekeeper could remove frames full of honey, extract the honey, and then reuse the drawn comb over and over again to make more honey. This is really significant when you realize that bees must consume eight pounds of honey to have enough fuel to produce a single pound of wax, and it is this wax that they use to build new comb. By being able to reuse the comb, bees could instead use their resources to make more honey, faster, which in turn means more honey for the beekeeper. That's why beekeepers say drawn comb is as valuable as gold. You can't buy it because the bees have to make it, and once you have it, your bees will become honey-making machines.

Before Langstroth, beekeepers had to destroy a hive and crush all the honeycomb to extract the honey. Langstroth's hive meant the comb could be removed, replaced, and reused, ensuring the bees did not have to keep rebuilding it from scratch, helping a hive and its bees live and thrive year after year.

The best way to think of a Langstroth hive is as a filing cabinet. In each cabinet drawer, there are ten "file folders" or frames. Each frame is a wooden rectangle that holds one section of drawn out honeycomb. These ten frames are spaced three-eighths of an inch from one another and from the walls of the hive body. Continuing with the file cabinet analogy, an established colony of bees requires two "file cabinet drawers" or boxes. The bottom most box is their nursery, and it is where they raise their young. The next box up is their pantry, and this is where they store the honey *they* need. Bees will then instinctively continue to fill any "extra" space they have in their hive with honey. Beekeepers utilize this instinct and keep adding additional boxes on top of what the bees need for themselves. This system also works well because a beekeeper can easily track which honey belongs to the beekeeper and which belongs to the bees. On my hives, I paint all of *my* honey boxes white, and the bees' boxes a variety of colors. It looks nice, and is easy for me to see how much honey the bees are making for me.

The bottom two boxes the bees need for themselves are larger than the boxes the beekeeper uses for his honey. Because these boxes are bigger, they are generally called "deeps." The smaller boxes for the beekeeper's honey are called "supers," because they are placed above and on top of the deep boxes. Since the frames in each box are all equally spaced apart, as you put box on top of box, the frames line up, as does the bee space, creating vertical walls of honeycomb and "hallways" from top to bottom of the hive, allowing the bees to move freely up and down the hive in the same way they would if they had built their nest in the wild. In addition to the boxes and frames of comb, a hive also utilizes a bottom board, or a floor. The bottom board allows a space between itself and the boxes above, as it is also the entrance to the hive. On the top of the hive is the inner cover, or interior ceiling, and last, an outer cover or roof. The outer cover is generally flat, creating a working area for the beekeeper to use when he is inspecting his hives. Other outer covers, such as the garden hive top, can be more aesthetically pleasing, as they have gabled roofs that are made of copper. There are several variations and additional add-on hive components, but the basic hive is a filing cabinet-style wood box holding evenly spaced frames. The logical elegance and usefulness of this layout is why Langstroth's design has remained virtually unchanged and is currently used throughout the world.

A modern Langstroth hive was inside one of the two boxes now sitting inside my garage, along with the other bee gadgets and "essentials" I thought I needed or was told that I needed. It was the end of May, and I knew I didn't have much time to get everything assembled and in place before my bees arrived.

The first thing I had to do was figure out where in my yard I should put my hive. It's always best to face your hives south, so as the sun rises and travels across the sky, it will light up the hive entrance, signaling to the bees that it is time to get to work. Also, a southern exposure helps protect the hive from northerly winds during the winter months. Luckily, the back of my property faced south, so I chose a spot in the southwestern corner of my yard, behind a shed that got plenty of sun and was away from where my son liked to play. Plus, I thought it was a good location because it was out of sight from most of my neighbors as I had no idea how they were going to react to the new tenants I was planning on bringing in.

I had read that the more sun a hive can get the better, and full sun is ideal. The back of my yard had a lot of trees and bushes, because like most people in suburbia, trees and bushes were how you defined your property and maintained some privacy. However, for the bees, I decided to break out my Edward Scissorhands skills to trim and cut away as many branches as I could, allowing more sun to reach the future home of my bees. Now, I've never been accused of being a lumberjack, and no one would ever say I was graceful on a ladder, yet there I was, high up on a ladder reaching, pulling, and sawing every branch I could reach, just so my future bees could get that extra bit of sun.

Now when I look back, I realize I'm lucky I didn't fall and break my neck, or at least fall and land on my prized hive and smash it to pieces. But at the time, I felt invincible because I was doing it for the bees.

> **BEE NERD ALERT:** Always make sure your hives face south, and get as much sun as possible. A good rule to follow is to place your hives where the snow melts first. If you live in suburbia, getting full sun is nearly impossible, so don't be an idiot on a ladder. A little shade is better than a broken back.

I made the home of my future apiary look as official as I could. First, for my hive stand, I used cinder blocks, because every photo I ever saw of beehives showed them sitting on top of cinder blocks. It's important to have your hive off the ground for a few reasons. First, it keeps the moisture from the ground away from your wooden hive. Second, it helps the bees better defend their hive from natural predators such as skunks.

Skunks like to eat bees. Their face and paws are sting-proof, so they will scratch at the front of the hive and when the bees come out to investigate, the skunk grabs the bees and eats them. However, the skunk's belly is sensitive and not sting-proof, so when your hive is on cinder blocks, the skunk has to stand on its hind legs, exposing its abdomen. The bees seem to understand this and go for the skunk's belly, causing it to run off.

Then I had to paint the hive to protect the wood from the elements. The Badger had said that it was not necessary to paint my hive white, so I decided to paint it the same color as my house. I thought it would look nice to have my hive match my house, but mostly I did it to save a few bucks, since I already had the paint on hand. And after paying for the expedited shipping on two huge boxes of bee supplies, I really needed to save a few bucks.

My hive was ready. It was painted, sitting atop a cinder block stand, facing south, and now all I needed were the bees.

So I waited for the bees.

Two weeks came and went, but still no bees. Anxious to get started, I emailed the Badger. He didn't have my bees yet. He explained to me that another member, a longtime member, was doing an extraction from a house, and he was waiting for the homeowners to set up a date.

An extraction is when you remove bees that have taken up residence inside the wall of a house. Honeybees always live inside some sort of cavity, like inside a tree or inside a hollow wall. Honeybees never live in the ground or in a paper nest hanging from a tree or in a bush. Those are wasps, or yellowjackets, the stinger-happy warlords of the insect world.

When a beekeeper removes honeybees living inside a wall, it's a big job. You have to break open the wall, pull out the comb piece by piece, then cut and secure it in empty wooden frames so you can transfer the bees into your Langstroth hive. Now, you can imagine how happy a wall full of bees would be to have the outer wall of their house opened up, then have their comb broken into pieces and reassembled in a strange new wooden box. It's also important to realize that at the peak of summer, a hive can contain up to sixty thousand bees. That's sixty thousand stinging insects, none of which are happy with what you are doing. Last, for the extraction to be successful, you must make sure you have the queen; otherwise she and any remaining bees will just start from scratch and rebuild their home again inside the wall.

So I waited some more.

Finally, the Badger called. I was told that tomorrow, June 4, was the day, and they needed my hive so once they removed the bees from the wall of the house, they could place them directly into their new home. I was invited to go with them and help, but as luck would have it, I couldn't take off from work that day. So while my bees were being placed into their new home, I would be stuck in a company-wide meeting listening to non-bee-keepers talk about non-bee things.

The Badger said he would bring my hive back to my yard once the bees were transferred so they could acclimate to the neighborhood.

My plan was to make it home before my bee delivery so I could give my bees a proper bee welcome to their new home. However, NJ Transit had other plans, and all-too-common delays made it a very slow trip home.

Instead of being part of installing my first hive in my backyard, my official start to beekeeping came via a series of text messages from Sara, my son's babysitter.

Days before, when I told Sara that I was going to become a beekeeper and start keeping bees in the backyard, I got "the look," something I would see time and time again when I told someone about my new hobby. "The look" is the facial expression that, regardless of one's native language, is understood to mean, "Are you f%#king kidding me?!"

Sara was overly dramatic about everything from breakfast foods to coordinating her outfits with my son's crayon selections, so my news about getting bees really sent her over the edge.

As I sat stuck on a train somewhere outside of Secaucus, the texts from Sara went something like this:

> There's a BRIGHT YELLOW car in the driveway & 2 strange men in the backyard!

> *They must be the guys from the bee club bringing me my bees!*

> Eeeeeeekkkkkk!!

> Are all the windows closed? Can bees fly down the chimney? ACK!!! What should I do!

> *Relax, you have nothing to worry about. Nothing bad is going to happen.*

> Now there is a HUGE cloud of smoke in the backyard! They're burning down the yard!

> *No, they lit their smoker. You use smoke to keep the bees calm.*

Hummmm, what kind of smoke makes bees mellow? What are they really burning???

Probably pine needles.

Oh . . .

Now they're carrying a box with a shiny silver top through the backyard!

The fat guy is yelling at the old guy saying he's using too much smoke!

The old guy is telling him to relax AND he's puffing even more smoke at him!!!

The old guy just pulled a screen off the box and he's puffing even more smoke!!!

The fat guy is dancing around slapping himself!

He's yelling about waiting till he wasn't standing in front of the hive!

Now the fat guy is running through the back-yard screaming I'm hit! Got my ear!!! Got my ear!!!

The old guy is laughing!

Now they are both leaving the backyard!

Someone's ringing the front doorbell!

It's them! They told me to tell you that the beehive is in and they're leaving!!!

I CAN SEE THE STINGER HANGING FROM THE FAT GUY'S EAR!!!

Eeeewwww!!!

At about the same time Sara was hyperventilating on the living room floor, I received a single text from the Badger:

Bees are in your backyard. It was a piece of cake & everything went smoothly. Tomorrow, tilt your hive so it's slanted forward. Good luck.

At last, I had a hive in my backyard and it made me smile. It was something I wanted for so long, and now I could finally call myself a beekeeper.

CHAPTER 2

Bee Cops

Buzzzzzzzzzzzzzzzzzzz

My alarm went off and I was wide awake. Today would be my first day as a beekeeper, or at least the first time I would be doing something with my bees. I had only one task to complete: I had to make sure the hive was level and then tilt it slightly forward. In addition to the Badger's direction, everything I had read had emphasized the importance of keeping your hive level.

The inside of a beehive, natural or man-made, is completely dark. Unless worker bees are foraging, or a queen bee is on her mating flight, bees live and work in complete darkness. Honeybees are constantly working and when a colony moves, or is moved to a new location, their top priority is constructing the honeycomb they will use to raise their young and produce honey. They build their honeycomb with wax that is secreted from glands on their abdomens, and they demand order, always building the comb in straight vertical lines. Constructing the comb in complete darkness, they can't rely on vision to make the lines straight; instead they lock legs to make a plumb line. The first bee goes to the top of where the comb building will begin, and then one by one, the bees lock legs and hold on, using their bodies to make a straight vertical line from top to bottom. Once the plumb line is complete, the rest of the bees build the comb straight from top down.

BEE NERD ALERT: The beekeeping term for bees linking themselves together by their legs is called festooning.

That's why it's important to make sure your hives are sitting level; if your hive isn't square, its comb will be crooked, making it difficult for you to move the frames and pull them out of the hive.

It's also important to remember that moisture is an enemy of the bees. If the weather gets bad, there's always a chance of rain getting into a hive, and it's not like the bees can just go and shut the window. But by slightly tilting your hive forward, any water that does get inside will just run out the front entrance instead of pooling inside the hive and causing a problem.

I went out back by my hive and watched the bees darting around. I wasn't going to be opening my hive, so I didn't bother to put on my veil. Theoretically, I shouldn't need it, and now that I was a beekeeper, I should get comfortable being around my bees. When I had placed the cinder blocks in their current location, I used a level to make sure they were as square as possible.

I now put the level on top of the flat hive cover, and the bubble sat neatly between the two hash marks. "Perfect," I thought. Now, all I had to do was lift up the back of the hive and slip a wood shim underneath so the hive would slightly tilt forward.

I could hear the bees buzzing away inside the hive. It sounded like an electric motor. "Hummmmmm."

It had a soothing quality to it. I carefully put my hand on the base of the hive, and taking a deep breath, I gently lifted it. Instantly, the sound of the hive went from "hummmmmm" to "RRRRRR."

I prepared for the worst.

Then, after a moment, nothing happened, so I slipped the wood under the hive and s-l-o-w-l-y lowered the hive down.

"Hummmmmm."

The hive returned to its normal frequency. I stepped back, happy that I accomplished my first job as a beekeeper.

Other than watch the bees come and go from the hive, I didn't touch it for the first seven days it was in my yard. I was told that since this colony was previously living inside the wall of a house, I should let the bees get acclimated to their new home before opening it up and poking around.

Even though my bees were living inside the wall, most likely, they were originally bees that had swarmed from another beekeeper's hive. A honeybee colony will swarm as a way to reproduce. If you think back to high school biology and remember that single-cell organisms reproduce by splitting in half and becoming two distinct organisms, then also think of a colony of honeybees in the same way. The colony prepares for a new queen, and just before she hatches, the old queen and half the bees leave to find another place to live. It's always the old queen who leaves the hive and the new, younger queen who remains. Their current home has been proven to be a safe place to live, and since the younger queen has a longer life expectancy, she gets the safe house, as it is a better bet to ensure that the colony's genetics will continue to survive.

Removing honeybees from inside a wall of a house takes both beekeeping and carpentry skills. Over the years I would develop my beekeeping skills, but my carpentry abilities peaked a long time ago at the boardwalk, when I was hammering away at Whac-A-Mole. The Badger, on the other hand, claimed to have the skills necessary to open up walls, remove the bees, and repair the walls, good as new. It required a lot of work, and like all beekeepers who extract honeybee colonies living inside people's houses, he charged a premium for his services.

Usually, when homeowners realize that they have honeybees living in one of their walls, they call an exterminator. Thankfully, all but a few unscrupulous characters will quickly tell the homeowner it is illegal to kill honeybees and they'll need to call a beekeeper. (And the last thing you want to do is kill a colony of bees. Having a wall filled with honey and dead bees is like opening an all-night diner for rodents, flies, cockroaches, and other disgusting beasts that thrive on death and decay.) Of course, when they hear an exterminator can't help them, most homeowners panic. They have bees in their wall, and how the heck do you find a beekeeper?! Your best bet in this situation is to go online and search for a local beekeeping club. Most clubs have a website that lists members who are willing to catch a swarm or extract colonies from inside walls. And don't freak out! You're not in danger. Most of the time, the bees are minding their own "beesiness," and simply flying in and out of a hole on the outside of the house or building. Now I realize a beekeeper's point of view is different from most, but if bees took up residence in a wall in my house, I'd think it was pretty cool, and as long as the hive entrance was safely away from foot traffic, I'd let them live there for as long as they wanted.

If honeybees are living inside a wall, then you can expect that they have built comb that's several feet long, as the average size of a wild or feral colony of bees is fifteen gallons. That's the size of three, five-gallon buckets standing end-to-end. In order to remove three, five-gallon buckets' worth of bees and comb you will have to open up a fairly large section of a wall. Then, after opening the wall, the beekeeper has to pull out all of the comb and transfer it into the frames. As you can imagine, the beekeeper has to be fully protected from head to toe while removing a colony of bees. Most important, the beekeeper has to always be on the lookout for the queen, because if he gets the queen, then all the bees will accept the new hive as their home. If he misses the queen, then the transplanted colony will not survive. Once all the bees are out, the cavity needs to be filled with insulation, the wall has to be repaired to look like new, and the hive entrance needs to be plugged so no other bees or other insects can start the process over again. It is an intense process that can be fun to watch on YouTube, but something that very few beekeepers have the desire and the know-how required to successfully do. As for the typical homeowner, I don't think many of them realize the extent of the work involved, or the hefty price tag. It can easily cost a thousand dollars or more. Truthfully, I don't think it matters to them. Most are just thinking, "*Get these bees out of my house!*"

ONE OF THE REASONS the Badger liked to do cutouts was because it was a good source of extra money. He'd do a dozen or so every year, and with the added disposable income, he could afford to buy more hives and more bee supplies. Since I was new to the club and eager to learn, the Badger invited me to go along with him to meet with a few people who had called him about removing some unwanted bees. It was another way for me to immerse myself in the world of beekeeping and a new way for him to show off in front of a "newbee," so I gladly accepted his offer to ride along.

I was excited to have an opportunity to learn more about bees, but equally important was finding out if bee people were for me. When I had tried other hobbies in the past, I never felt a connection with the people around me. For instance, when I gave golf a try, I was always more comfortable around the people who worked at the course than with the other golfers. Hopefully, my beekeeping experience would be different.

The first address we stopped at was a recently updated, expanded cape with an immaculately manicured lawn and squared-off shrubs running across the front of the house. The homeowner was in his driveway when we pulled up.

"Did you call about some bees?" asked the Badger.

"YES! Yes, I did! Please come, come with me!"

The homeowner, a jumpy little guy, led us around back, through a white picket fence that looked like it was pulled from a 1950s TV sitcom. Then pointing up at a tree, he said, "There! Up there! There it is!"

And sure enough, about twelve feet up was a knot in the trunk of the tree with lots of activity going into and out of it. The closer you looked, the easier it was to see the fuzzy little bees returning to their nest, many with loads of colorful pollen on their hind legs.

"You can get them out of my tree, right?" asked the homeowner.

"Well, I can cut down the tree," the Badger responded in an authoritative tone.

"No, oh no. I love that tree. It looks good in my yard."

"Well, I can try to make the hole larger so I can get the comb out," the Badger suggested.

"No, I don't want the tree damaged. Can't you vacuum them out or something?"

While it is true that beekeepers can use a special bee vacuum to remove bees, they still need access to the comb for it to work. Compared to a regular vacuum, bee vacuums use less suction and have a two-chamber system so it does not harm the bees. Think of a regular shop vac, only instead of the bees getting sucked into the chamber that the motor is attached to, they are diverted into a separate, secondary chamber, which is like sliding into a pillow of air instead of getting slammed into a wall. The bees aren't happy getting sucked out of their home, but it's an effective way to remove and contain the bees without injuring them. The advantage of the vacuum is that you can capture all the bees, which exposes the comb and makes it easier to secure the comb into the frames and then place it into a hive. After the comb is in the hive, the bees can be poured into their new home, and since they can smell that it's their comb, they will easily acclimate to their new surroundings. Even though beekeepers do sometimes use a vacuum during bee extractions, one thing is for sure: you can't put a vacuum hose up to a hole in a tree and suck out fifteen gallons' worth of bees, comb, and everything else that's inside.

After listening to the Badger and the homeowner go back and forth for a while, I finally asked, "Why do you want the bees gone?"

"Because I am afraid my kids will get hurt."

"But they're twelve feet off the ground. How are they going to get hurt?" I asked, followed by, "Has anyone been stung by the bees?"

"No, no one has been stung, but I have to protect my babies… keep them safe in the backyard."

As the homeowner was talking, the Badger grabbed a ladder that was lying nearby and set it up by the tree. He climbed up four or five steps so he could reach the hole in the tree, and then cupped his hands around the entrance to the hive.

"Look, look at my hands. Now, look at the bees. Are they stinging me? Do they care that I'm this close to the hive? No, they don't care that I am this close to their hive. And if they're not stinging me and I'm this close, they're not going to swoop down into your yard to sting your kids."

"But I can't take that chance. No bees!"

The Badger then climbed the rest of the way up the ladder, turned around, and put his face a few inches from the hive entrance. The bees just kept flying into and out of the tree, not fazed by the Badger's antics.

"But you are beekeepers, that is why the bees don't bother you. They know."

At that point it was clear that the homeowner was not going to listen to logic. It was also at this point that I first realized that too many people want a perfectly manicured yard so they can experience nature without nature getting too close to them. It doesn't occur to most of these people that they have a beautiful yard because of the bugs, worms, and dirt, not in spite of them. Many would just prefer an artificial yard if it looked like the real thing and came without any of the mess.

As we were pulling away, the Badger said to me, "I bet he poisons that hive tonight." It was a shame, but that's probably exactly what happened.

It is amazing to think about how much our society has changed. Not too long ago, a tree with bees living in it—called a bee tree—was considered a prized possession, and people used to seek them out.

Honeybees are not native to North America; our country's founding fathers brought honeybees from Europe to the New World. To this day we refer to European honeybees simply as honeybees. **BEE NERD WORD:** *Apis mellifera* The early settlers used to keep their bees in skeps, which looked like upside-down woven baskets. They would pack the skeps in hay-filled crates for their long ocean voyage. The hay served two purposes; first, it would keep the bees warm and protected. Second, it would keep the bees inside their hives. It's also interesting to note that most of the fruit that grows in the United States is also not native to North America. Apples, pears, oranges, watermelon, and also almonds were all brought to the United States to be cultivated in the New World. That's why they brought bees; they needed the bees to pollinate their crops the same as the bees had done back in Europe.

Once the skeps were settled in the new land, the bees began to thrive. Early beekeeping practices welcomed the natural instinct of bee colonies to swarm, as swarming meant more bees, which also meant more honey. Much like the European settlers, the European honeybee moved from the East to the West until there were honeybees all across the future contiguous United States and just about all of North America. During their western expansion, the Native Americans referred to honeybees as, "the white man's fly," because the bees, through swarming, settled the country in advance of European settlers.

Since honeybees need to live inside a cavity, they will build their nest inside something, be it inside a wall of a house or inside a tree.

> **BEE NERD ALERT:** Honeybees will never live in the ground. If someone says they have a bee's nest in the ground, those are not European honeybees.

Since there were not a lot of buildings in our country's early years, but there were a whole lot of trees, the bees usually found a home inside a hollow tree. People known as bee hunters would find these bee trees and claim them as their own. Bee trees were such an important part of early beekeeping that as far back as the nineteenth century, there were laws governing who had legal rights to a bee tree. The expression, "make a beeline" dates back to these early bee hunters, as they would follow bees, which always fly in a straight line—beeline—back to their nest. The bee hunters would lure bees with honey and then put them in special bee-hunting boxes. The bee hunter would release one bee at a time and follow it for as long as he could see it. Once he lost sight of a bee, he would release another bee, and another bee until he had arrived at the bee's nest. If the tree were unmarked, the bee hunter would leave his mark on the tree and claim those bees as his own.

Today, when bees swarm, some will still find a hollow tree, but especially in suburban and urban areas, bees usually end up taking residence inside a wall of a building, or inside some kind of man-made structure, which is why the Badger had a steady stream of calls.

Our next stop was an old Victorian house. The bees were supposedly coming out from underneath an upstairs window. The house looked tired; paint was peeling in spots, and some of the latticework was missing. We knocked on the door because the doorbell wasn't working. When the homeowner opened the door, the Badger asked in a monotone voice, "Did you call about some bees?" The way he said it reminded me of Sergeant Friday from *Dragnet*. Only instead of, "Just the facts, ma'am," it was, "Just the bees, ma'am." I couldn't tell if the Badger was bored or if he was putting on an air of authority to keep the homeowner calm. After what happened at the last call, I suspect he wanted a homeowner with a cool head so he could do what he came to do. Or it could be that he took his role as bee extractor too seriously, and saw himself as something of a superhero, arriving to protect and serve the community.

In any case, the owner of the Victorian didn't seem flustered at all. "Right up there, under that window," she said, pointing at an old wooden window with white paint peeling from its edges. And sure enough, there were hundreds of darting dots going back and forth from an opening between two broken cedar shingles.

Many times when a beekeeper gets a call from a homeowner saying that they have a "beehive" on their property, it turns out to be a wasp nest. Wasp nests are out in the open, and often look like a papier-mâché ball hanging from a tree branch or the eaves of a house, although sometimes it can be a palm-size bit of comb in a light fixture or under a piece of siding. Because most people don't really know the difference, the Badger was here to confirm they were honeybees and not wasps that had made their home in this old Victorian.

Years later when *I* started getting calls about unwanted bees needing to be relocated, I would always ask two questions: First, I'd ask it they could see the hive and if it looked like it's made of paper. Ninety-nine percent of the time, the answer was yes. If the person calling wasn't sure, I'd say, "Does it look like something from *Winnie the Pooh*? A round ball hanging from a tree?" And if they said yes, then I'd tell them that Winnie the Pooh lied to them. They had a wasp nest, because a honeybee nest never looks like that. And no matter the person's age, they were always sad to hear that Winnie the Pooh was a liar.

The second question I would ask is, "When you look at one of the bees, does it look fuzzy or is it smooth and looks like it's made of plastic?" Fuzzy means it's a honeybee and plastic means it's a wasp. Or as I like to say, fuzzy is good and plastic is bad. If possible, I ask if they could send a photo of what they are seeing just to confirm that the insect is indeed fuzzy or plastic.

By asking these two questions, I have been able to determine what's taken up residence and offer advice. Since most calls end up being a wasp's nest, I recommend finding a good exterminator, or if the homeowner was feeling brave, I'd offer advice on when and how to get rid of the nest themselves.

The Badger, on the other hand, would never rely on the homeowner; he liked to confirm everything himself. And if it were a wasp nest, he would tell the homeowner that he could remove the problem for a fee.

At the old Victorian, they were most definitely honeybees. In addition to being fuzzy, the sheer number of them coming and going said honeybees not wasps. Honeybees will make tens of thousands of flights a day, and during the nectar flow, the honey-making season, there are one hundred times more takeoffs and landings than there are at the busiest airport on its busiest day.

"I need to get a look at the wall those bees are living in," the Badger said.

The homeowner obligingly led us through the back door, into the kitchen, across the dining room, and into a short hallway that led to the stairwell.

"The bees are in my mother's bedroom, the last room on the left, at the top of the stairs." She pointed the way and motioned for us to go up. "I gotta finish dinner, so I'll be back in the kitchen," she said as she walked away.

We went upstairs and hung a left. The bee bedroom looked like a typical grandma's room: lots of figurines and knickknacks everywhere, a crocheted blanket on the bed and a crocheted cozy on the rocking chair that sat in the corner. The Badger went over to the window and knelt down next to the wall. He was knocking on the wall to see if he could get a sense of where the bees were, and also what the walls were made of. Then he went from knocking on the wall to laying his hands on it. I thought he was trying to summon the bees with some sort of beekeeper's mind-meld until he said, "Come here and feel this." I put one hand where he indicated. Then he instructed me to put my other hand about two feet away.

"Feel that heat? That there is the nest."

I was stunned. I could actually feel the difference in temperature. The spot where the bees' nest was located was noticeably warmer.

As the two of us were both on our knees, feeling the walls in this woman's house, I wondered what she would think if she walked in on us. Then it occurred to me that this homeowner let two strange men into her house and sent them upstairs, unsupervised. And now we were down on all fours in her mother's bedroom feeling the walls. The oddness of the situation started to make me uncomfortable, almost nervous. Then I freaked myself out as I started to get a Norman Bates vibe, and was worried "Mother" was going to jump out of the closet with a carving knife.

"Come on, let's go," the Badger said just as I was starting to scan the room for any taxidermic animals.

I led the way back to the kitchen and stood next to the back door. The Badger told the homeowner that he'd guess the hive was at least eighteen inches across, and because the house was probably built with balloon construction, the hive could run all the way down to the first floor. He said he'd have to open the wall in a few spots to be sure, and it was going to be a big job, especially because the walls were made of plaster.

The longer he talked, the more panicked the homeowner looked. You could see she was doing a mental calculation of what it would all cost, and with every sentence, she saw herself going deeper and deeper into debt. Finally she said, "The bees aren't hurting anyone, so let me think about it and get back to you."

It was clear there was no way she was going to pay thousands of dollars to remove the bees, but it was also clear that she was fine to just leave them be. The Badger struck out again.

The last stop we were going to make was a few towns away, and the Badger said, "This next one left me a voice mail last week. I haven't spoken to anyone, so we'll just ring the bell. They said the hive was close to the front door, so maybe we'll see it ourselves."

The house was a mid-century ranch, with a big glass window in the living room, and a painted wood front door with three rectangles of glass diagonally spaced across the top. We looked around, but didn't see any bees. After the Badger pushed the doorbell, he pointed on the ground, to the left of the front door. "Look, that's powder. I bet it's insecticide. They killed those bees."

From inside the door, we heard, "Who is it?"

"Did you call about some bees?" asked the Badger in a loud and official tone.

"Oh, he was already here. He took care of them," said the voice behind the door.

"Ma'am, what do you mean took care of? And, who's he?"

"You're not from the exterminators?" asked the homeowner.

"No, ma'am, we're not. We're beekeepers. If you're telling me an exterminator killed those bees, I need a name because he broke the law. Exterminators are forbidden from killing honeybees in the state of New Jersey. Now, please give me that name, ma'am."

"But they were right by the front door, we couldn't even come out of our house," said the voice behind the still closed front door.

"Doesn't matter, ma'am. Now give me that name and we'll be on our way." As the Badger was saying it, he noticed a piece of paper lying on the threshold at the bottom of the door. It was a note from a local exterminator company saying what time he had been there and had all the contact info printed on it.

"I found what I need. Now, I'll just take a few pictures, and we'll be on our way," said the Badger.

"What were we supposed to do?" was the last we heard from the voice behind the door.

"Call a beekeeper like you're supposed to do, ma'am!"

And with that we were off.

"That makes me so angry! I hate it when people break the law and kill honeybees. Don't they know that it's wrong? And just wait till the rats, maggots, and other scavengers find all that

honey and dead bees. Then they'll get what's coming to them."
It was the most worked up I had ever seen the Badger. While he
did get an income from removing bees, it was clear that it wasn't
just about the money; he truly cared about the bees, and that
people were doing the right thing. As he continued to rant, I felt
anger building up inside of me. Those bees were needlessly
killed. Bees can peacefully cohabit alongside people in suburbia.
But I guess most people want to sterilize their yards and elimi-
nate everything they don't understand. The Badger was trying
to help and educate people. The community and the bees were
lucky to have him. I looked over at the Badger and felt a newfound respect for him. And I also felt that same bee passion
starting to take root inside of me.

The whole day felt like a reality TV show. Riding around, re-
sponding to bee calls, it felt like we were "Cops: On Patrol!"
Make that, "Bee Cops: On Patrol." I envisioned getting bee
badges that we could flash as the Badger asked, "Did you call
about some bees?" Or we could say to someone, "Don't worry,
ma'am, we're Bee Police."

We could rework the theme song from *Cops*, only this time
the words would be:

> *Bad Bees, Bad Bees,*
> *What you gonna do when they swarm on you?*
> *Bad Bees, Bad Bees…*

Now all we needed was a TV network deal.

CHAPTER 3

Bee First

THE DAY HAD FINALLY COME. It was time for me to check on my bees. This would literally be my first time opening a hive, and inspecting it frame by frame. I was doing it solo, and even though I had read about it, and watched videos about it, I had no idea what it would actually be like. When I had ordered my hive, I also ordered the equipment that I thought I would need to be a beekeeper. I ordered a smoker, a hive tool, a bee brush, bee gloves, and a veil. Over time, I would end up replacing everything because as I would find out, everything I had ordered was wrong. The veil that I ordered looked like a large, soft-brimmed hat that you'd wear at the beach to keep the sun out of your face. A sturdy screen, one that resembled a window screen you'd have on your house, was sewn around the brim. The advantage was that you could see equally un-well in all directions. Below the screen was a soft fabric netting that would drape on and conform to the shape of your shoulders. At the bottom of the netting was a tie string that pulled the opening tighter together. The tie strings hung about three feet down on both sides. Since no directions came with the veil, I couldn't understand why the strings were so long, so I cut them down to about ten inches on either side, just long enough for me to tie them into a nice simple bow. In my not-too-distant future of beekeeping, I would find out just how big of a mistake I had made by cutting those strings. Their purpose, as I would learn the hard way, was to secure the veil by tying it securely around your chest, ensuring the veil remained tightly against your body, so no gaps—say large enough for bees to enter—would develop.

The Badger always took the cowboy approach to keeping bees, so he had told me that it was best not to wear any protective gear at all. He said you couldn't see what you were doing, and it was just "better" to get used to not wearing a veil or gloves. Some beekeeping books also recommend that you don't wear protective gear, but I believe it is best to wear, or don't wear, whatever will make you the most comfortable. If you're relaxed when you're wearing a veil and gloves, then that's what you should wear, because when you're relaxed, you will be at ease and can focus on your bees. I decided to wear my veil, but I chose not to wear my gloves, as I thought that might be overdoing it.

I walked over to my hive and stood about two feet behind it. Since bees come and go from the front entrance, they really don't care what's behind the hive. Think of it like an airport, and the entrance to the hive is the runway. As long as you're not standing in front of the runway, you are not in their way, so the bees don't care that you are there. Now, if you were standing in front of a hive, then as a bee was coming in for a landing, you might be in her way, so she might crash into you, or more likely, into your hair, and that could lead to you getting stung. But the old adage "leave them alone and they will leave you alone" is absolutely correct. One of the greatest joys for a beekeeper is sitting or standing on the side of his hives and watching the bees take off and land, coming and going, from the hives. The constant flow of worker bees, all with the focused determination to find, fill up, and carry nectar, pollen, or water back to the hive can be as relaxing to watch as being at the beach and watching wave after wave roll into shore. This is especially true during the nectar flow, the time when the bees are making honey and when the hive is at its busiest. In addition to watching the bees, you can hear them working in the hive, fanning the honey to reduce the moisture. You can also smell the honey—the sweet, sweet, smell of fresh, still in the comb, honey. And while I would come to appreciate how all my senses would come alive when I was close to a hive, since this was my first time, I was terrified. Terrified of what might happen when I took the cover off.

I had learned that bees communicate through smells, or pheromones. That's why beekeepers use smoke when they are working their hives. The smoke blocks the pheromones—the signals—that the bees might use to alert the hive that something is wrong. Think of it like this: when you hear a fire alarm go off, you know you have to leave the building. So imagine if there was a way to block you from hearing the fire alarm. You'd keep doing what you were doing and you wouldn't think anything is wrong. It's the same for the bees. The guard bees might let off a warning smell, but thanks to the smoke, the other bees don't know, and they keep doing what they're doing. "Hey look, a giant creature just ripped the roof of our house off, and is pulling everything apart. But, no one has sounded an alarm, so everything must still be O-K!"

You're supposed to use a natural fuel to burn in your smoker, nothing with harmful chemicals that might harm the bees. Many of the bee supply companies sell burlap, untreated twine, or pellets to burn, but most of the time, the only people who buy fuel for their smokers are beekeepers who don't know any better because no one has told them it's a waste of money. I bought wood pellets from the supply company, pellets that might work great in a grill or fireplace, but I would soon learn are more trouble than they are worth in a bee smoker. Once I saw other beekeepers were using pine needles, I dropped the pellets and made the switch. Pine needles are something you can rake up yourself from a pine tree in your yard or somewhere close by. I try to keep a large trash bag filled with pine needles in my garage. The longer they sit, the better they burn. But even if they're green, wet, or locked inside a flame retardant safe, pine needles will always burn better than those wood pellets I first bought.

A beekeeper's smoker is basically a metal can with a dime-size hole on its side, near the bottom. This is the back of the smoker. Also on the back, above the hole, is a bellow that sort of looks like a miniature accordion. The top of the smoker looks like a large funnel bent at a ninety-degree angle, facing toward the front. You hold on to the bellow and when you squeeze it, air gets blown into the hole at the bottom, providing oxygen for your fire. The bellow also pushes the smoke out the front, so you can control how much smoke you release, more squeezing equals more smoke, and you can aim and blow the smoke onto your bees where you need it. The most important thing to remember is that you must always use a cool, thick smoke on your bees. If any flames or sparks shoot out of the smoker, you could potentially singe your bees, and end up doing a lot more harm than good, because burning your bees to a crisp is the fastest way to stop all honey production.

I crumpled up a few sheets of newspaper, and stuffed one of them into my smoker and then used a BBQ lighter to light it. Once the paper was lit, I shoved another ball of newspaper inside and puffed on the bellow, so this second piece of paper would catch fire. Then, I added the pellets, and I kept puffing on the bellow, whoosh—whoosh—whoosh. I kept at it until...the fire slowly petered out with a whimper. After a few more tries and a whole lot of whoosh—whoosh—whooshing, I finally got the pellets to light, and stay lit. The smoke poured out in a thick pungent cloud, much like it would from a carload of teenagers smoking their first cheap cigars. I was now ready to go.

I dropped the veil on my head so the soft mesh rested nicely on my shoulders, and the brim of the hat was as flat and even as possible. I took my now smoking smoker and I puffed a few clouds of smoke across the entrance of the hive. The guard bees at the entrance of the hive looked just like bouncers standing guard at an exclusive nightclub, ready to alert the hive to any potential trouble. After a few puffs of smoke, even if they did try to alert anyone, the smoke would mask their pheromone alarm, so no bee would be the wiser. Next, I moved to the back of the hive, lifted the top, or outer cover, and puff—puff—puffed some smoke inside. After taking a few deep breaths to steel myself, I popped open the top and saw a few bees on the inner cover. Puff—puff—puff, and a few more deep breaths, then I popped open the inner cover. Now there was nothing between me and my bees.

Even though this was my first time, I could instantly tell which frames were the ones that I just ordered, and which ones were used to transport the bees and honeycomb over to my hive.

A frame is a rectangle of wood, hence the name "frame," and in the middle is foundation—a starter sheet of beeswax or wax-covered plastic. The foundation has hexagons imprinted on it, and is used as a "starter" for the bees to build their comb on. The foundation mimics what the bees would do naturally, and the end result looks exactly like comb built without foundation. The reason beekeepers use foundation is so the bees will build their comb even and straight inside the wooden frames. Building comb straight within the wooden frames ensures that the beekeeper can remove the frames without having to destroy any comb, allowing the beekeeper to check on the bees, or remove the frames with honey inside. The wax foundation is about as thick as a sheet of construction paper. The bees will use wax that they make to build out the comb, and each hexagonal cell will be at least a half an inch deep when they're done. Once the comb is drawn out, depending on where it is in the hive, it will either be used to store honey, or for the queen to lay eggs and the hive to raise baby bees.

The frames I ordered looked like fresh, new wood. It looked as if the bees hadn't even walked on them, as if they were trying to preserve their newness. The other frames looked old and worn. They were a dark, shiny brown, like an old wooden floor that has seen decades of wear and tear. Since my bees were extracted from a wall of a house, the comb on these frames was already drawn out, which made my new frames look even emptier and bare. The frames with comb were smeared with gunk on them, gunk that I would later learn was propolis. Propolis, or bee glue, is what the bees use like spackle to fill any nooks or crannies throughout the hive. If you have ever touched a plant or a tree and felt a sticky residue, this is what bees collect to make propolis. They collect it in much the same way they collect pollen, bringing it back to the hive on their hind legs, and then adding in some enzymes, which creates this wonderful putty-like substance that is antiviral and antimicrobial. So as the bees spread it throughout the hive, they are making the place sturdier and more hygienic. Once a hive really ramps up in population, you cannot even pop the top off, as the bees will have glued it shut with the propolis. That's why after the smoker, the hive tool is the most important piece of equipment for the beekeeper. Not every beekeeper will wear a veil or gloves or carry a bunch of bee gadgets, but no matter where on the planet they keep bees, every beekeeper will have a smoker and a hive tool.

A hive tool is basically a strong, flat mini crowbar. It's usually around eight to ten inches in length, and is used to get into your hives, and also pry apart and lift the frames from the wooden boxes. Because a lot of beekeepers love gadgets, hive tools come in all sorts of shapes and colors. Some have an extra-sharp edge, others are extra-long, or extra-skinny. Some even have a built-in screwdriver, just in case you open a hive and find that as a prank, the bees loosened all the screws inside.

I like to use what's called an Italian hive tool. It is long and skinny on one end, so you can easily slip it between the frames and use it like a lever to lift the frames up from underneath. I will use two, one on each end of the frame, so I can pop it up evenly, then by sliding my hands down can grab the frame by its ends, or ears as beekeepers call it. But on my first day, my hive tool was thick and bulky. If an Italian hive tool was built like Michael Phelps, this one was built like Frosty the Snowman.

The bees had not propolized the inner or outer cover, which is why I was able to just lift the lids off the hive. How much of a hive the bees propolize depends on what kind of bees they are, as some bees are more prone to propolize than others. How many bees are in a hive, and the time of year, can also affect how much a hive gets propolized.

While all honeybees are *Apis mellifera*, there are different breeds or subspecies of bees. Think about dogs; they are all canines, but they range from the German shepherd to the Jack Russell terrier. Bees are the same way, only they don't shed like dogs and they are housebroken when they hatch. But different types of bees do have different characteristics or dare I say, different personalities.

The most common honeybee is the Italian honeybee. These are the familiar fuzzy yellow with dark stripe bees you visualize when you think about honeybees. They tend to be gentle, and they are great honey producers! They usually keep a large population throughout the year, which means that you have to make sure they have plenty of honey stores for the winter. Beekeepers often say Italian bees eat a lot and have big families. There is a subset of the Italian honeybee called a Cordovan. These are also called blondes. They are much lighter in color than regular Italians, they are extremely gentle, and they are also great honey producers. (However, the other bees do make jokes about the blondes not being as smart, but they do have more fun!)

Another popular type of bee is called Carniolan, or Carnie, like circus carnie, for short. Carnies are better in cooler climates, and unlike Italians, the Carnies will limit their population when there is a shortage of food, thus not requiring as much honey stores to make it through the winter. Carnies are also known to propolize everything! It's like going to your grandmother's house and she's wallpapered everywhere, even the furniture! I have had a few Carnie hives, and the propolis looked like someone took spoonfuls of peanut butter and smeared it all over the inside of the hives.

Another specialty breed of bees is the Buckfast line. These bees are named after the Buckfast Abbey, a Benedictine monastery near Devon, England. In the early twentieth century, one of the monks, Brother Adam, decided he was going to breed a better bee. He wanted a bee that was healthy against pests, very gentle, and an incredible honey producer. In his lifetime, he traveled the globe seven times to find bees with characteristics that he wanted to include in his bees. His genetic breeding led to the creation of the Buckfast bee. What's interesting to note is that while another monk—Gregor Mendel—is usually mentioned when discussing breeding genetic traits, Mendel was unsuccessful in his attempts at breeding bees. What Brother Adam figured out that Mendel had not was that it was the drones, the male bees, that were the deciding factor when trying to breed specific bee traits. Beekeepers that keep Buckfast bees claim they are super-bees—very gentle bees that outperform all other types in honey production.

Another subspecies of honeybees are Russian honeybees. Lately these bees have been getting more and more popular. Russian bees are built for cold climates, which is one of the reasons for their popularity. They only require a small population of bees to survive the winter, so they don't require a lot of food. Russian bees are also prone to create supersedure cells, meaning they are always ready to overthrow their queen and put a new one in charge, slowing down honey production and increasing the chances of the hive becoming queenless. However, the main reason Russian bees have picked up in interest is because they seem to be better suited for fighting the honeybee's number one threat, the Varroa destructor, which is a parasitic mite that is the number one thing killing bees today.

For thousands upon thousands of years, Varroa destructor lived exclusively on the Asian bee. **BEE NERD WORD:** *Apis cerana*

While the Asian bee looks like our honeybee, the European honeybee, it is a different, smaller species, and is not found outside of Asia. In the 1960s, Varroa destructor jumped species to our honeybee, and first appeared in the United States in 1987. Since Varroa is not a native parasite, the European honeybee is not naturally equipped to fight it off, which is why it is devastating honeybee populations throughout the world. The mite looks like a little red tick, and an adult female mite will attach itself to an adult bee. If you took a Frisbee and held it up to your chest, that is how big the mite is next to a honeybee. Once in the hive, the mite will sneak into a cell with a developing bee larva and lay its eggs. The baby mites will feed off the developing bee, depriving it of nutrients so once it hatches, it is not as strong as an adult bee. Further, much in the same way that mosquitoes can spread malaria, the mites introduce deadly viruses into a bee's system, making the mites even more deadly to bee populations. Varroa is the number one threat to honeybees, which is why beekeepers, commercial farmers who rely on honeybee pollination, and scientists spend so much time and resources to find a way to combat it. One of the main reasons why it is so difficult to fight Varroa is that the goal is to kill a bug that lives on the bug that we want to keep healthy and very much alive.

Beekeepers have been working on genetic strains of honeybees that are able to naturally fight off Varroa. First, there was the Varroa Sensitive Hygiene (VSH) bee that detects and removes bee pupae that are infested with Varroa mites. So as the nurse bees are tending to the developing baby bees, if they can tell that mites are on one of the pupae, they pull that pupa out, so it and the mites die. A newer strain of Varroa-fighting bees is called the Purdue Ankle Biters. While one can imagine the name was derived from a Fighting Irish pastime, the reality is that these bees will bite the legs, or ankles, of mites that are on other bees' backs, so the mites fall off and die. This trait is interesting, as it would mean that when a bee flies back to the hive with a mite on its back that other bees would chew on and kill the mite before it has a chance to breed.

Beekeepers are like dog owners; we both think the breed we own is the best. Over time, and by trying different types of bees, you will find what's best for you. Over the years, I have tried many types of specialty bee, some I really liked, others I didn't, and most were just so-so. In the end, I mostly prefer "mutts" that overwinter well and makes lots and lots of honey.

I was initially drawn to beekeeping because I was interested and excited to have bees, and it was never about the honey. My first year, I knew that the chances of my hive making enough honey for me was very slim to none. My only goal was to get them to expand their numbers by drawing out the comb on the other frames that I had provided for them, so the queen could continue to lay eggs, and the workers could store honey for the winter. Standing over the hive was fascinating, but it was time for me to do a real inspection, and see what the bees were doing.

Since it was easy to see where the bees were, I pulled out the untouched, freshly lumbered frames. A hive has ten frames per wooden box, so a standard way to refer to frames is by number. The frame closest to you, or on the left side, since we read left to right, is number one. And the last frame, or far right frame, is number ten. The bees were on the middle frames, frames four, five, six, and seven. Frames one, two, three, eight, nine, and ten were all empty, the same as when I first put them in the bee-less hive.

I first pulled out frames one and two, looking at the frames, just to see if there were any bees on them, but just as I expected, not a one. Then, I took out frames nine and ten, and still no bees.

I puffed some smoke into the hive, just to make sure the bees stayed calm. Subconsciously, I was hoping the smoke would also keep me calm, but that would require me to use an entirely different kind of smoke. I then used the hooked end of my chubby hive tool, and pulled frame three away from the other frames, and pulled it over next to the side of the box, where frame number one would normally sit. Then I used the same technique on frame number eight. There were some bees on the sides of frames, but these bees were not doing anything except hanging out.

What I was hoping to see was the bees "working" the foundation, and drawing out the comb. The bees usually start in the middle of a frame and build out to the sides. The foundation is perfectly flat, so as the comb is being built up, it looks like wax hills rising from the flatlands. The whole process of building wax comb is amazing. The bees produce wax from glands in their abdomens, and when you see a bee with wax flakes, it looks like four tiny, very white, fish scales stuck on a bee's underside. It takes a lot of energy and resources for bees to make wax. Temperature is also a factor, as it needs to be at least ninety-five degrees inside the hive for the bees to work with and mold the wax. The bees have finger-like appendages by their mouths called mandibles. They use their mandibles to manipulate and shape the wax. Each hexagon cell is the same size, and each one is angled upward about ten degrees, so whatever is inside, an egg or honey, will not fall out. Bees use the hexagon as the shape of their cells because it is the most efficient shape to use. If you wanted to fit as many storage spaces as you could within a one-inch square, the hexagon would give you the most usable spaces, and also the least amount of non-usable space. For example, if you used circles, there would be voids between the circles where the circles did not touch. Bees are amazing architects. They always build comb with cells on both sides, and they slightly offset the cells, so that the back walls on one side act as support for cells on the other side. This is just as true in feral nests as it is in man-made hives. Because of their architectural prowess, one frame of beeswax can hold up to ten pounds of honey!

But the frames that I had removed from the hive only contained foundation. Now it was time for me to pick up and look at the frames with bees on them. I wanted to see if I could find the queen, or see eggs and larvae, which would be a sign that the queen was there and doing her job. I also wanted to see if there were signs of nectar coming in that the bees were turning into honey. I was ready. I just had to reach in, barehanded, and pick up a frame that was covered with a few thousand bees and hold it about six inches away from my face.

CHAPTER 4

All Hail the Queen

ALL I COULD THINK was Don't drop it. Don't drop a frame with a few THOUSAND bees on it. Because, even with a lot of smoke, I don't think they'd be too happy.

Thankfully, I didn't drop it. (While I have made many mistakes as a beekeeper, dropping a frame full of bees has never been one of them.) Staring at the frame, I was in awe. At that moment I knew the true meaning of "busy as a bee." The bees were doing what bees do, and they were totally disinterested in me. I was holding the frame by the ears, the outer most ends of the frame that stick out on either side, like ears on your head. It's best to hold a frame this way, as it is where there is the least amount of bees, and you can easily hold on to and move the frame around to look at it from any angle.

Since this was my first time in a hive, I didn't have a solid plan about what I was going to do. I knew I just wanted to look at every frame and see what I could see, and try to assess how my bees were doing. The bees in my hands were calm as could be, and because they were calm, so was I, and I was really able to inspect the frame I was holding.

The first thing I noticed was that the bees kept going about their business on the comb. They moved with a purpose and they didn't seem to mind that a human—one who had no idea what he was doing—was holding a section of their house in his hands. The bees' disposition can tell you a lot about how the bees are doing. When a hive has a healthy queen who is laying eggs, the hive is happy, and it is what beekeepers call "queen-right." The queen gives off pheromones signaling to all the other bees that she is in the hive and she is healthy. As worker bees come in contact with the queen pheromone, they pass it to other bees in the hive, and soon the entire hive knows how the queen is faring. Although the queen pheromone is not detect-able by the human nose, by the lack of drama in my hive, I could tell the queen was healthy.

If something happens to a queen, or if she is removed from her hive, the other bees will know in about twenty minutes that something is wrong, as they can no longer smell her. If a hive goes queenless, it's like the other bees have a collective panic attack and their buzz gets extremely loud. It would be like a second grade classroom without a teacher. The typical classroom with the teacher is usually quiet and orderly, with everyone going about his or her business as you'd expect. But, a teacher-less classroom would be total anarchy. The kids would be loud, out of their seats, running all over the place. The buzz of a queenless hive is so different from a queenright hive that beekeepers refer to its sound by saying, "The hive was roaring."

But maybe the classroom analogy isn't quite right, because a queen bee is not a disciplinarian, and doesn't behave like a typical human queen. When most people think of a "queen," they think of Buckingham Palace, toothy smiles, the royal wave, and a monarch who tells the peasants what to do. Let them eat cake, honey cakes! But in the bee world, a queen is not the boss, so a better name for her might be egg layer or mama bee. The queen is the mother of all the bees in the hive, and the only bee that can lay fertilized eggs, and without her, the hive cannot survive. At the peak of the honey-making season, a queen can lay up to two thousand eggs a day. She is working twenty-four hours a day, laying eggs and doing nothing else. She is so important that other bees do whatever they can to maximize the number of eggs she is laying, which is why she has attendant bees taking care of her every need. They feed her, they groom her, they remove her waste, and they share all the latest gossip about what's happening in the hive with her. The queen lays one egg per hexagon wax cell. An egg looks like a tic tac, but it's smaller than a grain of rice, and stands on end until it hatches into a larva. Honeybees are similar to butterflies. A butterfly starts out as a caterpillar, makes a cocoon, and emerges as a butterfly. Bees do the same, only they start as a larva, and while inside their honeycomb cell, they make their own cocoon. An adult bee emerges from its cell the same way a butterfly emerges from a cocoon. This is why you never see a little baby bee flying around, only adult, full-size bees.

The queen "decides" if she will lay a male or female egg. The male eggs are not fertilized, so they only have the queen's DNA and will become drones. **BEE NERD WORD:** The males are *haploids*, meaning they only have half the chromosomes, all inherited from their mother.

Drones do not have a stinger and don't gather pollen. Their only job is to mate with a queen. No work and just mating? What a life! Unless you consider that mating takes less than five seconds and drones die immediately after doing the deed.

The female eggs are fertilized, and they will develop into either a worker bee or a queen bee. Even though a queen and a worker bee both start out as the same egg, they are very different types of bees. The queen lives for two to three years, while a worker bee only lives for five to six weeks. A queen hatches after sixteen days, while a worker bee needs twenty-one days. The queen bee is larger, and she has a fully developed reproductive system. The worker bee's stinger is barbed like a fishhook, and the queen bee's stinger is straight like a syringe, meaning a worker bee will die if she stings you, but a queen will not.

So how does one egg become a queen bee and another a worker bee? There are two factors: food and space. A queen bee is exclusively fed royal jelly. While some may think royal jelly is a magical elixir, it is essentially bee's milk, a whitish fluid secreted from a gland in a bee's head. The worker bees are fed from "beebread," which is a mixture of pollen and honey that the bees blend together in the hive. Second, for an egg to develop into a queen, it needs more space to grow, so the worker bees will add extra wax onto a cell so a normal hexagon cell now looks like a wax "peanut in the shell" is stuck onto the comb. Beekeepers call this peanut in the shell a queen cell.

A queen bee lives a busy life, laying eggs all day, every day. Toward the end of her life, as she starts running out of steam— or eggs in her case—the worker bees build new queen cells so they can replace their failing queen before it's too late. Worker bees would be excellent professional gamblers, as they are always playing the best odds. When they need to create a new queen, they build multiple queen cells to ensure the hive has at least one strong enough to survive. Since there is only one queen per hive, the first queen to hatch finds the other queen cells and kills her unhatched sisters by stinging them while they're still inside their queen cells. If two queens hatch at the same time, they will fight to the death, leaving only one as the victor. The queens will call to one another and let each other know where they are in the hive by "piping," which is a trumpet-like noise they produce by rapid contractions of their wing muscles. The piping, which can be heard by the human ear, sounds like a trumpet or flute, and is essentially one queen smack-talking the other queen by saying, "I'm over here! You're going down, so bring it on!" This gladiator-style fight is exactly why queen bees' stingers are straight and not barbed like worker bees' stingers. The victor must live to see another day! A queen bee only stings other queen bees, and never to defend the hive from intruders, as that task falls to the worker bees.

While queens killing queens might sound barbaric, imagine if the human body could grow another heart when the old one starts to fail. Only, to play it safe, our bodies grew several hearts, knowing the strongest would survive. Since our life depended on it, we would want the strongest heart to be in use, and we'd want the weaker contenders to be disposed of, permanently.

It is amazing to stop and think about how sophisticated nature really is. The queen bee—the only bee that the hive needs to survive—takes the least amount of time to hatch. She is the only honeybee that has a straight stinger because it's used for royal duels, not stinging invaders. And while the queen might be the mother bee, she's not the monarch, as it's the worker bees that decide when she needs to be replaced.

Once a queen has hatched and whacked her sisters, she will go on her mating flight. The queen will fly up to nine miles from the hive looking for what is called a drone congregation area, which is like a bee singles bar about fifty or more feet up in the air and the size of a soccer field. All afternoon, drones will fly back and forth looking for a virgin queen to put the moves on. And just like human singles bars, there are hundreds of desperate males for every one virgin queen.

The queen flies so far from her hive because drones stay closer to their hives, and by flying farther away, she's less likely to end up in an awkward situation with one of her drone brothers. Once a virgin queen arrives at a drone congregation area, she will mate with up to twenty-four drones before heading home.

After her busy flight on the town, the queen bee will have accumulated enough sperm to last her lifetime. As a keepsake from her one and only flight of passion, she stores the sperm from all the drones she has mated with, and soon begins her life as an egg-laying machine.

The more you learn about the drones, the more you'll see they have a lot in common with their human equivalents. They are larger than worker bees and fatter than a queen bee. (Think Dad body vs. runway model.) Plus, they have huge eyes that are so big that it looks like they are wearing goggles. Also, drones don't have stingers; instead, they have penises. Drones do nothing in the hive, and they can't even feed themselves, which is why many think they should be called teenagers instead of drones. They live a bachelor's life of leisure, hanging out in the hive all day waiting to eat, only leaving the hive when they get the urge to try to mate. (Sound familiar?)

Drone bees are built for only one thing: mating. Like an insect mile-high club, bees do the deed midflight. That's the reason why drones have such big eyes: to quickly spot a virgin queen flying through the air. Once he has spotted a queen, the drone will fly as fast as he can, hoping he can catch her and be one of the lucky twenty-four. If he *is* lucky enough to "connect" with her, as a precautionary measure in case they hit any air pockets or their nuptial flight experiences any turbulence, his penis is built with special equipment so he can hang on until the nuptial flight is consummated. Their copulation lasts for just a few brief seconds. The drone bee ejaculates with such force that it ruptures his penis, and without his penis, the drone falls to his death, happy, satisfied, and still smiling.

Since a drone's sole purpose is to mate, if one does not mate, come late summer or early fall, the worker bees will first stop feeding him, chew his wings, and then throw him out of the hive to die. Yes, the hive is all girl power, and if a male isn't flying around trying to get his penis blown off, then he's of no use to the hive and he might as well be dead.

The last of the three types of bees in a hive is the worker bee. When thinking about worker bees in a hive, think of a big factory with an expanding and contracting workforce. When a factory has more jobs needing to get done, it hires more workers. The population in a hive fluctuates in much the same way, and the number of workers in a hive depends on the time of year and what needs to be done. At its peak, a hive will have upward of 60,000 bees; one queen, 3,000–6,000 drones, and over 54,000 worker bees. Worker bees are by far the most plentiful type of bee, and the only type of honeybee that most non-beekeepers ever encounter. Bees are born to work, but all 54,000 worker bees are not leaving the hive to collect nectar and pollen. A worker bee's age dictates what job she will do, and as she gets older she will also change jobs. Throughout her life, a worker bee will hold many different jobs. When a worker bee hatches, her first job, like any young child's first job, is to clean her room. She will tidy up her cell and get it ready for the queen to come back and lay another egg inside. At this young age, she is a house bee and her job is to clean cells, fix broken comb, and straighten up the hive.

Next, she will transition to a *nurse bee*, taking care of the "babies"—the larvae—until they are capped (in their cocoons) and waiting to hatch. Nurse bees bring "helicopter parenting" to a new level, as they will visit each individual larva approximately 1,300 times a day, or more than 10,000 times throughout the larval development. The nurse bees are examining the larvae to make sure they are healthy, developing properly, and to feed them. Then, nine days after they were newly laid eggs, the nurse bees will cap the cells so the larvae can take their metamorphosis journey and develop into adult honeybees.

There are also many specialty jobs in the hive. *Mortician bees* take dead, sick, or injured bees out of the hive. Honeybees are meticulously clean, so anything that could spread disease is removed from the hive. That's one of the reasons why people can use beeswax in food and cosmetics, because bees are so hygienic and keep their hive so clean. *Guard bees* are the police force within the hive. They protect the hive from intruders and robbers. *Comb builders* are the bees that construct the wax comb. *Heater bees* are the heat source that keeps bees, and especially the brood, warm no matter the outside temperature (regardless of the weather, they keep the brood between 92°F and 97°F). Bees can uncouple their wings and use their wing muscles to generate heat. Once a heater bee is up to temperature, she will dive into an empty cell, warming all the bees or brood around her. Heater bees are able to keep a colony warm, even during the coldest nights of a Swedish or Russian winter.

One of the last jobs a bee has is *forager*, and for the first time she will leave the hive to collect nectar, pollen, or water. It's a job that only the older bees do toward the end of their life span, because leaving the hive is always a dangerous adventure. Bees will travel, on average, up to three miles on their foraging trips. Bees live up to their reputation of always being busy, and in a single foraging flight, a honeybee will visit up to five hundred flowers! Bees always take multiple foraging flights a day, and on a good day, they will take about ten foraging flights. That's a lot of flowers!

A honeybee's entire body is covered in tiny, little hairs; even her eyes have hairs on them! As a bee flies through the air, she picks up a static charge, much the same way we do when we walk across a carpet. Then, when she lands on a flower, instead of a zap, the static charge makes the pollen from the flower cling to the bee. She grooms herself, cleaning the pollen off and storing it on her hind legs where she has saddlebag-like appendages for carrying the pollen back to the hive. By pushing all the pollen down into her saddlebags, she creates two big pollen balls that look like brightly colored beach balls on the sides of her hind legs. Pollen is the bees' source for protein. Pollen is like little walnuts, as it has a hard shell on the outside and the "meat" on the inside. Once the foragers return to the hive with their loads of pollen, other bees will use their mandibles to crack open the pollen. Then, they mix it with honey to make beebread, and store it in the brood's nest, as only the larvae or baby bees depend on pollen. Adult bees eat honey, nectar, or other forms of carbohydrates.

To collect nectar, a bee will use her straw-like tongue, which is called a proboscis, and she'll stick it down into a flower to

suck up the nectar. She'll store it in her honey gut, which is like
a storage tank that is not part of her digestive system. Then,
she'll fly back to the hive. If the nectar is plentiful, a bee can
carry a load as great as 85 percent of her body weight. Once
back at the hive, she will pass the nectar, straw-tongue to straw-
tongue, to a *receiver bee*, and then head back out to collect more
nectar. The receiver bee will either pass the nectar to another
receiver, or she will deposit the nectar herself into a honeycomb cell. For all of the work it takes collecting and hauling
nectar back to the hive, in her lifetime a worker bee will collect,
in total, enough nectar to make ¹⁄₁₂ of 1 teaspoon of honey.
Which means it takes twelve bees' lifetime work to sweeten the
average cup of tea.

When nectar comes into a hive, it can contain up to 80 percent moisture/water, and the bees need to bring it down to less
than 19 percent moisture before it is actually honey. Like everything in the hive, the bees have a system for this too. As they are
passing the nectar from one receiver to another, they are "airing
out" the nectar as it makes its way into the comb. Additionally,
as the bees are passing the nectar between themselves, they are
adding valuable enzymes that break down the sucrose in the
nectar into fructose and glucose, which further turns it into
honey. Once it's in the honeycomb, the bees will increase the
surface area of the nectar by forming it into a bubble-like cap,
exposing it to more air, and allowing it to further dry out. The
bees will also use their wings to create airflow in the hive, and
remove all the excess moisture created by the honey curing process. The combination of bee enzymes, airing the honey, and
creating the needed temperatures in the hive turns nectar into
honey, and once it is finished, and less than 19 percent moisture,
the bees will seal the honey in the comb by putting a wax cover

over the comb. People must use a special tool called a hydro-meter to measure the moisture content of honey, but the bees just know when it is at the correct moisture level, proving once again that they are the experts of the honey world.

It is amazing to think about the "bee math" of making honey. If one bee will make 1/12 of a teaspoon of honey in its lifetime, that means:

- 12 bees = 1 teaspoon of honey
- 1,150 bees = 1 pound of honey
- 115,000 bees = 100 pounds of honey
- 250,000 bees = 200 pounds of honey

Let's look at how many flowers the bees have to visit to make honey. Extrapolating from a bee visiting 500 flowers on a single foraging flight means that bees visit 2 million flowers to make 1 pound of honey!

Which means:

- 2 million flowers = 1 pound of honey
- 200 million flowers = 100 pounds of honey
- 400 million flowers = 200 pounds of honey

The last thing to look at in our honey equation is time. How much time does it take bees to do all this work? In New Jersey, bees have from mid-April to early July to make all their honey for the year. Why? Because that's the period of time when everything is in bloom and there is nectar available to be collected. It is referred to as the nectar flow. April to July is only about 100–120 days to collect nectar and make all the honey the hive will need. A hive in New Jersey can make anywhere from 100 pounds to over 300 pounds of honey in a season. (One year, one of my hives produced a personal best of 340 pounds of honey, and at its peak, the hive stood over seven feet tall.) That means that on the low end of honey production, a hive is making about one pound of honey per day, and a super-hive on the high end is making about three pounds of honey per day.

The amount of bees it takes to make honey explains why the queen lays 2,000 eggs a day. During the summer an average hive has 50,000 to 60,000 bees in it, so the population of the hive has to turn over at least once just to be on the low end of production. If your hive produces 200 pounds of honey, that means the population turned over at least five times.

When you read how many bees and flowers it takes to make honey, you have to ask yourself, Why do bees go through so much trouble and spend so much energy? The answer is, to provide food for their unhatched sisters to eat in the winter. Yes, hundreds of thousands of bees spend their entire life working so their sister bees, who they will never know, as they don't yet exist, will have food to eat when there is nothing to eat outside the hive.

In tropical regions like Hawaii, where flowering plants provide nectar for nine or more months out of the year, an average hive needs between twenty and forty pounds of stored honey. In colder climates, like here in the Northeast, a hive needs 80–100 pounds of honey to make it through the winter. So before a beekeeper can start taking any honey for himself, he must make sure the hive has plenty of honey for it to survive. Estimating how much honey is in a hive is easier than it sounds. Going back to the filing cabinet analogy, the second box up is the pantry, and this is where bees store their honey. The frames in this box can each hold about ten pounds of honey, so by looking at how many frames are capped, you can estimate the honey stores by multiplying by ten. Also, when you pick up a box full of honey your back will also scream out how heavy it is.

Once a hive has capped at least eight frames for itself, you can put your honey boxes, or supers, on top. Since honey weighs so much, most people use a medium-size box for their honey supers, and their lower backs generally thank them for it.

It's worth pointing out that hundreds of pounds of honey are being stored in wax comb that is about as thick as a piece of paper. It shows what masterful builders honeybees are, as the storage spaces they've created from wax their bodies produced are strong enough to hold such a heavy load. In many ways, honeybees are the doomsday preppers of the insect world. They store food for the future and they've developed ways to efficiently keep it safe and secure until they finally need it.

Bees have a natural instinct to make honey, and as long as the nectar flow is on, the bees will keep making honey. In their hive, if there is empty comb, they will fill it with honey. If there's no comb, but room for comb, they will build more comb to make more honey. Beekeepers use this natural instinct to get the bees to keep making honey for them. As long as the nectar flow is on, as soon as the bees fill a box, the beekeeper puts another box on top. If the nectar flow was infinite, then you could put an infinite number of boxes on a hive. Bees don't have the "yeah, that's enough for now" gene and they will keep doing what they're instinctually programmed to do for as long as they can do it.

When you first start a hive, it's rare to get a surplus of honey. The bees first need to build all of their comb, and then fill it with honey. Because there is less drawn comb available, they also need to provide the queen with space to lay eggs, which will increase the workforce, so they, too, can build more comb, and then make enough honey for the hive to survive the winter. It's a lot of work with only a short period of time to get it done.

Since it takes so many resources to make comb and fill it with honey, beekeepers like to feed their hives so the bees have what they need to produce the wax and draw out the comb in the hive. The food beekeepers use is sugar syrup. If you have ever made simple syrup for a cocktail, then you know how good bee food can taste. By using equal parts sugar and water, the syrup will be the same consistency as nectar, stimulating the bees into making more wax comb. Feeding your bees syrup helps them work 24/7, as they don't have to depend on when they can forage to get something to eat. Bees can only forage during the day, and when it is not raining. Feeding your bees means they don't have to depend on good weather or daylight to eat, therefore making it easier for them to build up the comb faster. Also, if the bees use sugar syrup as energy to build the comb instead of relying on nectar and honey, then they can store that "extra" honey for themselves and for you.

AS I STOOD by my hive holding the frame of bees, I did see some capped honey on the first frame I looked at. It was exciting! But what I really wanted to see was my queen. The Badger told me she would be difficult to spot, but I was hopeful.

After examining both sides of the frame, I slowly lowered it back into the hive. I moved on to the next frame. On this one I saw what looked like capped honey, only the cappings had a brownish, fiberish look to them instead of the opaque wax-covered honey on the first frame. I realized what I was looking at was capped brood, not honey.

BEE NERD ALERT: Brood is a general term that encompasses all stages of developing bees. The four stages of a bee are: egg, larvae, pupae, and adult. Uncapped brood refers to eggs and larvae, while capped brood refers to pupae.

This was a good sign, as it meant that the queen was laying eggs a few weeks ago, and the nurse bees were caring for the developing pupae. As I flipped the frame over, inside the cells, I saw dozens of glistening, white blobs in the cells. I was looking at larvae. When I looked closer, I could make out the C-shaped larvae at the bottom of the cells. They were big, and looked cramped in the cells, which meant they were eggs about a week and a half ago, which also meant, these were laid before the bees were put into my hive. So I still had no clue what the queen had been doing lately and if she was healthy. I put that frame back into the hive and pulled out the next one. This frame was the centermost frame in the hive, and since the queen is usually in the middle, this was where I would find her. As I lifted the frame, I was extra careful to hold it above the hive, so if any bees, and especially if the queen, were to fall off the frame, she would fall back into the hive. On this frame, I could see that the larvae were much smaller than they were on the previous frame. I scanned the one side, and then carefully flipped it over to look at the other side. This side of the frame looked the same as the first, with the larvae looking even smaller, but still suggesting they were laid before the bees were moved into my hive. I flipped the frame over several times, just to see if I could spot the queen, but I was not able to find her. I put it back in the hive, next to the other frames I had already inspected.

The next frame I picked up had comb that looked empty at first, but then as I took a closer look, I saw the smallest larvae I had seen. These looked less than seven days old, which said the queen was somewhere in the hive and she was depositing eggs in the wax cells. It felt great to know the hive was queenright! I flipped the frame over, and in the upper corner of the frame, something seemed different. Every frame up to this point was covered with bees, and all the bees moved around the comb in more or less the same way. It looked like organized chaos, but it was consistent organized chaos. But the movement on this frame was different. Then, among all the other bees, I saw her in all her glory: the queen bee! She was a beautiful, big, majestic reddish-yellow queen, who was about one and a half times bigger than the other bees. What struck me was not how she looked so much different from the other bees, but how she moved so differently from the worker bees. The queen has a longer abdomen, so as she walks it looks like she is rhythmically swaying her tail behind her. And as she walked, the other bees always moved out of her way. When it's just worker bees, they climb over one another, but these bees were clearing the path for their queen.

The queen was headed for the far side of the frame, and she climbed over to the backside. When I flipped the frame so she was on top, she would head back toward the down side, away from me, and out of sight. I soon realized that since the inside of a hive is dark, the queen was now trying to move out of the sun and move to the backside of the frame that was more shaded. I waited until she had walked to the middle of the frame, and then I slowly put the frame back into the hive. I wanted to make sure she was away from the edges of the frame, as I put her back where she belonged. Then, I carefully pushed her frame and the one next to it together, so she was safely between two frames. Once I knew she was safe, I put all the frames back where they belonged, and I made sure the frames were all equally spaced.

I had seen the queen, I had seen tiny larvae, and all the bees were calm, so I knew the bees were doing what they were supposed to be doing. Now, before I put the inner and outer covers back on the hive, I put a hive top feeder on the hive. The feeder was a shallow box that looked like it had two swimming pools in it, and a space between them that the bees use to crawl up from the hive. In the swimming pools were wooden rafts that fit snugly inside the pools. I filled the feeder with sugar syrup, and the rafts floated to the top. The way it works, the bees would climb up from the hive and stand on the raft. Then the bees suck up syrup and bring it back down to the hive. The rafts in the feeder ensure the bees don't drown in the sticky liquid, and as the level of syrup goes down, so do the rafts. The feeder holds about three gallons of syrup, and since the feeder sits directly on the hive, it's super-efficient for the bees to go up and get a drink. It's the same as a food truck that goes to a construction site, since the food is at the work site, the workers don't have to leave to bring back food. Since the bees had not drawn out any comb on any of the new frames, it was important that I feed them, as I needed to make sure they had the resources they needed to produce wax and build comb. Once I had filled up the feeder, I put the covers on top of it, and I closed up the hive.

It was a successful first hive inspection, and I felt good about what I had seen. I felt exhilarated to know that moments before I was immersed in a colony of stinging insects and nothing bad happened. I was proud of myself for what I had accomplished, especially since I didn't know anyone who had ever done what I had just done, and if given the chance, most people would never want to get this close to a colony of honeybees. For the first time, I understood why some people like to climb mountains, run marathons, or read James Joyce's *Ulysses*; the thrill is mastering something that very few people have done. I was eager to do more, to talk about what I had seen, and to meet other people who were equally as excited about bees.

CHAPTER 5

Bee Club

IT WAS THE THIRD FRIDAY of the month, which meant that tonight was the monthly bee club meeting. The bee club met in the Badger's hometown of Stone Valley, and it made me wonder if they held our meetings in Stone Valley because the Badger was the president of the club, or was he president because the club meetings were in Stone Valley.

I wasn't sure what to expect, because I hadn't been a member of any clubs since Boy Scouts, and I certainly hadn't been to any bug-themed meetings before. I wondered if they were going to teach me a secret bee handshake, or if I was going to have to go through some sort of insect initiation ceremony to be part of the club. As it turned out, all I had to do was pay twenty-five dollars for my yearly dues and take a seat.

The meeting space was a seldom-used town hall that had the charm of an abandoned elementary school's cafeteria. The space was set up so there was a rectangular ten-foot folding table at the front of the room with four chairs behind it. Facing the table were four rows of four chairs on the right, an aisle down the middle, and four rows of four chairs on the left.

I arrived about fifteen minutes early, but the room was already set up and many of the people had already settled in. The Badger had not arrived, even though he lived just a stone's throw away. When I walked in, there were about nine people standing around talking to one another, and what struck me the most was that everyone seemed to be about three hundred years older than me. Until I heard someone talk about bees, I thought I was in the wrong place and had stumbled into a nursing home's escape committee meeting.

About two minutes before the start of the meeting, the Badger showed up. He walked in and immediately started glad-handing the other members; he looked over at me and gave me a nod of approval for being there. He stood by the table at the front of the room and asked that everyone find their seats. I stood and waited for the others to sit down, as it was obvious they each had their favorite place to sit. I ended up in the third row back, on the right side of the room, an ideal spot as it was close to the door in case I needed to make a quick exit.

The Badger said he'd like to call the meeting to order, and someone seconded it. Two other men, who turned out to be the club secretary and the club treasurer, also went to the front of the room and took a seat alongside the Badger, leaving one empty seat at the folding table.

Including me, there were nine people sitting in chairs facing the Badger, for a total of twelve people at the meeting. Even though I was the only new person in the room, no one had said a word to me, and other than the Badger's nod, no one had acknowledged I was there. I was beginning to think it was an age thing, and all these old-timers thought kids, even forty-year-old kids, should be seen and not heard.

It was apparent that the Badger enjoyed calling the shots and directing the flow of the meeting. It was also clear that the Badger enjoyed the bureaucracy of conducting a meeting, and he did his best to make every step in the process as official as a meeting about bees could possibly be.

After the meeting was called to order, he asked the secretary to read the minutes from the last meeting. The secretary, Jack Flanagan, was a younger yet graying senior citizen with a pronounced potbelly who was wearing a faded flannel jacket, circa JCPenney 1992. He said about two sentences' worth of words and bulleted phrases. "Read minutes, treasurer's report, what's blooming, how's your bees, mites, and adjourn." He was half smirking as he spoke through his tightly pursed lips, and once he had finished, he folded his hands and gave a tight smile. He had been reading from an old cloth-bound bank ledger, and during the meeting, he appeared to be taking detailed notes, writing down what was being said, yet, every meeting I've been to since, his minutes were always just the same few bullet points. Based on the facial expressions he'd make when the Badger or the treasurer spoke, I always wondered if he was writing down what he thought of people's comments instead of what was actually being said. Inspired by *The Shining*, maybe he just wrote, "Bullshit" over and over again, page after page of "bullshit, bullshit, bullshit..."

Then the Badger simply said, "Treasurer's report," and it was Earle's turn to speak. A big grin appeared across Earle's face, as he knew he had the floor. He reached under the table, grabbed an old briefcase that looked like a prop from *Madmen,* and put it down on the table in front of him. "Pop-Pop" went the locks as the case sprung open, and Earle fumbled around until he finally brought out a small cardboard box. He opened the box, pulled out a checkbook, and flipped through it until he came to the ledger page he was looking for. Still grinning, Earle said, "No deposits, no expenses. Our balance is $284.76." Earle then said, "We really need to get some funds into our account, otherwise some day when the club needs money, we won't have it. Maybe we should have a bake sale. We could sell cookies like the Girl Scouts, only we could sell honey cookies instead. Everybody loves honey and everybody loves cookies, so we should sell honey cookies."

Jack rolled his eyes, shook his head a few times, and feverishly wrote his meeting notes, "bullshit, bullshit, bullshit..."

Earle was a lovable guy with a heart of gold, but he was about as sharp as a marble. He always meant well and wanted what was best for the club, but most of all, he liked to hear himself talk. For someone who had been keeping bees from when *The Brady Bunch* was still in prime time, he really didn't know that much about bees or beekeeping. He once stood up at a meeting and told everyone that before the worker bees push the drones out of the hive, the worker bees feed the drones a hearty last meal—just like prisoners on death row. Now, knowing how efficient honeybees are and that everything they do is for the good of the hive, it defies all logic that bees would waste food needed for the colony to survive the winter on a drone whose days were numbered. Plus, every book about bees will tell you that worker bees first starve the drones so they're weak, then they chew the drone's wings so they can't fly, then they physically toss the drones out of the hive to die. But in Earle's perfect world, the worker bees prepared a special "going away" meal for the boys to eat, then stood at the entrance of the hive and waved good-bye to the drones like they were servicemen leaving to fight for their country in the war to end all wars.

To get Earle to stop talking, the Badger fidgeted in his chair and said, "Andy, what's blooming right now?" His question was directed to a heavyset, older gentleman sitting in the second row on the center aisle so he was precisely dead center in the room. Andy looked like he hadn't bothered to shave for the last week or so, and at the mention of his name, he unfolded his arms that had been tightly crossed since he sat down, cleared his throat, and said, "Black alder and milkweed are just starting to bloom, so keep an eye out for them, that's what the bees will be working on for the next few weeks." Everyone else in the room nodded their heads and a few mumbled, "Yeah, black alder and milkweed. Got it, black alder and milkweed." Since bees and plants go hand in hand, many people who keep bees are also into plants. Andy was clearly the group's expert. He had a working knowledge of all the plants in our area that bees would go to for nectar and pollen. He knew the plant names, when they bloomed, and where they liked to grow. Everyone, including me, was always impressed with his knowledge of plants, but I never really knew how any of it would help me or my bees. If I moved my hives around to chase whatever was blooming, or if I could convince all my neighbors in a three-mile radius what they should plant, then I could see the benefit of memorizing the blooming cycles of plants in my area. Truthfully, I was never into plants, but many other people are. One of the great things about beekeeping is that it's connected to so many other interests that a passion for bees can lead in so many different directions.

Many people who are concerned about the environment are also drawn to beekeeping. Knowing that one-third of all the food we eat is thanks to the honeybee helps folks understand the important role bees play in nature. But it took a crisis to really make people come to beekeeping in droves. In 2006, beekeepers began reporting high colony losses where adult honeybees simply disappeared from the hives, and there were few, if any, dead bees found in or around the hives. To understand what they were finding, imagine a large apartment building where thousands of people lived. Then one day, all the adults simply vanished, leaving the apartment building in perfect condition, completely filled with food, and all the kids (capped brood and larvae) left behind, unattended. That's what Colony Collapse Disorder (CCD) is described as; the unnatural disappearance of all the worker bees from an otherwise normal looking hive. CCD's mass disappearance of worker bees is different from colonies that swarm or when bees abscond from a hive, as only with CCD are bees leaving unattended brood/babies behind. CCD caught the public's attention because it was in the news, and had a catchy, buzz-worthy name. The cause of it was unknown and many scientists scrambled to find answers. The conspiracy theorists had a field day with it, and came up with more convoluted plots than they did for who shot JFK. Some of the craziest theories included: cell phone signals were killing bees as they flew through the air; the chemtrails the government was secretly spraying from commercial airliners was toxic to bees; aliens from another dimension were communicating to honeybees through interstellar vibrations warning the bees they are in danger and to stay away from humans. The truth was that there were many factors contributing to CCD, and it was not as simple as discovering a single culprit that was behind it.

As the public became more and more aware of the honeybee crisis, countless people joined the beekeeping ranks to "save the bees." Colony Collapse Disorder not only brought a lot of public attention to bees, it motivated people to pay attention to the environment around them. CCD made more people aware of the dangers of pesticides and the importance of knowing what is being sprayed on our lawns, plants, and the food we eat. Regardless of the impact many of these pesticides are having on honeybees, the more people who are paying attention to what chemicals get in our ecosystem, the better it is for all of us and our planet.

Another reason people get into bees—and a common motivator throughout the history of humankind—is booze. Yes, alcohol, the other kind of buzz, draws people in to beekeeping. One of the oldest alcoholic beverages is mead, which is created with honey and water. Alcohol is basically the by-product of yeast consuming sugar. Honey is sugar, so using it to make alcohol is a natural combination. Originally, people would pour a bunch of honey into a pot of boiling water, let it cool, and wait. The natural yeasts in the air would find the watered-down honey mixture and get to work. Also, since honeybees are native to such a large and diverse geographic area (Europe and Africa), for many people, honey was more accessible than other possible alcohol sources, say grapes for making wine. This made it easier for people to get their drink on, and why mead was found in so many different cultures and societies. Today, mead is made the same way wine is, and many people refer to mead as honey wine. Unlike wine, mead can take on many different flavors, depending on the recipe, how it is aged, and what type of yeast is used. Some meads are made with fruit juices, adding another level of complexity to its taste, others are aged in oak barrels giving it a similar taste to wine, and some are carbonated like champagne. Many home brewers are attracted to mead because it is relatively easy to make, and because there are so many variations and recipes you can try. However, since mead is only as good as its ingredients, and honey is the main ingredient, many mead makers want to use their own honey to ensure it is pure and all natural. Plus, it takes a lot of honey to make mead, and if you don't have to pay for the honey, making mead becomes even more attractive, as it means you'll get more buzz for your buck.

While mead is just one of the many uses for honey, honey is probably the single biggest reason why people get into beekeeping. It's great to be at a fair and watch someone try a spoonful of local honey. Honey is nature's joy in a jar. For everyone from little kids to grumpy grandpas, once the honey hits their taste buds, it produces a smile. Most people have a sweet tooth, and nothing is sweeter than honey, so it's easy to understand why honey has such a following. Honey is essentially liquid flowers, so natural honey is so much more than just sweet. Real honey is rich with floral notes, and describing how it tastes can be as complex as describing varying varietals of wine. Since there are so many different types of flowers, just like wine, there are infinite variations on how honey can taste.

One of the main benefits of being a beekeeper is the honey your hives will produce. Besides all the honey you and your family will eat, no matter where you live there is always a demand for local honey. Once people find out that you're a beekeeper, one of the first things they'll ask is, "Do you have any honey to sell?" One of the great things about having beekeeping as your hobby is that often it can pay for itself. Depending on how many hives you have and how successful you are, your honey sales could easily cover the costs for all your beekeeping equipment and possibly even develop into a substantial revenue source for you. Just keep in mind that if you haven't kept bees before, it's never a good idea to get dollar signs in your eyes and think you're going to get rich selling honey. Instead, it's always better to start off slow, with two hives, and learn the art of beekeeping before trying to be the next honey tycoon. Your bees will thank you, and in the long run, you'll end up being much more successful.

Even for those who get into beekeeping for reasons other than honey, how much honey you get in a season is still the measure many beekeepers use to judge success. Healthy hives make more honey, meaning good beekeepers get more honey, which is why, hive for hive, honey is a valid measure of success. So no matter why someone gets into beekeeping, sooner or later honey will be a sweet part of having bees.

Of course, honey isn't the only thing you can get from your hives. Many beekeepers save the wax they get from harvesting their honey to make everything from candles and lip balms, to soaps, hand creams, and furniture polish. Beeswax is very versatile, and it can be used in many natural products. Candles made from beeswax are so desirable because beeswax candles last longer than common—derived from petroleum—paraffin candles, giving you more candlelight for your dollar. Beeswax also burns brighter than paraffin, as beeswax has a naturally higher melting point. Pure beeswax also burns cleaner—naturally dripless, smokeless, and sootless for better indoor air quality and a cleaner home.

Homemade creams and lip balms are a great way to use wax and make products that people want and are more than willing to pay for. The company Burt's Bees was started by a beekeeper, who along with his business partner, turned two hundred dollars from their first craft fair into a multimillion-dollar corporation. Not everyone is going to make the kind of money that Burt's Bees made, but making your own line of handmade products is another way keeping bees leads to other endeavors.

Even if you're only interested in the bees and nothing else, beekeeping can still lead you down many different paths, and there is always something new you can try. Some beekeepers like to try less traditional types of hives, such as the top bar hive or Warre hive. A top bar hive looks like a wooden watering trough with a lid on it. It is horizontal instead of vertical, and the bees start in the front and build toward the back. The Warre hive is similar to the traditional Langstroth hive, only when you need to add another box, you add it at the bottom instead of the top. It's supposed to better mimic how bees would build a natural hive inside a tree, but having to add empty boxes to the bottom can be problematic, especially when there is a lot of honey in the hive, as each box can weigh over forty pounds and you have to take all the boxes off, put the empty box on, then re-stack all the boxes you just took off.

Other beekeepers raise bees for themselves or to sell to other beekeepers. Since all hives have the same needs, one queen, plenty of workers, brood, and food, a beekeeper can split his or her hives to create additional colonies. Pull out some frames with brood, making sure there are some eggs or very young larvae, a frame with just comb, and another filled with honey. Put the four or five frames into a new hive box, then shake plenty of nurse bees into it, keep it closed for twenty-four hours, and presto, you have a new hive. As long as there are eggs or one- to two-day-old larvae, the bees will create a new queen, and in about thirty days, you will have a fully functional, new hive. If you don't want to wait for the bees to create a new queen, you can buy a queen to add to the hive, and since they are no longer around their queen, after a few days the bees will accept the new queen as their own.

When you want to add a new queen to any hive, she will come in a queen cage that is about the size of a matchbox car. It's a small wooden rectangular box that has a screen across one side of it. The queen and several attendant bees are inside the cage. On each of the smaller ends of the cage, there are holes drilled through the wood. One of the holes is plugged with a cork, and the other is filled with a sugary candy. When you put the queen cage into the hive, the worker bees will smell the queen through the screen. Since they don't immediately recognize her as their queen, initially they will try to kill her, but she's safe inside her queen cage. It just takes time for the colony to familiarize itself with the new queen's pheromones, and while they're acclimating to their new monarch, the worker bees start eating the candy from the hole on the side of the cage. In the few days that it takes them to consume all the candy, the hive becomes accustomed to the queen's pheromones, and accepts her as their queen. Once the candy is gone, the queen and her attendants just walk out of the cage as members of the colony, and the queen soon gets to work laying eggs.

Just as some beekeepers like to raise bees to sell, other beekeepers continually like to try new and different breeds of bees to find the variety that best fits their style of beekeeping. There are plenty types of bees to choose from, and no matter what traits you prefer, whether it's honey production, gentleness, or overwinters well, they're all still *Apis mellifera*. However, every once in a while you may come across a beekeeper who believes in honeybee segregation. At one bee club meeting, after the Badger asked how everyone's bees were doing, a loud-mouthed beekeeper—who was from another bee club but decided to give our meeting a try—announced that he was looking for a second bee yard because he wanted to try Carniolan bees. He said all his current bees were Italian, and there was no way he was going to put Carnies in the same bee yard as the Italians, since "that would lead to trouble, 'cause you know, you can't let the two mix. They're different, so you have to keep them apart." I'm not sure what he thought happened on the flowers, but it was clear how he looks at the world didn't mesh with the rest of our views, nor did it match reality, science, or common sense. Thankfully that was the only meeting he attended and we didn't have to mix with his kind again.

At that first meeting, when I heard the Badger ask, "How's everyone's bees?" all the answers were normal—at least normal for beekeepers. The members who spoke up said their hives were getting heavy, and talked about how many honey supers they had on. Someone said he was worried about swarming, and the other beekeepers replied that he was always worried about his hives swarming.

After everyone who looked like they wanted to talk had spoken, the Badger said, "I'd like everyone to meet our new guy. He got his bees a few weeks ago. Rusty and I did a cutout, and Rusty rubber-banded the comb into the frames. It was a solid four-frame of bees when we got done." Then he looked at me and said, "How are your bees doing?" So I told everyone how I waited a full week before I went into the hive, and when I went in they were calm, and that I saw tiny larvae and the queen.

When I said that I saw the queen, I could tell that the old-timers were impressed. "Oh, saw the queen. Good, good, saw the queen," was the murmur from the members. I also said how the bees had not drawn out any comb on my new frames so I put a feeder on the hive, and when I said this, it sparked a lot of questions. "What kind of feeder did you use?" "Did you use one-one syrup?" "How long ago did you put the feeder on?" "Have you checked to see if they are taking the syrup yet?" I answered the questions as best I could, and when I didn't understand what they were asking, someone would explain what they were trying to find out so I could give them the information they wanted.

This was my first taste of it, but I was beginning to understand the power of the bee club. The room was filled with over five hundred years' worth of experience, and when I would describe what I saw, or what I did, they could use all their experience to help me learn what I should be doing, and what I should be seeing. I could also tell that they were enjoying helping me. It is a trait that most beekeepers I have met usually have, a desire to help. Often a beekeeper will help another beekeeper, and many times they will generously offer to help before you have a chance to ask. The desire to help must be tied to the same gene that makes a person want to keep bees, as you usually don't see one without the other. The bee club was the first group where I felt comfortable asking for help because I knew I could get it with no strings attached. Even among this bunch of odd and amusing characters, they all had a good heart and a willingness to do what was best for the bees. I felt connected to this group, not so much because of their eccentricities, but because of their never-ending devotion to the honeybee.

We ended up talking about my bees for about twenty minutes that first night. Finally, the Badger said, "Okay, this month's meeting is adjourned." Instead of leaving the building, everyone just stood up and moved over to another table that was set up in the back of the room. On the table were some store-bought cookies, a tray of homemade brownies, a percolating coffeepot, Styrofoam cups, and napkins. Everyone grabbed a few cookies, a cup of coffee, and started talking about their bees. Some repeated what they had said during the meeting, and others who had said nothing started talking about their bees. I was quiet because I was listening to what everyone was saying and I was trying to absorb as much knowledge as I could from everyone.

After a while, Andy asked me, "So, what do you think of Rusty, Rusty Spoonauer?" I said, "Rusty? I'm not sure if I met him. Was he here tonight?" Andy started to chuckle and said, "Oh, if you met Rusty, you would certainly remember it. There's only one Rusty, and he always makes a strong impression." I nodded, and said if that's the case, then no, I had not met him yet. Andy went on, "Oh, since he got you your bees, I just thought you would have met him, that's all." I explained how I was stuck at work when Rusty and the Badger dropped my bees off at my house. Andy's response with a wink was, "Well, when you finally meet the famous one-eyed bee guy, you let me know what you think."

One-eyed bee guy? Andy had me curious. But it wouldn't be long before I encountered the eccentric legend of the bee world.

CHAPTER 6

One-Eyed Bee Guy

RUSTY SPOONAUER, the one-eyed bee guy, had to be the most unique person to ever keep bees. When I first met him, he was already in his late seventies. In his younger days, he would have been about six feet one inch tall, but like a balloon losing air, he had been shrinking about a quarter of an inch a year for the past decade and now stood closer to five-seven. He must have hit his prime in the 1950s, because he still had that '50s look. He always dressed as if he was heading to the office, with a collared, button-down shirt, slacks, and black leather shoes. It was as if he stepped out of one of those black-and-white TV sitcoms such as *Leave It to Beaver* or *Father Knows Best*. The type of show where the man of the house would wear a suit to mow his front lawn. His clothes might have been fashionable when he bought them, but now they were decades old, faded, and worn.

A funny thing about Rusty was he had to make alterations to everything. Nothing that was store-bought was good enough so he'd "Spoonerfy" everything he owned, from his clothes to his car. He would take a perfectly good-looking dress shirt and remake the breast pocket so it was longer and could hold more stuff. As Rusty would say, "A shirt pocket should be deep enough so your pens and pencils don't fall out every time you bend over." Based on how much stuff he could pull out of his pants pockets, he must have had pockets inside of pockets that went down to his knees.

Rusty had a full head of jet-black hair that was always parted on the side and combed toward the back. He had all of his teeth, a fact that he was very proud of, especially because he had a bee-keeper's sweet tooth and he would eat honey just about every day. Rusty was also hard of hearing, but he refused to wear hearing aids. He'd say that he wasn't going to put anything inside his body, especially not a device that could be used to listen in on his conversations. When he attended our meetings, he couldn't hear what anyone was saying, so he would wear these giant, camouflage, amplifying headphones that were meant to be used to hunt wild turkeys. And yes, Rusty only had one eye. Or should I say that he was blind in one eye? Only instead of getting a glass eye or wearing a patch, Rusty wore a pair of Buddy Holly, black horn-rimmed glasses with one of the lenses blackened to cover his bad eye.

How Rusty lost his eye was anyone's guess, because depending on who he was talking to, he would change the story to fit the occasion. If he ran into someone wearing a military uniform, Rusty would talk about how the Germans in World War II were responsible for him losing his eye. Sometimes he'd say he was an electrician and took a ten-thousand-volt jolt to the eye, so now it glows in the dark. Other times he was a plumber and some toxic juice got him as he was heading off a major catastrophe by closing a drainage pipe from an undisclosed nuclear storage facility. Other times, it happened when he was still a boy, defending the honor of his childhood sweetheart, and he ended up in a rock fight with a bunch of hooligans from the other side of town.

My favorite story was what he would say whenever he'd catch a young child staring at the blackened lens on his glasses. Rusty would explain that he was a pirate with buried treasure. He'd open his good eye as wide as he could and let out an "Aaaarrrrgggghhhh!!" and then say, "Aye, aye, now where's me parrot be? Who's seen me parrot? Did ye take me parrot?"

After you've spent less than a minute with Rusty, you totally forgot that he only had one eye, because you were so distracted by all his other outlandish attempts to be different and draw attention toward himself. He might have been known as the one-eyed bee guy, but people always remembered him because of all his other antics.

Rusty liked to drive in style—Spoonerfied style. He drove a 1959 Cadillac Eldorado Seville that he had custom painted a bright bee yellow with black racing stripes and black trim. He said it was the best car money could buy because its tail fins made it look like it could fly. It was a massive boat of a car, and being painted bright yellow, you could see it flying from far away—which was a good thing as it gave you plenty of time to get out of the way of Rusty and his one good eye zooming down the street.

The trunk in a 1959 Cadillac Eldorado was bigger than some New York City apartments, and Rusty had personally outfitted his trunk for his beekeeping adventures. Since he liked to catch swarms and cut out hives living inside the walls of houses and buildings, Rusty had everything he would ever need inside his trunk. He had created a custom rack within his trunk that held dozens of boxes and cabinets. He meticulously cataloged where everything should go so he could easily find it at a minute's notice. His trunk was a virtual workshop.

Of course, Rusty didn't trust anything that was too modern and he didn't believe in battery-operated tools. Instead, he had a five-hundred-foot, industrial-grade extension cord in his trunk. Anytime he needed to use his drill or a power saw, he'd simply pull everything out of his car and get to work. Personally, I couldn't imagine letting a seventy-eight-year-old, one-eyed man, who showed up in an old car painted like a bee anywhere near my house with a power tool, but people paid him to work on their homes all the time. Rusty also devised a way to mount two commercial-size extension ladders onto the roof of his car, along with a pulley system that allowed him to easily load and unload them from his car. Why two? "Because why stop at one if you can fit two?"

Rusty liked to catch swarms, and I don't know if it was corralling the bees or the attention he got that he liked more. Many times, when a beach ball–size swarm of 15,000–20,000 bees suddenly appears, it's covered by the local news, as it makes for great photos and video coverage. When bees decide to swarm, after leaving their hive their first stop is simply a gathering place for them to bivouac until they can find a more permanent home. In urban areas, swarms often bivouac on light poles, street signs, mailboxes, bicycles, cars, and sides of buildings. It's usually a big commotion, with the police roping off the area and some people simply freaking out. Beekeepers find the whole thing hilarious because they know the bees' secret: honeybees are the most gentle when they swarm.

Before they leave the hive, bees gorge themselves on honey, as it might be several days before they will have something to eat. After they've swarmed and are bivouacked in a big ball, bees are like people after a big Thanksgiving dinner; they just want to hang out and relax. Also, honeybees only become defensive if they are defending their home or their lives. Since they do not have a home while they're bivouacked, they're not defensive. So as long as you don't try to start crushing bees in your bare hands forcing them to defend their lives, they will not sting you.

Catching a swarm is always exhilarating. Imagine there is a huge ball of about fifteen thousand bees hanging from an elementary school's swing set. People are terrified for the children, wondering what they will do for recess. A crowd gathers. The police section off the area with police tape. Then, as lunchtime approaches, and kids are wanting to get outside, in strolls the beekeeper. Or, when it's Rusty to the rescue, in zooms the bee mobile, momentarily taking the crowd's attention away from the bees.

A typical beekeeper wouldn't wear any special equipment to catch a swarm; he'd just wear whatever he had on when he got a call, even if it's just a T-shirt and shorts. He'd walk over to the bees carrying a cardboard box, a spray bottle, and a yellow-bristled brush. If there's an audience watching, he will gently place his bare hand directly on the ball of bees. The crowd gasps. The mindful beekeeper knows that it's important to show people how mellow honeybees really are, plus, he likes to hear the gasp of the crowd. Next, he sprays sugar syrup on the bees. This does two things: It provides more food for the bees so they will be preoccupied with eating, just like when dessert is served after that huge Thanksgiving meal. Second, it makes the bees sticky, so they are less likely to fly around. After spraying the bees, the beekeeper will position the cardboard box about six inches underneath the cluster of bees. He will then use the brush to sweep the bulk of the bees into the box with one or two quick and long sweeps. The goal is to get the queen and most of the bees into the box, and once they're inside, close up the box.

Many beekeepers have a cardboard box specifically set aside for catching swarms. They cut out ventilation windows on all four sides of the box, then cover the "windows" with screen, so the bees have plenty of air, and you don't have to worry about the bees overheating or getting out. You can reinforce the box with duct tape to keep it sturdy. When it's not housing the swarm, the box can hold everything one needs for the capture: garden sheers to cut branches, Gorilla tape to seal the box once the bees are inside, a bottle of sugar syrup to spray the swarm, an old bed sheet to wrap around a tree or poll to catch any bees that fall, and some old honeycomb to make the bees feel at home.

Another good thing about having a special swarm box with ventilation windows is that it's easier to "catch" the bees that don't make it inside. Since the worker bees are attracted to the queen's pheromones, the screened windows allow them to find her more easily. Any bees flying around trying to find where their sisters and queen went will smell the queen and fly to the screens and hang on, trying to get inside the box. After about fifteen or twenty minutes, all the bees will either be inside the box, or clinging to the outside of it.

Worker bees have a gland on the bottom of their abdomen called a Nasonov's gland. The Nasonov's gland releases a pheromone that is like a homing beacon that signals, "Here's our new home. We're over here." Bees will put their butts in the air and use their wings to fan this pheromone out to their sisters, so any stragglers can follow it back to their new location. Once the bees begin to land on the screen windows, you'll see them, butts in the air, fanning away so more bees can find the swarmed colony.

After the beekeeper has all/most of the bees, he'll pick up his swarm box and walk it over to his car. Many beekeepers drive a car, not a truck, so the box of bees will just go in the backseat. One of the greatest guilty pleasures of being a beekeeper is watching people's reactions when they see you place a box covered in bees in your backseat and then get into the driver's seat. One time when I caught a swarm, the police officer on the scene asked me what I was going to do with the box, and when I said, "Put it in my car and take it home," he reacted like he was Moe from the Three Stooges. He ran his hands over his head and face, and then his whole body shivered like he was just pulled out of a snow drift. It's always funny to see people's reactions, but to see a six-foot-four-inch-tall, heavily armed policeman get the willies was absolutely hilarious.

Since catching a swarm generally attracts a crowd, and since Rusty loved being in front of a crowd, he would go after any swarm he could. He was a constant showman, and in another life he could have been a barker for a circus sideshow, or a traveling medicine man who went from town to town with his horse and wagon amazing the locals with newfound inventions and modern medicinal elixirs, then he'd hightail out of town before they figured out they've been had.

Rusty had his own special swarm box, one that he painted bright yellow with black vertical stripes. He also painted the words *Bee Jail* on each side of the box, along with cartoon bees behind bars. He liked to work the crowd as he was collecting the swarm, and he'd shout out things like, "I've never seen this many bees before." Or, "I sure hope this works." He lived for the crowd's reaction, and getting the swarm was almost secondary for him.

Beekeepers like to catch swarms because it's free bees. If you want to buy a colony of bees, you will pay between $140 and $200, so catching a swarm is like free money. When you're buying bees, they're sold in one of two ways: packages or nucs. A package is a wire-screened wooden-framed box filled with three pounds of worker bees (approximately twelve thousand bees), and a queen bee in a queen cage. The queen is not the mother of the worker bees, which is why she is in a separate cage, inside the wire-screened wooden-framed box. Buying a package of bees is similar to catching a swarm, as it's just adult bees, without any brood or comb. An interesting fact about packages is that you can legally ship them through the U.S. Postal Service. I have yet to meet a postal worker who was a bee-keeper, so getting your bees delivered generally makes for a good story that usually involves a lot of pointing ("they're over there") and getting invited (or told) to get the bees yourself from the back of the post office or from inside the postal truck.

The other way to buy bees is to buy a nuc. Nuc is short for nucleus hive, and it is simply a smaller working hive. Nucs are usually four or five frames of bees instead of the ten per Lang-stroth hive, and have a queen who is already laying eggs and is the mother of the adult bees in the nuc. Additionally, there are frames of comb that have brood, honey, and pollen. Since a nuc has brood and drawn out comb, it can grow significantly faster than a package. Additionally, since the queen is the queen of all the bees inside the nuc, it is easier for the beekeeper to install the nuc and grow it into a full hive.

Rusty never bought packages or nucs; he relied on swarms to get his bees. He also saw swarms as a moneymaker, and while it is not a common, or even an acceptable, practice, Rusty would try to sell the swarms he caught to other beekeepers.

He'd say, "A swarm is just as good as a package. Actually it's better, 'cause all the bees are related, and from the same hive." Then his showmanship would kick in and he'd say things like, "Wait till you see this queen, she's huge! A monster ready to lay ten thousand eggs a day!" and "You're gonna get a great bargain, 'cause I'm gonna let you have this swarm for just seventy-five dollars! That's half of what you'd be paying for a package this size!" It was usually new beekeepers or the desperate-for-bees beekeepers who would take him up on his offer. Once he had the cash in hand he'd say, "Now remember it is a swarm, so no guarantees." If he couldn't sell it as a swarm, he'd put the bees in one of his oldest hive bodies with the oldest, gnarliest look-ing frames of comb. He would care for the bees, and once they took hold in the hive, and had brood and honey, he'd sell the whole hive for double what you'd pay for a nuc. While it's still never a good idea to buy bees this way, Rusty would say, "The good thing about buying a hived swarm is that you can look at the bees and see how productive the queen is *before* you buy it." If there was an angle, he was always working it to make a few dollars.

Rusty wouldn't just try to make a buck off of beekeepers; he'd try to take money from anyone. If a swarm would fly away before Rusty could get to it, or if it turned out it was not a swarm but a yellowjackets' nest, Rusty would bill the home-owner for his time, and he would use the going rate for buying bees as his hourly rate. He had three-sheet, carbonless invoices printed up, and a special portable metal case to carry and dis-pense them from. The invoices said across the top, "One-Eyed Beekeeping Services" along with a post office box and his phone number. Across the bottom in red ink, it said, "PAYMENT DUE IN 30 DAYS. NO EXCEPTIONS." When I once asked him why

he had a post office box, he said, "I don't want any of these weir-
dos knowing where I live!"

Most people just threw away bills for One-Eyed Beekeeping
Services, but every once in a while somebody would pay him,
and when he got a check, he'd tell everyone. "Look here, I got
paid for my beekeeping services. You know what that means?
By definition, I am a professional beekeeper." Being able to call
himself a professional beekeeper was why he had all those invoices printed up, and why he loved giving them out to people.

Rusty also used the invoices for the bee-related business he
ran out of his house—his apitherapy practice, which is better
known as bee sting therapy. Charles Mraz (1905–1999) was a beekeeper from Vermont who is credited as being the grandfather
of bee sting therapy. Mraz claimed that bee venom could be
used to treat certain conditions such as multiple sclerosis, rheu-
matoid arthritis, tendonitis, back pain, gout, and lupus.

Bee sting therapy supposedly works because it stimulates
the body's immune system so that it can begin to heal itself. Bee
venom stimulates the human body's adrenal glands, and the adrenal glands react by releasing cortisol. Cortisol is the natural
version of the man-made steroid cortisone, which is commonly
used by physicians to treat arthritis and other types of inflam-
mation. However, because cortisol is naturally produced by one's
own body, it is supposedly better for you. The way apitherapy
works is that the patient will tell the apitherapist where his or
her body is hurting. Then, together, they will find the exact spot
that hurts the most. Once the spot is found, the apitherapist will
mark the spot with a magic marker. Next, the apitherapist will
use forceps to hold a live bee by its wings, and rub the bee's abdomen on the mark until the bee stings the patient. Once the
bee stings the patient, the bee is held in place for at least ten sec-

onds to ensure the stinger has lodged into the skin. Then, the bee is pulled away, leaving its stinger and venom sacs in the patient. The stinger is left in place for at least two full minutes to ensure all the venom has been pumped into the patient. Depending on the patient and how many previous treatments he or she has had, the apitherapist will sting the spot with up to five bees in one treatment session.

There are quite a few people who prefer alternative medicine to more traditional methods, so Rusty always had a steady stream of patients who would pay him to get stung by his bees. Rusty loved playing bee doctor, and he would wear a white lab coat that, instead of his name, had "One-Eyed Bee Guy" embroidered on it. He would charge $25 for the consultation, and $25 per bee that was used, so each visit could cost up to $150. He'd perform the stinging procedures in his dining room that was set up to look like an api-doctor's office. He had made a deal with a medical supply store that was going out of business for an old dentist chair, brought it home, and placed it where a dining room table would usually stand. He also installed a row of cabinets and a countertop on one wall to hold all his api-supplies and his invoices, stamped "For Services Rendered." Rusty also had built a hive specifically for his apitherapy business. The hive was the size of a nuc, could hold five frames of comb, and it was permanently attached to a wall in his dining room. He used PVC pipe for the bees to get through the wall and in and out of the hive. He ran the pipe on the outside of his house, all the way up past the rooftop, so that any people stopping by his house didn't have to worry about stepping in front of the bee traffic of a busy hive. The hive was made entirely of Plexiglas, so you could look inside and see the bees. Attached to the back of the hive was a small three-inch by three-inch

Plexiglas box extension with a sliding door on it. Rusty built this extension on the hive so that he could lift its sliding door up and reach inside with his forceps to grab a bee. The extra box allowed him to lure bees away from the comb with a drop of honey, but kept most of the bees away from his little sliding door, ensuring bees would not be flying around his office. Rusty believed that having a supply of bees in his apitherapy office was much more efficient than having to continually go outside and get them from one of his hives, even if it meant keeping a hive in his dining room.

Converting his dining room into a pseudo doctor's office didn't seem out of place, as Rusty's house was a cross between MacGyver's and Buffalo Bill's from *Silence of the Lambs*. He had Rusty-made gadgets everywhere, and the house gave off a creepy, do-not-go-down-into-the-basement vibe. So, while having a bee-hive and a dentist's chair in your dining room would look odd in most homes, in Rusty's house, they fit right in. The house was an American Foursquare built in 1929, the same year Rusty was born. He had lived there his entire life, as initially it was his parents' house and they had it built for their growing family. His parents had long since passed, so Rusty had decades to decorate the house to his liking. The outside was originally painted bright yellow to match his car, but over time, its color had been sun-bleached to a less obnoxious shade of yellow. In his living room, he had dozens of cobalt blue bottles hanging from the ceiling and filling his windows, because he liked the reflections they scattered through the house in the afternoon light. His kitchen looked like it was straight out of the 1955 Sears & Roebuck catalog, complete with a Formica and chrome kitchen table with matching chairs. Since Rusty only had one eye, he had poor depth perception, so to minimize spills and accidents while he was cooking, he used stockpots to cook all of his meals no matter what he was making. There were dozens of them, in all sizes, sitting on his stove and around his kitchen. Off the kitchen was a half bath, and the toilet sat atop a six-inch pedestal. Years ago, Rusty had to do some plumbing work, and instead of tearing the floor open, it was easier for him to work on the pipes above the floor and then build the pedestal around the pipes when he was done. Unless your legs were five feet long, it was a bit precarious to use, and you'd wish there was a seat belt to buckle yourself in.

I was always amazed that people would get out of their cars when they got to Rusty's, let alone go inside and pay an old one-eyed man to sting them with bees. Rusty's yard was a menagerie of items he had found or built that were too big to bring inside. He thought having a front lawn of grass was a waste of space; so instead, his front yard was one big garden, where he grew jersey tomatoes, jersey corn, blueberries, and any other local fruits and vegetables that he had appropriated throughout the past seven decades. He had also acquired a full-size Bob's Big Boy statue that stood six and a half feet tall. The Big Boy statue stood in the middle of his front yard garden, and with so many of his possessions, Rusty had Spoonerfied it, connecting it to a garden hose and turning the hamburger into a sprinkler that he used to water his Jersey Fresh garden.

Rusty was a lifelong bachelor, and the more time you spent with him, the easier it was to understand why. Rusty was a flirt, and he would flirt with any woman who didn't immediately walk away from him. He was never crude or overbearing, but he had a way to let the ladies know that if they were interested, he was available to pollinate their garden. In his younger years, he may have had a few takers, but now, most women just laughed and chalked it off to an eccentric old man.

Rusty has always lived his life how he wants and is like no one else you're ever going to meet. Bee people might be a unique bunch, but by anyone's standard, comparison, or measurement, Rusty Spoonauer, the one-eyed bee guy, stands alone, as he absolutely is one-of-a-kind.

CHAPTER 7

Smoke a Little Smoke

THE OFFICIAL START TIME for the bee meetings was 7:30, but I soon learned that they unofficially started at 7:00 P.M. People would start showing up before 7:00 P.M., waiting for Earle, who had the key to open the building. The Badger also had a key, but he and Rusty were usually the last two people to arrive. When Rusty arrived, he was always exasperated from his drive to the meeting. He'd make an entrance by letting the door slam closed behind him, and as everyone looked over, he'd let out a big sigh and tell the tale of sadness he had to navigate to make it to the meeting. Then he'd shuffle over to the front of the room and plop himself down into his chair. The Badger always moved with a purpose, and no matter when he arrived, he'd march himself to the front of the room and immediately get down to business. His late yet determined entrances seemed planned and dramatic, until you got to know the Badger and you realized he was driven by his disorganization and lack of social graces.

The bee meetings began to feel like *Groundhog Day*, as every meeting seemed like a rerun of the last meeting. The Badger would call the meeting to order, then the reading of the minutes, which were also a preview to the meeting that was about to take place: "Read minutes, treasurer's report, what's blooming, how's your bees, mites, and adjourn." As a new beekeeper who didn't have any idea what he was doing and was looking for knowledge, the meetings were not very fulfilling. It was frustrating because the meetings were more about following a set structure, not the content that should be within the structure. I was eager to learn from all the experience in the room, but too many people never spoke up, and they were never given a chance to say what they think. Instead, the same questions were repeatedly asked for the same few people to answer.

I had been going into my hive about every three to four days. It's actually better for your bees if you go into your hives every seven to ten days, as it's less disruptive for them, but I would not learn this and a lot more best bee practices until many months later. I was constantly looking to see how much sugar syrup the bees were taking and if they needed more. Unfortunately, the bees were not consuming the syrup like I had hoped, so about once a week, I would dump it and refill it with fresh syrup, thinking the bees would drink more if it were fresh. I had seen a YouTube video that claimed if you added a few tablespoons of herbal tea to your syrup and some natural sea salt, the syrup would more closely resemble real nectar, enticing the bees to more excitedly consume it. But that, too, didn't work.

Many new beekeepers, like myself, look to the Internet for advice for their bees, but unfortunately the most prolific sources offering online advice are the least reliable. Through the years I have been amazed at the crazy and absolutely wrong advice that is available online. Thankfully, while the herbal tea was new-age-nutty advice, it didn't hurt my bees. The most unscientific advice, which was also the most-likely-to-kill-your-bees advice, ever posted online was from the non-smokers. The don't-smoke-your-bees-because-smoke-is-bad-for-your-bees non-smokers.

Since the beginning of time, Man has had a sweet tooth, and ever since the very first Neanderthal tasted honey, Man has been collecting honey. In ancient cave paintings, people depicted how they collected honey, and in their paintings, they used smoke to calm the bees. The ancient Egyptians were some of the first beekeepers, and their hieroglyphics tell how they kept bees in hollow logs stacked on one another, and that they would blow smoke into their hives to calm the bees. Every beekeeping book you read will tell you that you should use smoke while working your bees. *Apis mellifera* is the most studied insect on the planet, and every scientific article on the topic will tell you to smoke your bees. Commercial beekeepers, who spend every single day working with thousands upon thousands of hives, will tell you that the single most important tool they carry is their smoker. The simple reason all of these sources say the same thing about smoking your bees is that bees communicate with pheromones and smoke blocks bees from smelling them. If a guard bee releases an alarm pheromone, no bee can detect it, so all the bees stay clam. It's that simple. Smoke works.

But even though smoke has been used for tens of thousands of years, and scientists have studied its use, some people still disagree and think they know what's best for their bees. There is a small group of people who believe that smoke is bad for the bees.

Some try to compare beekeeper's smoke to unfiltered cigarettes, and since cigarette smoking has been proven to be bad for people, then any smoke in a hive could hurt a bee's little "lungs."

BEE NERD ALERT: Bees don't have lungs, they have tubes called "tracheae."

The tracheae bring air deep inside the bee's body, carrying oxygen to muscles and organs, and carrying carbon dioxide away from them. Running down the sides of their bodies, bees have a series of small holes called "spiracles" that are like portholes on the side of a boat. These portholes are connected to the tubes and are how bees draw air into their bodies.

Defying all logic, and to make matters even worse, some of these non-smokers say they "found a natural alternative to smoke." Instead of using what every beekeeper, in every country around the world uses and has been using the past twenty thousand years, these non-smokers use essential oils. They claim it's more natural and it's "so calming." The only issue is that any oil—including an essential oil—will coat a bee's body and clog up its breathing portholes, making it impossible for any air to get into the breathing tubes. So while an essential oil might smell nice, it will suffocate your bees. Also, because it's an oil, the bees cannot remove it, so once they're coated, that's it, they're done for. The non-smokers might think their bees are calm when they are using essential oils, but the reality is that their bees are not flying around because they're too busy gasping for air, trying to breathe.

Other non-smokers believe that the smoke freaks out the bees because the bees think their hive is on fire. They believe that every time you use smoke, you are disrupting the bees' normal routine for the next twenty-four hours. They believe the bees are so worried about catching on fire that they cannot think about anything else and actually stop working. These non-smokers feel that by not smoking their bees, the bees will not lose any productivity, causing the bees to produce more honey than if they were regularly exposed to smoke. It baffles me that people actually believe this when every single credible source refutes every part of this theory.

Not smoking your bees definitely does not increase honey production. And this practice can actually be dangerous for you, your family, and your neighbors. Non-smokers will wear full one-piece bee suits, gloves, and boots when they are working their bees. They make sure they are completely covered, because they know the bees are going to get upset and that the bees will try to sting them. Every time they go into their hives, the bees are releasing alarm pheromones, fear pheromones, and attack pheromones. Since there is no smoke to mask these pheromones, the entire colony smells them, gets agitated, and is on high alert. When the non-smoker is done, he or she will close up the hive and walk away, but the pheromones remain in the hive, and the bees *stay* on high alert. The result is what beekeepers call a defensive hive, meaning that the bees are very quick to defend their hive by either buzzing, or stinging, anything that comes close to the hive. This is the bees' normal response to its natural predators. For example, skunks love to eat bees, and at night they will scratch at the front entrance of a hive, so as the bees come out to see what is going on, the skunk grabs the bees and eats them. When visiting a hive, if a beekeeper notices it is more defensive than normal, the first thing he will do is look for muddy scratch marks at the front entrance to see if anything is bothering the bees. If he does find signs of a skunk, raising the hive higher off the ground will solve the problem, and after several weeks, the bees will calm down and not be so defensive. Since the non-smokers are always fully protected when they are around their hives, they have no idea how defensive their hives are when other people happen by them.

The bee club used to have a member who was a non-smoker and caused a lot of trouble. Her name was Rut (pronounced root). She'd say her parents named her that because they knew she'd be close with Mother Earth. We'd say it was because she was usually covered in dirt. Her clothes, her minivan, and her house were always filthy. She was the living equivalent of Pig-Pen from *Peanuts*, as she seemed to travel in a cloud of her own filth.

Rut had a leathered, unnaturally round face with a toothy grin, sported Jim Carrey's haircut from *Dumb and Dumber*—and she was a self-serving, self-absorbed, manipulator. Most beekeepers are kind and nurturing people, and Rut played on many beekeepers' good natures for her own benefit. If during a meeting someone said they had more "——" than they knew what to do with, Rut would say she needed it and asked if she could have some. It didn't matter what "——" was, if she could get it for free, then she NEEDED it. A lot of beekeepers are pretty handy and build their own hive boxes, frames, and other beekeeping gadgets. If someone was proud of what they made and brought it to a meeting, Rut would ask if it was hard to make. If the person were modest and said anything to the effect of, "No, it wasn't too bad," she'd say, "Well, could you make one for me?" It put most people in an awkward position, forcing them to say, "Yeah, I could make you one, sometime, I guess." Then every time Rut would see that person, she'd ask if "———" was finished, and remind him that he said he was going to make it. And she'd keep asking until she finally got it. Al Sturgis was an old-timer in our club and was a decorated veteran of World War II. He was withering away because he had prostate cancer, and yet at one meeting, he brought in a solar wax melter he had built from scratch.

Beekeepers use a solar melter to render the wax from their hives. It's basically a box with a glass top on it that works like a solar oven to melt the wax. The inside of the box is usually painted black or is lined with metal sheeting to absorb the heat from the sun and raise the temperature. The melter is angled, so as the wax melts, it drips down through a filter and into a holding pan. The filter takes out any impurities, leaving the beekeeper with a solid block of beeswax.

Al had brought the wax melter to the meeting to prove to everyone, especially himself, that he was still the same ole Al and that cancer wasn't going to stop him. Rut played her gimmee-gimmee game with him until he finally made her a solar wax melter of her own. Since his health kept deteriorating, it took him six months to build it, but he made her one because Rut made him feel like he owed it to her. Three weeks after delivering the solar wax melter, the cancer finally won and Al passed away.

During the time that she was a member of the club, Rut would volunteer to help new people get started in beekeeping. Rut and the Badger never got along, and since he had brought me into the club, Rut always stayed away from me. On the surface it seemed like she was being good-natured when she offered to help someone, but her motives were always self-serving. When she'd go over to someone's house, she would size up what she could get from him or her. If she was helping

someone feed their bees, she'd say how she needed to get some
sugar for her bees, but she hasn't had time because she was always helping so many other people. The new beekeepers would
feel bad that Rut was helping them instead of taking care of her
own bees, and they'd give Rut pound after pound of their sugar.
Other times, Rut would talk about how much the price of gas
had gone up, and how expensive it was to always be filling up
her minivan until the "newbee" would fork over some cash to
"help her pay for gas." She was a shyster who played the martyr
and used pity to get what she wanted.

No matter how inexcusable her manipulative tricks were,
Rut's beekeeping advice was much worse. Since she preyed on
the new beekeeper, many people would take her advice as gos-
pel. She was very vocal about why people shouldn't smoke their
bees, and for a time there were a number of non-smokers in the
club. Plus, she wasn't really interested in helping people become
better beekeepers, so she usually was the one who went into the
hives while the new beekeeper just stood back and watched her
work. Not allowing the new beekeeper to get any hands-on experience had two outcomes. First, because they weren't going
into their own hives, they didn't really know what they were
doing and usually ended up making a lot of mistakes when they
tried something on their own. Second, many people grew tired
of just standing around watching her be a beekeeper and they
would lose interest in keeping bees and just ended up selling or
giving Rut all of their bees and equipment.

This finally came to a head when Rupert, a beekeeper who
for over two years had been paying Rut $50 an hour for beekeep-
ing lessons, lessons that consisted of him watching her work his
hives, decided he was ready to go solo. Rupert was having a
dinner party that night, and he thought serving some of his

honey would be a nice touch. He knew he didn't need a lot, and was looking for just one really nice frame of honey for his dinner party. He thought he would cut out a big block of honey still in the comb and put it on one of his finest serving plates. Then, if any of his guests wanted fresh honey, they could simply scoop out as many spoonfuls of honey as they desired. Since it was to be a showpiece at his nice dinner party, Rupert wanted to be certain he found the best looking frame of honey that was in his hive. Rupert wasn't the sharpest knife in the drawer, and he never bothered to learn even the most basic of beekeeping skills. He always wore a full one-piece bee suit like Rut, but when the outside temperature was hot and humid like the day of his dinner party, he didn't wear a shirt or pants underneath, just his one-piece bee suit, tighty-whities, and sneakers. Rupert didn't own a smoker, because Rut told him he'd never need it. Instead, he headed out to his hives with his hive tool, and a Rubbermaid container to put the frame of honey in.

Beekeepers talk about the importance of using smooth, fluid motions when working with bees. The best beekeepers look like they're practicing a form of tai chi as they smoothly pull a frame from the hive, spin it, and put it down all with one Zen-like motion. Beekeeping can be very meditative, because you are hyper aware of slowing down your motions, focusing on what is happening in the moment, and remaining calm and relaxed as you are inside a hive, working your bees. Unfortunately, the Zen of beekeeping was lost on Rupert, because he was about as deep as a tub of butter. Rupert ripped open the cover of his hive and tossed it to the ground with a loud thud. He jerked the inner cover off with his hive tool, and flung it to the ground, as he hummed "Pour Some Sugar on Me" to himself. He stuck his face right on top of his now open hive, seeing if he could see what would be the best frame to take. He pulled on the frames with the hive tool, and got the outer few to move from away the other frames. Then, he broke two frames apart with his hive tool and pulled them out one at a time. He'd look and flip each frame to see which one had the most honey on it. After he looked at a frame, he would lean it against the hive, down by his feet. Frame by frame he looked until he had six frames out of the hive and leaning against the hive or sitting on the hive top he had tossed on the ground. Having so many frames scattered about, and because of how carelessly they were handled, there were bees flying everywhere. They were buzzing all around Rupert, and the longer he was banging around inside the hive, the more agitated they became. Rupert didn't expect it to take more than three minutes, as he envisioned that he would open his hive, the perfect frame of honey would be waiting for him, he'd grab it, and get back inside his air-conditioned house. He still had a lot to do for his party and he was rushing to get everything done. As he was rushing, he had neglected to check and confirm that he had zipped his suit all the way shut.

With so many bees flying around Rupert, eventually one found its way inside his suit. Suddenly, Rupert saw a bee flying in front of his face, inside his veil. He was worried he'd get stung and he wouldn't look good for his dinner party, so he did the only thing he could think of doing. He stood up and unzipped his veil to let the bee get out. Only, instead of one bee flying out, about a dozen bees flew in. Apparently, one of the beekeeping tips Rupert never bothered to learn was that if you ever get a bee inside your veil and you'd like to remove it, first make sure you walk away from your hives.

Now standing over his hive with twelve angry bees buzzing around his face, Rupert started to panic. Since his genius idea of unzipping his veil to let one bee out worked so well the first time, he thought he'd try it again. Only this time, instead of a bee, it was Rupert who was going to get out of that suit. He unzipped his suit and flung the bee-filled veil off his head. As the veil fell against his back, he realized he was still standing by his hive with all the bees getting more and more worked up. Rupert decided it was time to run. As he started to move past his hive, his veil caught on a frame he had partially pulled out of the top of the hive, and in that brief moment the veil was stuck. Rupert pulled with enough force to pull himself out of his one-piece bee suit. As his suit fell below his knees, his veil became unstuck. Now that he was free, Rupert started running as fast as he could. He made it twenty yards before he tripped over his suit that was bunched around his ankles and dragging behind him. He fell forward, hit his head on the Belgian block at the edge of his driveway, and he knocked himself unconscious.

Rupert's neighbor hadn't seen what happened with his bees, but he did see Rupert run nearly naked across his yard, trip, and fall. So as Rupert was sprawled out on the ground, with his bee suit wrapped around his ankles, his BVDs exposed for all to see, his neighbor called 911 to report Rupert for parading around in his skivvies.

The officer who responded to the scene happened to be a beekeeper and a member of our beekeeping club. He closed up Rupert's hive, got him off his front lawn and back in his house, then ticketed him for being a nuisance. After his public humiliation, Rupert quit beekeeping faster than he jumped out of his bee suit. Rut also disappeared once the story made the local news. She had always bragged about Rupert being her star pupil who always followed her directions to the tee and did his best to keep bees exactly the same way she did. Rut stopped coming to the bee meetings because she was mortified about Rupert being practically naked under his bee suit, as she thought people would think she told him not to wear any clothes, and would hassle her for being some kind of depraved, man-ogling pervert. So instead of having to face everyone, she just stayed away and kept to herself, disgraced not by her own actions, but by a nearly naked man found lying spread-eagle on his front lawn.

BACK AT THE BEE MEETING, I mentally followed along with the predictable sequence of events, and waited for the Badger to say that the meeting was adjourned. Once the meeting was over, and everyone moved over to the refreshment table for cheap cake and coffee, I started talking with a few of the experienced beekeepers about my hive and asking them for their opinions. I explained that the bees were not taking the syrup, and after six weeks they had only built up comb on one side of the two frames closest to the comb that came from their original hive. When I said that I was dumping the syrup every week and re-placing it with fresh syrup, I thought Andy was going to choke on his cupcake. He said, "You never have to change the syrup, the bees don't care how old it is." And he went on to say, "If your bees aren't taking the syrup, there is something going on with them, not with your syrup. Don't waste it, stop dumping it." Then he asked me if I had seen the queen, and I said, "Yes, I see her almost every time I go into the hive." So he asked if I saw eggs and larvae. I told him the truth—that I couldn't see eggs, but I did see larvae. He was skeptical when I told him I always saw the queen, but once I said I couldn't see eggs, he knew I was telling the truth and that I wasn't making anything up. Seeing eggs is very difficult, and they're like the *Magic Eye* illustrations, first you can't see them, then, you still can't see them, but then one day, BAM, you see them! And after you finally do see them that first time, you see them so clearly every time you look that you wonder why it took you so long to see them in the first place. Eggs are so hard to see because each one is smaller than a grain of rice, standing at attention at the bottom of a hexagon cell and you can only see the top end of each super small egg. The trick is to make sure the sun is at your back, and you hold the frame up so the sun is shining over your shoulder and down into the comb at just the right angle. The light will reflect off the back of the comb, backlighting the eggs, illuminating them so they really pop, and making it easy for you to see them. It can take months or even years to become good at seeing eggs, but once you get the trick down, seeing them becomes something you can do just about every time you go into a hive.

Andy and the other beekeepers I was talking to thought it was good that I could see the queen and larvae, but they were puzzled over why the bees were not taking the syrup or building out the comb on the other frames. Andy suggested that I get a spray bottle, and spray the sugar syrup onto the other frames. He thought that since I was using plastic foundation instead of wax foundation that the bees might need to be coaxed on it. He thought that by spraying sugar syrup onto the other frames, the bees might venture over to those frames to eat the syrup and then once they're on the new plastic foundation, they would start to draw it out into comb. The Badger came over at the tail end of the conversation, and he agreed with Andy's plan and thought it might work. Andy looked over at the Badger and said, "You should go over there and see if you can tell what's going on in his hive." The Badger looked at me, then looked at Andy, then back at me and said, "Yeah, I should. Look for my call. I'll stop over sometime this weekend." I smiled, because I knew it would be great to have an experienced beekeeper tell me what I was looking at. Also, I wanted my bees to be okay, and having the Badger inspect my hive seemed like it would be good for my bees and for me.

CHAPTER 8

That Stings

SATURDAY WAS A BEAUTIFUL JULY DAY, sunny, warm, and not too humid. All day, I kept my phone close by my side, waiting for the Badger to call, but not a peep, a ring, or a buzz. Then Sunday morning as I was in the middle of my fried eggs and pork roll breakfast, the doorbell rang. It was the Badger.

"I was driving back from my girlfriend's house and I thought I would stop by." The Badger seemed both nervous and proud to utter the words "my girlfriend."

"Come on out and meet her," he said through his big smile. We walked over to the driveway where his car was parked, and I could see a middle-aged woman sitting inside. He opened the door and said to her, "Here's my apprentice." His girlfriend seemed a bit embarrassed, which I initially thought was because she was with the Badger, but after he said, "See, I told you it would be all right if we just stopped by," I realized she was embarrassed about stopping by someone's house unannounced on a Sunday morning.

After she was out of his car, the Badger held her by the hand and said, "His hive, the one I set up, is 'round back." Then he led the way through my backyard to my hive.

The Badger was in his glory. He had a hive in front of him and an audience by his side. He was wearing a baseball cap, and as he spun the brim to the back of his head, he looked over to me and said, "Shall we open her up?"

"Sure!" I said. "I'll go grab my smoker and hive tool and stuff."

But the Badger replied, "That's okay, we don't need all that, we'll just open it up and take a quick look." The Badger was always the cowboy, cutting corners, and always looking for shortcuts. He knew the rules and the proper procedure, but he still liked to push the limits more than playing it safe.

"Well, at least let me go grab my hive tool," I said.

But the Badger reached down to a side pocket on his cargo shorts and pulled out a hive tool. I thought to myself, "Who carries a hive tool with him, on a Sunday morning, when he's riding around with his girlfriend?"

Besides the bees and a hive to put them in, the two most important pieces of equipment every beekeeper needs is a smoker and a hive tool. A hive tool looks like an eight-inch, flat crowbar. It is so important because the bees make bee glue, officially known as propolis, that they use to spackle everything in their hive. A colony of bees will propolize every frame in place, the bee boxes together, and cement-shut the inner and outer covers. The propolis is so strong that it is impossible to pull the hive apart without a hive tool.

Bees make propolis by collecting resin from plants. If you have ever touched a tree or plant and gotten a gooey substance on your fingers, that's resin and you know how sticky it is and how difficult it can be to clean off. Bees collect this sticky stuff, and then, back in the hive, they add enzymes to it. When they're finished, the propolis has the consistency of a dark, creamy peanut butter. They'll use the propolis throughout their hive to seal up any small cracks or crevices, and glue everything into place. In addition to securing everything, propolis also serves a more important function in the hive; it protects the health of the honeybees. Propolis is antiviral and antimicrobial, so by spreading the propolis throughout their hives, it reduces the number of pathogens inside their home. I am always amazed by the relationship between bees and plants. Plants produce resin as a way to protect themselves from disease; when their outer layer gets cut open, they produce a thick, sticky goo to seal the cut shut, stop anything from getting into it, and kill any potential germ that comes into contact with it. At some point along their evolutionary journey, bees learned that the sticky stuff plants produce to protect themselves could also be used to keep honeybee colonies healthy.

When bees make their nests inside of trees and other non-man-made cavities, bees will coat the inside walls with propolis to act as a barrier around the nest. Bees don't propolize the inside of man-made hives because the inside walls of the hive are too smooth for the propolis to stick to it. Marla Spivak, PhD, a professor at the University of Minnesota, has done a significant amount of research on bees, including the impact propolis has on bee health. Spivak found that in hives where the bees have created a propolis "envelope" around their nest, the bees have quieter immune systems, meaning the bees' bodies are not working as hard to fight off disease as bees in hives that are not lined with propolis. Since propolis does seem to keep bees healthy,

Spivak recommends coating the inside of your hive bodies with propolis. One way to do this would be to paint the inside of your hives with a propolis extract. (Propolis dissolved in 70 percent ethanol alcohol.) Another would be to use a router to "rough up" and create grooves on the inside of the hive bodies for the bees to apply propolis. Yet another recommendation is to staple window screen against the inside walls of the hive bodies so the bees can plaster their walls with propolis, mimicking what they would do in a non-man-made cavity like the inside of a tree.

Propolis has also been shown to have health benefits for people. Since it is antimicrobial, it is used in at least one brand of commercially available toothpaste. Additionally, some people will use the same propolis extract that Spivak applied to the inside of her hives as a topical treatment for cuts and scrapes.

Since my hive was less than a few months old, the bees hadn't been collecting a lot of propolis, so my hive wasn't as stuck together as a hive that had been occupied for a couple of seasons and would be relatively easy to open. The Badger was eager to show off and he popped open the outer cover without a hitch. Then before he took off the inner cover, he said to me, "Come a little closer, and let's get a good look at what we can see." He slid his hive tool under the corner between my inner cover and the hive body, then twisting his tool, he raised up the inner cover about a half an inch. Then he put it back down, looked over at his girlfriend who was standing behind me, and said, "What? Don't worry, this won't take too long." Standing twenty-five feet away from him in a stranger's backyard was not how she wanted to spend her Sunday morning. This didn't seem to bother the Badger because he quickly turned his attention back to the inner cover, and this time, he just used his hands to pull it off, tilting the underside—the side with all the bees on it—

away from him and facing me. Within a millisecond of him pulling the inner cover off, I heard a loud, "Zzzzzzzert!!" and felt a slight thud on my forehead, between my eyebrows. I instinctively swiped at the spot where I felt the thud, and when I did, I felt a fuzzy little pellet under my finger. That's when I realized it was a bee, and then I realized that the thud I felt was the bee stinging me. Like most first-time beekeepers, the anticipation of getting stung was a lot worse than the actual sting. Most people think a sting is going to hurt a lot more than it actually does, and they spend so much time worrying about it that when they finally do get stung, the universal reaction is, "Oh is *that* it? It wasn't as bad as I thought it would be." In reality, the sting feels about the same as getting stuck by a thorn on a rose bush. And, as beekeepers and anyone who grows roses will say, the longer you're around them, the less you'll notice it. Truthfully, I didn't feel the sting itself, but I'll always remember the loud kamikaze noise the bee made as it crashed into my face with a loud, "Zzzzzzzert!!!"

The Badger glanced over at me and said, "Looks like one got you there. That's why it's always a good idea to have your smoker going. You can smoke it to keep other bees away from the sting. You'd better go get that smoker now."

Thank you, Mr. Obvious. Thank you for telling me what every beekeeper knows, and what I already knew: use smoke, and keep your bees calm. My first sting as a beekeeper and it was not from anything I had done, other than letting the Badger open my hive without first lighting my smoker. I was frustrated that the president of the club would not want to set a better example and follow beekeeping's most basic best practices. I knew I had a lot to learn, but I still felt that a president should focus on helping his club's members.

I went over to my garage, grabbed my smoker, veil, and hive tool. I lit my smoker as I was walking back to my hive so I'd have more time to try to learn something from the Badger's hive inspection. "Smoke your face, smoke your face," the Badger said, instructing me to mask the pheromone from the sting.

When a bee stings you, the venom sac also releases a pheromone that acts as a bull's-eye for other bees to aim for. If a bee stings an intruder, then its sisters will smell the pheromone and try to sting the predator in the same spot. It takes the guesswork out of where to sting, and makes it easier for bees to find the target. By blowing smoke on the sting site, you are masking its smell and decreasing your chance of getting additional stings. The sting pheromone also alerts the other bees that there's a threat in the area, so they become more alert and potentially more defensive. The Badger also said to me, "Scrape your hive tool over the sting to make sure you got the stinger out." When someone gets stung, their natural reaction is to use their thumb and forefinger and try to grab, pinch, and pull the stinger out. But as you grab a stinger by pinching it between your fingers, you are actually squeezing more venom into your body. If you use a hive tool, however, or something with a hard edge like a credit card, you can scrape the stinger out of your skin and remove it without it pumping additional venom into you.

A honeybee's venom sac is fully developed at sixteen days, and if necessary, she will start defending her hive at fourteen days. This is another reason why bees don't leave the hive when they first hatch; their venom sacs are not developed and they cannot defend themselves or the hive. Additionally, this is why beekeepers are not worried when they are holding frames of bees, as most of the bees are house or nurse bees, and they are much less likely to sting you. It's the older bees that are fully armed and more likely to pay the ultimate price to defend their hive.

Honeybees die when they sting you, so stinging is an act of last resort, and they only sting to defend their hive or to defend their life. Bees know they can scare off many intruders, especially humans, so first they will buzz you, flying close by so you can hear them. Next, they will fly into and bounce off your hat, or veil if you're a beekeeper. I call this "popcorning," since it looks like popcorn popping off your veil as they try to intimidate you. Then, only if their primary defense tactics have failed will bees move to DEFCON 1, the very last stage, and sting to defend their hive.

The reason bees die when they sting is because their stinger is barbed like a fishhook, and after they sting you and try to fly away, they literally tear themselves in two, leaving the stinger, venom sac, and part of their abdomen with you, as they fly away to their impending death. One of the many things that separate honeybees from yellowjackets and wasps is that only the honeybee's stinger is barbed. The yellowjacket's and wasp's stingers are straight, like a doctor's syringe, so they can repeatedly sting you over and over again and not suffer any ill effect. (That's also why they are more likely to sting you; they won't die if they do.)

The venom of each type of bee and wasp is also different, meaning that how your body reacts to one insect's venom could be very different from how it will react to another's. Honeybee venom contains a multitude of enzymes, peptides, and active organic compounds. The major component in honeybee venom is the peptide melittin, which upon injection releases histamine and ruptures red blood corpuscles, causing pain and swelling.

It's important to remember that it's totally normal to have a reaction at the sting site. You may experience some pain, redness, or even swelling, but as long as it's at the site of the sting, then it's just a natural local reaction. This is true even if you experience a significant amount of swelling. It's actually more important to note *where* the reaction is happening rather than *how big* it happens to be. A good rule of thumb is to count how many body joints are between the sting and the reaction, and know that any more than two joints apart could mean an allergic reaction. So, if you were to get stung on your hand, but you had a reaction on your chest (wrist + elbow + shoulder = 3 joints away) then, you are having an allergic reaction. If your hand blows up to a watermelon-size lobster claw, however, then you are still having a normal local reaction. It is also important to note that less than 3 percent of adults, and less than 0.05 percent of children will ever develop an allergy to bee venom. As a point of comparison, according to the Centers for Disease Control, 8 percent of children have food allergies, so that means someone is five hundred more times likely to be allergic to peanuts than to bee stings.

BEE NERD ALERT: Bee's stingers evolved from ovipositors, a tubular organ some insects use to deposits eggs. That's why only female bees can sting: it was originally part of the female's reproductive system.

People will sometimes ask if any of the old-time home remedies for bee stings work, and the answer is a big, simple N-O. If you want to do something to reduce the local reaction you're having, the best thing you can do is to take Benadryl to reduce the swelling and redness, then just give it some time. After a few days, all of your symptoms should be gone, which for many beekeepers means that by the next weekend they're as good as new and ready to go back into their hives.

If you're going to keep bees, you have to accept the fact that you will get stung. When an experienced beekeeper gets stung, instead of being afraid or starting to panic, he will feel sad because one of his bees just died and he probably did something wrong that caused the bee to sting him. If the beekeeper uses smoke, opens the hive, and moves the frames with smooth fluid motions, and doesn't bang or knock the hive, the bees will stay calm. If a colony of bees is having issues, though, such as a skunk bothering them at night, or if there is a lack of food available, or if a disease is overwhelming a colony, it will increase the chances that the bees are more likely to sting. But even if you do everything right, and your bees are healthy, sooner or later you will get stung, which is why getting your first sting out of the way is always a good thing.

After I smoked my face, and used my hive tool to scrape the stinger out, I was back in business. The sting didn't hurt, but it did feel like a very mild sunburn. It felt hotter than the skin around it, and also tighter. But other than that, I was fine. And I was excited and energized, which was actually a by-product of the sting. When the Badger had interrupted my breakfast, I hadn't had a chance to drink my coffee, but now I felt like I had downed a quad shot of espresso, and I liked it.

BEE NERD ALERT: Melittin stimulates your body's production of cortisol. Cortisol is best known for its role in the "fight-or-flight" response and producing a temporary increase in energy.

I was buzzing, my blood was pumping, and I was ready to learn from the Badger. He used his hive tool to move the top feeder a little to the side so he could get a grip and lift it off the hive. He sat it down on the grass and he did a decent job of not letting too much syrup splash out. Once the feeder was off, and you looked down into the hive, you could still easily tell what frames the Badger and Rusty had brought with the bees, and which were the new frames that I had recently purchased, but things had progressed more than the last time I had looked at them. The bees now had drawn out the comb on both sides of the frames that were on either side of their original drawn comb, and they were starting on the next frame out. The Badger pulled the first newly drawn frame out of the hive, and he could see that the bees were starting to store nectar in the newly formed, pure white comb. The same was true for the drawn-out frame on the other side.

The Badger was going every other frame, and he pulled out one of the frames that was almost dead center in the hive. On the frame you could see brood. In the middle of the frame was the oldest brood, and it was capped, or was in the process of being capped. As you scanned from the middle of the frame and looked toward the sides, you could see that the brood was getting younger and younger, all the way to the edges, and then you could see what was one- to two-day-old larvae. This is typical for how a queen will lay. She will usually start in the middle of a frame, and make larger and larger concentric circles, laying eggs as she goes. Or, she'll start on one end of a frame and work her way to the other. There is always a systematic and efficient pattern she follows to lay the most eggs in the least amount of time. If you start with the oldest brood, or largest larvae, and follow it to the smallest/youngest larvae, you can trace the pattern the queen followed to lay the eggs. It's also fun to guess where she went after she finished with a frame, and by using the youngest brood as a clue, you can usually figure out what direction she is moving in.

So much of beekeeping is educated guesswork, or looking for clues like a detective, and then make assumptions based on what you are seeing. The best beekeepers are like Sherlock Holmes; they quickly see the clues and they're able to properly deduce what is going on in the hive. It can take years to hone your skills to the point that you can instantly map the pieces of information you see, smell, and hear to what is going on in your hive. This is why it's invaluable for a new beekeeper, to watch someone with experience, especially when he or she points out what they are seeing.

Once, when I was still fairly new to beekeeping, I had the privilege of having Bob the Beekeeper, an old-timer who had been keeping more than one hundred hives for over forty years, over to my house to inspect my hives. I had just been in my hives four days before, and everything looked okay to me. I saw brood, the bees were making honey, and they seemed mellow and peaceful. But on the day I was with Bob and when we were still about ten feet away from the hives, he said, "Those hives are queenless." I was skeptical since I had just inspected them several days before. So one at a time, we opened both hives up, and masterfully he was able to show me rather quickly that both hives were indeed, queenless.

Bob was able to determine the hives were queenless by the sound the bees were making. He said, "Their buzz doesn't sound right. Listen. Both those hives are roaring." When he opened the hive up, he went immediately into the bottom deep and found multiple queen cells on several of the frames, proving that the old queen and half the worker bees had swarmed. The cells were mostly chewed away by the remaining worker bees, so Bob was able to guess the queens had hatched more than a week ago, and if one had survived her mating flight and was back in the hive, the bees would not have been acting "off," and instead, they would have been calmly working throughout the hive.

In *Outliers: The Story of Success*, Malcom Gladwell writes about the factors that contribute to high levels of success in everything from computer programming to sports. One aspect he discussed was the ten thousand hours rule, which essentially says that for someone to achieve expertise in any skill, they have to practice, and correctly repeat that skill for a total of ten thousand hours. This is certainly true in beekeeping, and is proven by how effortlessly the really experienced beekeepers are able to "just know" what is happening with their bees. For a new beekeeper, it might take forty or more minutes to inspect one hive. But for an experienced beekeeper, especially a commercial beekeeper who has thousands of hives and decades of experience, he can inspect a hive in less than sixty seconds. Why? Because he has perfected his mental checklist of what he needs to see, hear, and smell in order to tell if a hive is okay or has something wrong with it. This is one of the reasons beekeeping appeals to me: I can always be better. No matter how long I keep bees, or how much I know, there is always more for me to learn and additional ways I can improve. I like that the longer I keep bees the more attuned I will be to what's happening in my hives, and how my time with the bees is what will help me to be a better beekeeper.

Since the bees in my hive were using the new frames for making honey, that meant the queen was limited to laying her eggs on her original frames of drawn comb. Instead of filling the new comb they just built with honey, it would have been better if it were being filled with eggs and larvae. More bees means more honey, and by limiting where the queen was able to lay, the colony was limiting how big and how fast it could grow. The Badger said, "I don't like how the bees are blocking the queen by using those new frames for honey. Let's mix things up, so she doesn't get honey-bound."

"Honey-bound" is when the worker bees store nectar or honey in every available open honeycomb cell. The issue is that if there is limited room, or no room, for the queen to lay eggs, then the population of the hive will dwindle over a few months as there are not enough new bees hatching to replace all the ones that are dying of old age. Since a worker bee's life expectancy is about six weeks, the queen must constantly lay eggs to sustain the population needed for a colony's survival. In some cases, a healthy honey-bound hive will die, all from a lack of bees.

The Badger moved the two newly drawn out frames in closer to the middle, and then moved two frames of the bees' original comb out closer to the sides. So now, two of the colony's original combed frames were in the middle, followed by the two newly drawn out frames, followed by the other two original comb frames, leaving four of the newly purchased frames on the outer most positions on the right and the far left sides. The Badger's idea was that if the newly drawn out comb was next to the comb where the queen was laying, there was a greater chance she would move over and start laying in the new comb, before the worker bees had filled all the cells with nectar.

As the Badger was reassembling the hive, and moving the frames all around, I kept an eye on the frames to look for the queen and also to just see what the bees were doing. As he pulled out one of the last frames with comb, I saw a bee shaking back and forth as it was walking around the middle of the frame. When it would shake, its whole body would excitedly twitch and flutter. The Badger could tell that I was intently looking at something, so he looked down to see what had caught my eye. He smiled and said, "The waggle dance. Looks like somebody found some tasty flowers around here."

The waggle dance is another way bees communicate. A worker bee does a dance to tell her sisters about the location of a food source and gives directions for how to get there.

BEE NERD ALERT: The only other species that is able to give directions to a food source is humans.

If the food source is less than a football field away, the bee's dance is in a circle. If it's farther away, even three to five miles away, the dance is in a figure eight. The dance will communicate the quality of the food source and how much food there is to be had. Bees navigate by the position of the sun, and the directions given through the waggle dance is related to the sun's location in the sky. Inside the hive, for the purpose of the dance, the sun's position is always represented by straight up, or twelve o'clock. The bees will always do the waggle part of their dance, quickly shaking their body back and forth, in the same direction and at the same angle as the food source is in relation to the sun. If a bee is waggling at forty-five degrees facing left, then, outside of the hive, the food source is forty-five degrees from the sun, and to the left as you're leaving the hive. The waggle part functions as if it's a big neon-flashing arrow pointing in the direction to where the food is located and telling all the other bees to fly in that direction. As the bee does its dance and hits the angle and direction from the sun, it will waggle away. Much of the rest of the dance is a reenactment of the flight. It is almost like they are showing all the movements needed to fly to the food. It would be the same if people gave directions and instead of saying, "Turn left at the corner, then go straight for ten miles, then hang a right onto Maple Avenue," they mimic everything they would do to drive a car to get to their destination, such as how they'd move their hands on the steering wheel, move their feet like they're pressing the gas and brake, and flicking the turn signal up or down. The bees also cover distance by how long the waggle takes. The longer they shake and waggle their bodies, the farther away the food is. The more excited the bee, the better the food source. The whole goal of the dance is to get other bees excited about this location so they, too, will check it out and come back and tell more bees how great it is. Sometimes, more than one scout bee will come back to the hive to tell her hive mates about a food source. In these cases, it's like a dance-off, where the bees are competing to see who has the best food source. Comparing the dances to one another, the other foraging bees will choose a winner, and that food source will be the one that most of the foragers travel to and stock up on supplies for the hive.

Bees are able to give directions to food that is over five miles away, and they will be accurate to within one meter. Think about giving detailed directions and information about food that's waiting to be eaten by dancing, in the dark, without words or maps. All this from a bunch of bugs, while we humans, the more intelligent species, need to plug an address into our GPS and listen as it tells us step-by-step which way to go.

CHAPTER 9

•᷐•᷐•᷐•᷐•᷐

Death and an
Autopsy

IT'S ALWAYS AMAZING TO SEE a bee communicating with its
sisters, but watching a beekeeper communicate with other
beekeepers can be quite a sight to behold. Just like the various
movements a bee makes during its waggle dance, beekeepers
have specific gestures they use while telling a story. Holding
your arms up to make a big circle means, "The swarm was this
big." Leaning over and holding an imaginary box in your hands
while saying, "This sucker is heavy" represents how much
honey a hive produced, and the more someone struggles with
the words, "*is heavy*," the more jars of honey that hive produced.
Many beekeepers also like to use innocent-sounding words
when talking about their bees because they think it makes
them sound like they're cool. Since I'm anything but cool, I've
always found that many of these cool-kid phrases are like fin-

gernails on a chalkboard. For example, when a beekeeper says, "I went out to my bee yard today and got kissed a few times," they're saying they got stung a few times. Now, whoever thinks barbed stingers and venom is the same as pressing lips with a loved one must have a very bizarre home life. As for me, I'd rather call a sting a sting and a kiss a kiss.

Still even more annoying is when a beekeeper will refer to his bees as "his girls" and say something like, "My girls are really working. They've been coming and going all day. Can't wait to see how much honey my girls have made for me." If you refer to your bees as "your girls," it sounds like you're some kind of creepy bee pimp talking about his crew out hustling on the streets. "I checked on my girls today. They weren't too happy to see me. I ended up getting kissed a few times." What? Does child services know about this? Are you still allowed within one thousand feet of a playground after saying things like that? Yes, worker bees are female, but that does not give you the right to call them "your girls," or for you to talk like you're their proud pops. Needless to say, my bees are always "my bees," and if I'm in the mood to anthropomorphize something, I'll let a dog lick my face and call it love. Because calling dog slobber "love" makes more sense than calling sixty thousand stinging insects "your girls."

Summer went by fast, and my bees built out the full ten frames. I added a second deep on top, and was still trying to coax the bees to move up, build out the comb, and fill it with the honey they needed for winter. It was now late September, and I was looking for advice on what to do and what I should be seeing. It had been a few months since the Badger was over to look at my hive, and since then, things had really slowed down. I kept my feeder on, and every week instead of dumping the syrup, I would spray some syrup on the frames like Andy told me to do. I knew time was running out and before long the temperature would drop to freezing and the bees would not have the weather they needed to make honey. I was eager to talk with Andy and the other club experts so I could figure out what I should be doing. I was looking forward to this month's bee meeting so I could learn some real beekeeping skills over a cup of percolated coffee and a few stale cookies.

The night of the meeting, things were humming along and following the same schedule as the other meetings, until it was time for the Badger to ask, "How are your bees?" Only this time he said, "Let's talk about honey. How did everyone do this year?" Instantly, you could see that the regulars were uncomfortable with the question. The struggle for many of them was while they'd love to tell a good story about how many hundreds of pounds each of their hives had produced, they also didn't want to publicly say how much honey they had and were going to sell.

One of the benefits of beekeeping is that it is one of the few pastimes that can actually pay for itself, and that's significant when you consider all the beekeeping equipment and cool bee gadgets you end up buying. Even with a few hives, it is possible to get 150 or more pounds of honey, and with six hives or more, you could easily get 500+ pounds of honey a year. Depending on where you live, one pound of honey can sell for $10 or more. In New York City and the surrounding suburbs, a one-pound jar of local honey sells for between $15 and $20, which means that 500 pounds of honey can be worth $7,500 to $10,000.

Once a beekeeper's initial expenses for the hives and other equipment are paid off, the yearly costs of keeping bees drops significantly. The only ongoing expenses are for sugar (food), mite treatments, cool new bee gadgets, and if needed, new bees.

After a few years, each bottle of honey may only cost the bee-keeper a few dollars' worth of supplies, meaning that most of the money he makes per bottle is money in his pocket. However, the one part of this equation that is *not* included is time. Bee-keeping takes time, and bottling honey takes a lot of it; so if an hourly wage is included in an actual profit and loss calculation, then a beekeeper's profit is closer to pennies on every jar he sells. But still, when compared to a hobby like golf, which also takes a lot of time and a lot of money, it's nice to know that bee-keeping can put money back into your pocket instead of forcing you to pay any time you want to enjoy it. If you're a gol-fer, imagine if after a few years, you'd make enough money from playing recreational golf to pay for all of your clubs, balls, clothes, cool golf gadgets, and all your tee times. From a financial point of view when you compare the two, dollar-to-dollar, it's golf that seems like the crazier of the two hobbies.

Most of the guys in the club didn't want to announce how much honey their bees produced because they didn't want ev-eryone to do the math and figure out how much cash they could be bringing in. Andy in particular was super paranoid and he didn't want anyone to even know how many hives he had. He was especially worried that someone would report him to the IRS for not claiming all the cash he made from his honey. So when the Badger asked his question, Andy sat with his arms folded across his chest, then he slightly turned his head and out of the corner of his mouth he mumbled mostly to himself, "Not your business. Never know who's listening."

The thing was that all the members, including Andy, kept bees as a hobby, so it's not like anyone was making big money. Most were selling their honey out of their house and by word of mouth. A few set up a table at a neighborhood yard sale or a town fair, but everybody was selling the honey directly to their customers and not through any stores or local markets.

Yes, on paper you could calculate how much honey you could sell to become the next honey tycoon, but the reality is that you would have to sell thousands of pounds of honey at full retail price to get rich from selling honey. Realistically it's never going to happen for a backyard beekeeper, because year after year, you'd need tens of thousands of customers all paying full retail price for the tens of thousands of jars of honey your bees would have to produce in your backyard. It can't be done, which is why commercial beekeepers sell their honey at wholesale prices to supermarket chains that are equipped to sell thousands of jars of honey.

Nonetheless, a husband and wife who were not fans of reality once joined the club with dreams of getting rich from keeping bees. The Poseurs were both in their mid-thirties and they had that crunchy granola, wannabe artist, "I'm smarter than you," vibe about them. They liked to talk, a lot, about themselves. Like characters from a made-for-TV movie, they were tired of the corporate world. They wanted "to get back to nature, to simpler times, and farm the land." The only thing was, they wanted to realize their dream in their backyard, while living in the New Jersey suburbs.

They had spent the good part of a year watching every YouTube video they could find on beekeeping. Afterward, they would tell everyone that they knew everything there was to know about beekeeping. Most longtime beekeepers recommend that you slowly grow your beekeeping operation, start with a few hives, and then increase by a few every year. Still, Mr. and Mrs. Poseur went all in, because after all, they were experts. They bought equipment for thirty-six hives, veils, smokers, commercial-grade honey-extracting equipment, honey jars. They even designed and printed their own labels for all the honey they were going to sell. And they bought all of this before they ever had a single bee.

When it came time to buy their bees, they bought twelve nucs for their thirty-six hives. Since they had learned that bees can create their own queen, they had decided they would take the standard-size starter colony of bees—the five-frame nuc—and split each nuc three times to have enough bees to fill all of their thirty-six hives. They brought the twelve nucs home and immediately put them into twelve hives. Three weeks later, after the bees had started to expand into the other frames in the hive, they took half of the frames with bees on them and put them into twelve new hives. Then after another three weeks, they took one frame from each of the twenty-four hives to fill their remaining twelve hives. By splitting the bees this way, they said they were able to save $3,600, which is how they justified buying all the other equipment. Plus they said, "Buying it all at once saved us a bundle on shipping."

They had decided that each of their hives would produce ninety pounds of honey, so they would be harvesting over 3,000 pounds of honey—3,240 pounds to be exact—but they preferred to use 3,000 pounds, "just in case a few hives didn't quite produce the ninety pounds we're expecting." Their plan was to sell each bottle at $20 apiece, which would make them $60,000 and allow the missus to quit her office job and start living the dream of being a suburban backyard, back-to-nature farmer. Then the following year, they would double their hives again, get 6,000 pounds of honey and make $120,000, allowing *both* Mr. and Mrs. to quit their office jobs and work full-time at their backyard-farming operation.

They had it all figured out, and the only way they could have developed a plan like this was by smoking something other than pine needles in their smoker. First, trying to put seventy-two hives in a suburban backyard makes about as much sense as trying to have seventy-two toddlers quietly sit still in your backyard. Any town official or beekeeping authority would provide a laundry list of reasons why this is simply not a good idea. Second, even if they were able to produce 6,000 pounds of honey a year, where would they sell it? If they sold it every day of the year, they'd have to sell 16.5 bottles a day, every day, 365 days a year to make $120,000. Unless the plan was to convert an old ice cream truck into a honey truck and drive around all day, every day, I'm not sure how anyone could sell 16 bottles of honey a day, 365 days a year. Plus, I'm not sure how big the honey market is on Christmas and New Year's Day.

If they were going to sell it on the weekends at farmers' markets, then they'd have to sell 115 bottles every weekend for fifty-two consecutive weekends, meaning they'd need to find fifty-two locations that would each attract 115 people to it who would each be willing to pay $20 for a jar of honey. They also didn't factor in any of the added costs they'd incur from having to pay for things to sell all their honey, like the booth space at the farmers' markets, or gas for the ice cream turned honey truck they'd be driving around every day. They continued to spark up their smoker and dream about all the money they were going to make, but they made one fatal flaw: they had no idea what they were doing.

Beekeeping, like so many other things in life, is something that is best learned from the experience of others. If you're brand new to something and think you know better than everyone else, then chances are you will probably fail. In the

United States, people have been successfully keeping bees since the colonists first brought bees to North America; so learning what has worked over the past few centuries is probably more reliable than thinking you can find a better way. The second rule of beekeeping that applies to so many other things in life is: if YouTube is your primary source for information, then you will definitely fail. While YouTube may be great to watch to see how to perform a skill like nailing something together or changing a tire, it is not a great place to go for advice on how to learn a craft like beekeeping. This is especially true if you're not looking at people's credentials and listening to anyone and everyone on the Web who has posted a video. Obese Eddie might have a large presence on the Web, and at the all-you-can-eat buffet, but that doesn't mean he should be your go-to guy for bee advice.

The Poseurs' life as beekeepers was short-lived. As you can imagine, most of the nuc splits they made ended up killing both sets of bees. In other cases, some of the frames they moved to a new hive didn't actually contain any brood, just dark, capped honey. They were also trying to work as cheaply as possible, so they didn't feed their bees, severely limiting the growth or killing most of the other colonies. Out of the thirty-six hives they thought they'd have, six made it to the fall. But, because they didn't want to feed any of their hives, by the end of winter they, too, were dead.

Beekeeping is not something you're going to learn from YouTube. It may be easier to sit at home and watch videos, but if you really want to learn what you should be doing, you're going to have to go out and learn from local beekeepers. Beekeeping is not something you can do while sitting on the couch. It requires active participation, and just like the lottery commercial says, you have to be in it to win it.

No one answered the Badger's question about honey with an exact amount. Instead, it was a lot of "pretty goods," and, "about the same as last year." Then someone called out, "Enough so that my wife said I could keep keeping bees and come to these meetings." Everyone was laughing, and then Rusty stood up and started banging a hive tool on the table as he said, "Attention, attention members." Everyone settled down and then Rusty said, "It don't matter how much honey you got. Don't sell it and don't give it away. Keep all your honey. Store it in a safe place. Soon enough it's gonna be more valuable than paper money. Save your honey, 'cause when the governments fall and we're all living in anarchy, you can trade your honey for goods and services." Then he sat back down, happy he had enlightened his fellow beekeepers.

The Badger, always up for poking fun at Rusty, said, "So, Rusty, is that what you've been doing with all your honey for the past sixty plus years? Storing it and waiting for the governments to fall?" To which Rusty replied, "Not all of it, just enough to get me by when the time comes." And before the Badger could jump in with a follow-up question, Rusty said, "And with the rest of it I make mead. 'Cause people always gonna need a stiff drink." As he was saying his last few words, Rusty reached down into a bag and pulled out two blue wine bottles and punctuated his sentence with a bang as he popped them onto the table. All the members started to applaud and the Badger said, "Meeting's adjourned. Grab some cups and let's toast the governments. Long may they not fall!"

Making mead may be easy, and a good use for your honey. But making mead that actually tastes good is a talent. Rusty didn't seem to have a talent for taste, as he was only interested in how strong he could make his mead. Mead, like other naturally fermented beverages, such as beer and wine, get its alcohol content from the yeast. Basically, the yeast eats the sugar and the by-product is alcohol. But brewed beverages have a natural limit to how much alcohol they can have. As the concentration of alcohol reaches somewhere between 14 and 18 percent, it becomes toxic to the yeast, killing it and stopping the production of alcohol. But Rusty found a way around it, and his mead had a much higher percentage of alcohol. Rusty looked back to the original colonists for a solution to turbocharge his mead. The American colonists used to make a drink called Applejack, which was a strong alcoholic drink produced from apples. They would first make hard apple cider and then use a process called "freeze distillation" to increase the drink's proof. After making a barrel full of hard apple cider, they'd sit the barrel outside during the winter. As the cider froze, they would remove the ice from the barrel. Since water freezes before alcohol, they were removing the water and keeping the alcohol, which meant the more ice they removed, the stronger the Applejack would be. Rusty used this same principle on his mead. After his mead had reached its natural, maximum alcohol content, Rusty would pour it into a plastic bottle and then toss it in the freezer. After it was frozen, he would turn the plastic bottle upside down and sit it in a Mason jar. As the mead started to warm up, the alcohol would liquefy first, and drip out. Keeping a watchful eye, Rusty would remove the plastic bottle after all the alcohol had dripped into the Mason jar, but before any of the still frozen water had melted. The end result was a high-octane mead that was probably close to eighty-proof.

Rusty's freeze distilled mead tasted like charcoal lighter fluid with a hint of honey. Everyone had a few sips of it, but no one could take a drink without coughing. It was like drinking kerosene; your body knew you shouldn't be drinking it and was trying to tell you, "No, this stuff is *not* good!" The more people gagged and gasped for air, the prouder Rusty was. He believed "the bigger the kick, the better the drink." It was almost like he wanted to be the only one who could drink it so he could keep it all to himself. Either that, or he enjoyed watching everyone suffer as they tried to drink it. Since Rusty had created such a scene with his concoction, no one was really interested in talking about bees. Most of these guys had known each other for a few decades and they were more interested in having some laughs and reliving old times. Watching a room full of people who had bonded over a bug made me feel great about the club. I was happy knowing that being a beekeeper meant more than just having bees; it was a way to make many good friends. As the new guy, I didn't feel it was my place to try to butt into the conversation and steer it to my bees, so I waved good night to everyone and headed home.

Over the next few weeks, as September faded into October, I kept checking on my bees, but nothing was happening. They had stopped taking the sugar syrup and they never moved up into the top box. One Thursday night, about two weeks before the next bee meeting, just as I had gotten home from work, the doorbell rang. It was the Badger. He said, "I was headed over to my girlfriend's house, so I thought I'd stop by and see how you're doing." We walked out to the backyard, and as soon as he saw my hive he said, "Why's your feeder still on? You should have taken that off months ago. It's too cold to have it on now." I told him that I had kept it on because the bees still had not drawn out the top deep.

The Badger shook his head. "It's too late now. Take the feeder off, and also take the top deep off. You don't want the bees to have too much space, because it makes it harder for them to stay warm." Since it was dark outside, and it's always best to open your hive during the day, we didn't do it then, and I assured him that I would do it right away.

I was disappointed that I had made such a dumb mistake. I was also a bit frustrated that the Badger and everyone else always waited to tell me what I needed to do *after* I had already made a mistake. I was going to the bee meetings so that I could learn best practices, but it seemed like the experienced beekeepers liked to hear about the mistakes I had made, then tell me how they would have done it differently. When I'd ask questions about what I should be doing, their responses were never as detailed and thorough as when they were dissecting what I had done wrong.

That night, after the Badger had left, we were hit with an arctic blast, the temperatures dropped below freezing, and the wind was howling down from the North. I was worried about going into my hive while the weather was so cold, so I waited several days until the weather climbed back up above 45°F. When I walked over, I didn't see any activity. None of the bees were flying. I put on my veil, lit my smoker, and took the top off the hive.

I could see that none of my bees were in my feeder, and the level of syrup had not moved since I last checked it. I took the feeder off with the help of my hive tool and poured the syrup into the yard. I was thinking that Andy probably would tell me to pour it into a bucket and save it for spring, but I really didn't want to keep a bucket of sugar syrup in my garage all winter. I puffed my smoker so a cloud of cool white smoke washed across the top of the deep. I didn't see any bees, but I wanted to make sure I smoked them. As I looked between all the frames, I still couldn't see any bees, so I put my hive tool between my boxes and popped them apart. Then I removed the top deep. I looked down into the remaining deep, and still nothing. The hive was very quiet. I puffed some smoke down between the frames, but there wasn't any of the normal buzzing I'd usually hear whenever I smoked the hive. Now I was worried. I put my face down to the frames so I could look down deep between the frames, and there was absolutely no movement. I thought I'd better get a closer look and started removing the frames. I started on the left side with frame number ten, then number nine. That's when I saw them. My bees were motionless on the bottom of the hive. The more frames I took out, the clearer I could see that all my bees were laying on the bottom of the hive. Finally, I had to accept that my hive was dead. All of my bees were dead.

After I had all the frames out, I removed the bottom deep so all that remained was the bottom board of the hive. It was covered in dead bees. I brought the bottom board into my garage, found a paper bag, and poured the dead bees into the bag. I wasn't sure what I was going to do with them, but I wanted to, needed to, do something. Next, I put the hive back together, very aware at how quiet it was, which made me realize when your hive is filled with bees, how much life energy is buzzing all around you.

No matter how long you've been keeping bees, any time a hive dies, it's a sad day. Seeing frame after frame of empty comb where so many thousands of bees had once lived is eerily quiet. I was upset and angry with myself for not taking better care of my bees. I got in to beekeeping because I wanted to succeed and be good at something, but I had failed. I felt like I was entrusted with keeping my bees safe and now they were dead. I wasn't sure what I was going to do next, but I did know that I wanted to make sure that this never happened again.

When a hive dies, the only thing you can do is use it as a learning experience so that you can become a better beekeeper, and hopefully learn something that will help you better care for your future bees. The best thing to do when a hive dies is to do an autopsy on it to figure out what happened. Looking back at my first hive, I can now see that all the warning signs were there, only I didn't see them. The first clue was how slowly the bees were building up in the summer. This was a sign that the queen was at the end of her life and she was starting to slow down. As queens get older, they are running out of eggs, so they cannot lay as much as they could when they were younger. That's one of the reasons why I was always able to find the queen; there were not that many bees in the hive, so she was easy to spot. Second, the bees storing nectar in the new comb they built instead of the queen laying eggs in them was another sign that something was up with the queen. Third, the bees stopped taking the syrup. I have found that when a hive becomes disinterested in free food, and the bees refuse to take the sugar syrup on their hive, it's a sign that the hive will not survive. Sometimes it means that the queen is failing, or has died, and the worker bees are not interested in storing food in the same way that a healthy hive is. It's almost like the bees know that without a queen the colony is not going to last, so they lose interest in storing food for the future. Last, when I was going frame by frame, I never saw any brood, which is the surefire way to know that the queen is dead or gone. In hindsight, what I should have done was purchased a new queen to replace the old one before it was too late. This would have brought a resurgence to the number of bees in the hive and they could have built up and would have been ready for winter.

It's important to note that bees never die from the cold; they always die from something else. For instance, keeping a feeder full of liquid on top of the hive is never good because it brings extra moisture into a hive, and moisture in a hive will kill bees. In the winter you are supposed to vent the top of your hives to make sure any condensation can escape. Otherwise, the condensation will stick to the inside inner cover, and as it forms into water droplets, it will drip onto the bees, and since the bees cannot dry themselves off, the moisture will kill them. In my case, the colony died because of the sheer lack of bees; their numbers were just too small for them to stay warm. Leaving the feeder on for too long only exacerbated the already bad situation.

My experience with my first hive is exactly why every beekeeper and every beekeeping manual will always recommend that you start with two hives. Since I only had one hive, I had nothing to compare it to. If I had had two hives, then I could have compared them to one another and I would have seen that one hive didn't have the same amount of bees in it as the other hive did. Additionally, if you have two hives, you can use resources from one to use in the other. So, for example, if one hive is light on brood, then you can take a frame of brood from the other hive to equalize the population in both hives. Most important, by having two hives, and by seeing the similarities and differences between them, it's easier to learn about bees, and that will translate into you becoming a better beekeeper faster by being able to spot an issue while you still have time to correct it, and have a greater chance to keep your hives alive.

But my hive was dead. I realized that I needed to make a decision. Did I still want to keep bees, or did I want to give up? As I thought about what it was like to stand over my hive, holding a frame with a few thousand bees on it, watching them peacefully go about their business, I knew I was hooked and there was no turning back. I also accepted the fact that my first attempt failed because I didn't know what I was doing and if I was committed to becoming a beekeeper, I had to learn how to be a beekeeper.

CHAPTER 10

•°•°•°•°•

Varroa the Destructor

THE MOST SERIOUS AND DESTRUCTIVE killer of our honeybees, aka the European honeybee, BEE NERD WORD: *Apis mellifera* is a parasitic mite called Varroa destructor. In the 1960s Varroa began infesting the European honeybee colonies that had been brought into Asia, and has since spread worldwide and has become the leading cause of colony losses. These parasites depend entirely on bees to live, as they latch their mouthparts on to the surface of a larvae, pupae, or adult bees to feed. If you don't treat for varroa mites your bees will die, and dead bees cannot make honey.

For millennia, Varroa destructor had lived exclusively on another type of bee, the Asian bee. BEE NERD WORD: *Apis cerana* Bees that are part of the *Apis* genus share many of the same traits and physiological characteristics, but the Asian bee and the European honeybee are different animals as distinct from one another as a fox and a coyote. Varroa doesn't kill Asian bee colonies, which is true with most parasite-host relationships. The Asian bee adapted to Varroa and learned how to control the Varroa population in a hive. Additionally, Varroa had adapted so it doesn't overwhelm its Asian bee host population, and limits where the mother mites will lay their eggs.

All of this changed in the 1960s as Varroa jumped species and started to appear in European honeybee colonies. In just three decades, as infected honeybees came in contact with healthy honeybees, Varroa destructor has spread across the globe and is now a threat to European honeybees everywhere they live. There are currently only two places in the world that do not have Varroa, Australia and Newfoundland, both of which are obviously surrounded by ocean. However, New Zealand and Hawaii do have mites, which is why Australia and Newfoundland have to be extra diligent to keep mites off their shores.

Varroa has forever changed how we keep bees. If you talk with someone who kept bees pre-V, they will tell you how easy it was, especially compared to today. Back then, you set up your hives, put your honey supers on in the summer, made sure the bees had enough food in the fall, then just let them be until spring. Now, most beekeepers spend a great deal of time and expense to control Varroa in their hive. Beekeepers are so consumed with fighting Varroa that the big joke is that beekeepers talk more about mites than they do about bees.

Nowadays the question all beekeepers ask themselves is not *if* their hives have Varroa, but *how many* Varroa are in their hives. Varroa mites are the biggest threat to beekeeping because bee colonies that are overrun with mites are fighting to stay alive and are not healthy enough to produce honey or pollinate our crops.

Varroa destructor is a breeding machine. The adult females have two life stages: phoretic and reproductive. The phoretic stage is when the mites spread from colony to colony, by attaching themselves to an adult bee. When a bee from an infected colony comes in contact with a bee from a non-infected colony, such as on a flower or other food source, the mite will hop onto the other bee. The size of a Varroa mite compared to the size of a bee would be comparable to a Frisbee-size tick on you. The mites can be seen when they are on a bee's back, but mites also attach themselves to the underside of bees where it is much more difficult for the beekeeper to see them. Similar to a tick, the mites are feeding off the bee by sucking out its nutrients. Until recently, it was believed that the mites were consuming the bee's blood. **BEE NERD WORD:** Actually this is *hemolymph*, a fluid equivalent to blood that circulates in invertebrates. However, new and recent research now shows that the mites are actually living off the bee's fat body, which is sort of like a bee's liver.

BEE NERD ALERT: Bees don't have veins and arteries, instead their internal organs float around in free-flowing hemolymph.

Regardless of what the mites are sucking out of the bees, as they hop from bee to bee they are also spreading disease in much the same way a mosquito or tick spreads diseases to people. Only, the diseases spread by Varroa infect bees, never people. And while honeybee viruses have always existed, it wasn't until Varroa started spreading them that these viruses became so widespread and deadly to the global bee population.

When Varroa mites were first reaching across the globe, colonies could tolerate much higher infestations than they can today. Back then, colonies could survive with 10 percent to 20 percent of the bees being infected; but now, because of the diseases the mites carry, colonies can only tolerate having 1 percent to 2 percent of the bees being infected. These diseases are a major factor in the overall bee death we are seeing. One of the diseases the mites are spreading is called deformed wing virus. DWV stops a bee's wings from developing properly, and it looks like a bee's wings are shriveled up or melted. DWV prevents a bee from flying, limits the bee's contribution to the hive, and causes premature death. Another virus the mites spread is acute bee paralysis virus, which is exactly what it sounds like. It causes uncontrollable tremors, an inability to fly, and an early death for the infected bees. In much the same way that you can control malaria or the zika virus by killing the mosquitoes that spread it, by controlling the Varroa mite population, beekeepers can also control the spread of these deadly diseases.

Varroa mites are an even bigger concern when they enter their reproductive stage. Once the mites are inside the hive, they make their way to the brood chamber, as they reproduce exclusively on honeybee brood. The mites prefer larvae that are about five days old, and are only one day away from being capped so it can pupate into an adult bee. The mite will scoot into a cell and hide under the larvae, waiting for the bees to seal the mite in with the bee larvae.

Three days after the cell is capped, the adult female mite, or momma mite, **BEE NERD WORD:** *foundress* mite lays her first egg, which is male. After the male egg is laid, the momma mite will then lay an egg every thirty hours. All of these subsequent eggs are females. After the mites hatch, they all feed on the bee pupa, sucking nutrients from the developing bee and also infecting it with any diseases the mites are carrying. Since these bees don't have all of the necessary nutrients needed for their proper development, another impact of the mites is that when the bees hatch, they are not as strong as an uninfected bee. Think about prenatal nutrition and how important it is for a developing baby. Now imagine a parasite sucking these nutrients away from a developing baby and the lasting impact it would have once that baby is born. The end result is a colony of bees that is comprised of weakened adults infected with various viruses.

It takes mites six days to reach sexual maturity, and while still inside the cell with the bee pupa, the female mites mate with their brother. When the honeybee finally emerges from its cell, any surviving mated female mites exit the cell on the honeybee's body, while the male mite and any immature females die inside the cell. Depending on whether they are workers or drones, honeybees will emerge twelve to fifteen days after being capped. On average, about one to two new mites, along with the momma mite, emerge from each worker brood cell, and two to four new mites, along with the momma mite, are released from each drone brood cell.

When Varroa infects Asian bee colonies, the mites only lay eggs in drone brood, which is why they never over-reproduce and kill off the whole colony. The bees are able to control the mite population by limiting the amount of drone comb they build. Unfortunately, while Varroa does still favor drone brood in European honeybee hives, they also go after worker brood, which is a major issue for population control.

Since the Asian bee is smaller than the European honeybee, some people initially thought if they could develop smaller

European honeybees, this would control Varroa infestation. The bigger size of European honeybees is in part a man-made phenomenon. Beekeepers realized that the size of the honeycomb cells impacts the size of the bees. Back in 1857, when Johannes Mehring first invented a machine that could manufacture embossed wax foundation, others took his idea and experimented with different-size cells to see if they could grow a bigger and better bee. Of course, they needed to figure out the perfect size, the sweet spot between bigger and still efficient. If you think about bees as airplanes, then think about finding the sweet spot between having a plane big enough to carry more cargo (nectar), and how much fuel it requires to run (efficiency). If a plane is too big, it's not as efficient because it consumes too much fuel to operate. But if it's too small, then it cannot carry much cargo. The standard beekeeping supply companies settled on a cell size of 5.4 mm, which is the standard cell size of the foundation we use today. (If you look at feral colonies, where all the comb is built from scratch and not following factory-produced foundation, the cells tend to be slightly smaller than what you will find in a man-made hive.)

Now, with the Varroa problem, the thought was that since Varroa's original host—the Asian bee—was smaller, and since man has been growing super-size bees, we should perhaps try to develop smaller bees. So some beekeepers started using small cell foundation, which uses a 4.9-mm cell size, to see if smaller worker bees would incent the mites to only lay in the drone comb. Unfortunately, like everything about Varroa, it was not as easy as this, and the smaller cells did not have an impact on controlling Varroa like so many had hoped.

Beekeepers and researchers continued to try to find an effective treatment to control Varroa. The main issue with finding an effective mite treatment is that it requires killing a bug that lives on a bug. So any treatment needs to be deadly to the mites, but harmless to the bees. If it were a bug living on a mammal, like a flea on a dog, then developing a treatment would be much easier. Also, since honey is consumed by people, all treatments have to also be safe for humans, which means careful attention needs to be taken to ensure any treatment does not stay in the hive, is absorbed by the wax, and does not cause any ill effects or health issues.

The first compounds to combat Varroa were Apistan and CheckMite. Both of these synthetic miticides seemed like they were the answer, but in both instances the mites developed resistance to them, and after a few years these products proved to be virtually ineffective. Additionally, they were both very strong pesticides that contained some pretty nasty stuff, and were bad for the bees. Again, it was the bug on a bug dilemma.

Since the hard chemicals, or synthetic miticides, were short-lived in their effectiveness, people started to look at natural treatments to fight the mites. The first, and for a time, the most popular natural "treatment" was powdered sugar. The premise was that if you can get the bees to groom themselves, they will also pick off the mites. To accomplish this, you open your hives, and using a flour sifter, you rain down several cups of the powdered sugar onto your bees. Since it's sugar, it won't hurt the bees, and since it sticks to their fur, they will clean it off one another. The theoretical end result was that the powdered sugar, along with all the mites, will fall out of the hive through the screened bottom floorboard, and then you will have a mite-free hive. The big problem with using powdered sugar to treat for mites is that it doesn't work. Not at all, not even a little bit, not one iota. Several scientific studies have shown that using powdered sugar is as useful for controlling mites as doing absolutely nothing at all.

Other types of treatments used naturally derived chemicals, which are made from natural substances, only applied in higher dosages. For example, thymol is produced from the oils of the thyme plant. Another treatment, formic acid, is naturally found in honey and in honeybee colonies. The main issue with these treatments is that they really stink, and their vapor packs a wallop. Also, because the vapor is so strong, the treatments are tough on the bees. (Again, the bug on the bug conundrum.)

Currently, the most effective treatment is Apivar, which is a man-made miticide that has a very high success rate. The big issue with Apivar is how much it costs. To treat two hives, it will cost you $35. Also, most beekeepers have to treat several times a year, and the Apivar mite treatments do add up, especially when you have a lot more than two hives. Many commercial beekeepers are spending tens of thousands of dollars a year on Apivar treatments, which makes it more difficult for them to make a living from keeping bees.

Another treatment that is being used around the globe is oxalic acid, which is a naturally occurring substance found in some vegetables, like rhubarb and spinach. Oxalic acid is also commonly sold at hardware stores as wood bleach, so it's cheap and readily available. There are three ways to apply oxalic acid: (1) Mix it with sugar syrup and dribble it on your bees in the hive; (2) put the sugar syrup–oxalic acid mixture in a spray bottle and spray the bees; and (3) sublimation, otherwise known as vaporization, or vaporizing the hive.

The first time I heard about oxalic acid was at the first and only Natural Beekeeping course that I ever attended. It was being held at a biodynamic farm just a thirty-minute drive from my house. The course was team-taught by several people, some with more bee knowledge than others. They all had varying interpretations of what "natural" meant, and some of these views were, shall we say, bordering on the extreme. Before I continue, let me make one thing clear: I believe that everything should be as natural as possible, as it's better for everyone and everything. However, I also believe that you need science to back up and support what you do, otherwise it's just superstitious mumbo jumbo. For example, one instructor was explaining that her bees "know" where she needs to be stung, and when the bees sting her, they are sacrificing themselves to help her. If her back is hurting, BAM! She gets stung in her back. When her knee is sore, BAM! A few stings to her knee. But she said one thing in particular that will stick with me forever: "Every time I have needed to *see* something, really *see* something in my life, the bees have stung me in my *eyes!*" As I processed her words, I realized that "every time" meant that this had happened to her more than once! MORE THAN ONCE!!! And, "in my eyes" meant, IN-MY-EYES!!!! I thought, and still think, that if I get stung in my eye, I may give up beekeeping and instead start collecting soft and fuzzy teddy bears.

At this point during the course, alarm bells were going off in my head. I am skeptical by nature, but now I was on high alert. When the topic of honeybee pests came up, there was a discussion of biodynamic farming principles, which included—and I am not making this up—the following instructions: Collect as many of the dead Varroa mites as you can, and during specific full moons throughout the year, you burn them to an ash, then sprinkle the burned Varroa ash around your hive so as to frighten and keep away any remaining mites. The belief is that no animal wants to cross over its own dead, so when they encounter an ash line made from their own kind, they will not want to cross it. This is not exactly the type of mite treatment you read about in any of the scientific journals or hear that commercial beekeepers are using, and it made about as much sense to me as wearing aluminum foil on your head to get a better Wi-Fi signal.

It was also at this same natural beekeeping course that I first heard about oxalic acid, but because it was discussed alongside torching pests by moonlight, I didn't exactly embrace what was being said. To make matters worse, at that time, oxalic acid was not approved as a treatment for Varroa in the United States, and technically it was illegal to use in your hive. So hearing the words "illegal" and "wood bleach" didn't give me the confidence that this was a scientifically proven way to deal with Varroa. Further, when it was explained that you vaporize the wood bleach with a metal wand powered by a car battery, and you have to wear a respirator because the fumes could melt your lungs, I was thinking the only way this could sound more like Hogwarts was if you also sprinkled in some pixie dust and porcupine quills.

The reality is that oxalic acid works because it hurts the mites, but not the bees. While the research is not conclusive on all the ways it impacts the mites, it seems like the acid is absorbed by the mites' soft footpads, burning the footpads during the process, which also causes the mites to lose their grip on the bees and fall off. Note that oxalic acid only reaches the phoretic mites attached to adult bees, it does not reach mites in capped brood cells.

While using oxalic acid as a treatment for Varroa is relatively new and legal in the United States, it has been used for quite a while in Europe and Canada. I realized that if entire countries were relying on oxalic acid to keep their bees alive, this treatment was a lot less of a magical potion cooked up in the moonlight and actually had some solid science behind it. As I thought about colonies less able to tolerate Varroa, the need to alternate Apivar with other treatments, plus everything I had been reading, it seemed like all of these things were pointing me in the same direction, and "showing me" what I needed to do. I needed to start using oxalic acid. And, I would like to add, I "saw" this without having to get stung in the eye!

Even with all the information available on how deadly Varroa is to honeybees, and even though every beekeeping authority will tell you to treat, and even though every commercial beekeeper that makes their living from bees is treating multiple times a year for Varroa, there are still beekeepers who want to be treatment-free.

The treatment-free crowd believes that any type of miticide is bad, and they do not want to put anything "unnatural" into one of their hives, even if it means their bees will die without it. The thought is that bees are part of nature, so the only solution should be natural selection. The major issue that these people are overlooking is that Varroa destructor is *not* a natural parasite of European honeybees, so trying to naturally fight an unnatural enemy doesn't really work. Many of the treatment-free believers say that the only way European honeybees are going to survive is if they learn to live with Varroa in the same way the Asian bee has learned. The issue with this belief is that evolution takes thousands upon thousands of years, and a few people with just a couple of untreated hives are not going to have an impact on an entire species. Instead, what you're going to do is kill your bees and further infect other colonies in a three- to five-mile radius from your hives.

Since on average, honeybees will travel up to three miles from their hive, it is likely they come in contact with other bees from other hives that are traveling in an overlapping three-mile radius. Since people tend to live where other people live, that means one beekeeper's hives are almost always in proximity to another beekeeper's hives, and the result is what beekeepers call "mite bombs." A mite bomb is a hive that collapses from an exceptionally high mite load. These hives usually die in the late fall, after other beekeepers have treated for mites and think they are sending their hives into winter with a low to no mite count. However, one of two things will happen with the mite bomb hives. Either the surviving mite-infested bees abscond from the hive and find their way into the treated hives, or bees from the treated hives find the mite bomb hives, and since it is dead, they rob the honey from the mite bomb, and bring a lot more than just honey back to their own hives. The result is hives that were virtually mite free in September are exploding with mites in early winter causing many of these hives to die off. Dennis van Engelsdorp, a professor of entomology at the University of Maryland, and project director for the Bee Informed Partnership, said, "If you're opposed to treating, kill your bees and those mites because they're going to die anyway, and it's better for you to do that *before* they spread those mites to everyone else."

The treatment-free beekeepers are the anti-vaccine people of the bee world. They are not looking at science and they are not thinking about how their actions will impact the overall honeybee population. Further, what they are doing is cruel and unnecessarily stressful to their bees. Imagine if you had a dog that was covered with ticks or infested with fleas. Would you let your dog naturally find a way to deal with the infestation? Would you believe it's better to let half the dogs around the world die so the surviving dogs could build up a tolerance to ticks and fleas? Carrying this scenario one more step, if your home became infested and overrun with ticks and fleas, would you find a natural way to deal with them? The answer to all of these questions is of course a big N-O! If your dog was infested and its life was in danger, you would do everything you could to save your dog, and as a precautionary measure, you'd probably start using the strongest flea and tick collar you could buy. It's also safe to guess that if someone's home was filled with any kind of insect infestation they'd use the strongest stuff on the market that has been proven to work and they'd kill every bug as fast as they could. So if it's okay for dogs, and for people, why is it not okay for bees?

All beekeepers are passionate about doing what they think is best for their bees. Even the all-natural, anti-treatment bee-keepers want to believe they're doing the right thing; it's just they are using unreliable and nonscientific sources to base their decisions on. Other times they are anthropomorphizing their bees and projecting human emotions and believing their bees will react the same way humans would react. To be a successful beekeeper, you have to think of the whole hive as the living or-ganism and each bee is a cell in the larger organism. That's actually how the bees *do* think about it. They live their life for the benefit of the hive, not for themselves; that's why bees are willing to sacrifice their lives when they sting you to protect the hive, and why sister bees take care of their younger siblings instead of producing their own. **BEE NERD WORD:** Bees and ants are *eusocial*, meaning each individual puts the hive's best interest above its own interests.

A good example of how a beekeeper has to think about the hive and not any individual bee is when testing for Varroa. To test for mites, you have to scoop up half a cup of bees, which is about three hundred bees, and put them in an alcohol washer. The washer is basically two peanut butter jars that uses a special cap to screw both jars together with a screen between them. You put rubbing alcohol in one of the jars, and then dump in the half a cup of bees. Once the bees are in, you screw the other jar on top. Then you shake. And shake and shake, for about one minute. Afterward, you turn the washer over. The alcohol and the mites all flow into the bottom jar, but the bees stay in the top jar because they are too big to fit through the screen. Then, you count how many mites you see floating in the alcohol. Ideally, you never want to see more than two mites at any one time, and the more you see, the more urgent it is to treat your hive.

Without testing for mites, there is no way to know how many mites are in your hive, if past treatments are working, or if your hive is about to collapse because it literally contains more mites than bees. There are some beekeepers that don't want to test, as they feel bad for killing some of their bees. While it certainly isn't an enjoyable procedure, you always have to ask yourself, is it better to kill three hundred bees, or an entire hive of sixty thousand bees?

The Varroa destructor is aptly named as it could destroy so much if it is not stopped. Varroa has made life difficult for the honeybee, and beekeepers must continue to do everything they can to stop this pest until it is no longer a threat. Until that time, we can never give up; it's not an option, it's our responsibility to care for our bees, keeping them healthy, any way that we can.

Unfortunately, procedures like testing for mites are taken out of context by animal right activists who like to hold it up and say that beekeepers are cruel, uncaring, and enjoy killing their bees. They would rather see no intervention—no killing

This hive was my all-time biggest honey producer. It produced 340 pounds of honey in three months— 100 pounds for itself and 240 pounds for me! The white boxes are honey supers (my honey) and the gray boxes are for the bees. The yellow and orange stripes are secondary entrances.

THE LANGSTROTH HIVE

(A) The bottom board and entrance to the hive
(B) The bottom deep box, called the *brood box*, a.k.a. the *nursery*
(C) The top deep box, where bees store honey for themselves, a.k.a. the *pantry*
(D) The honey super is for the beekeeper's honey, and it is put on after the top deep is filled with honey
(E) The inner cover, which is notched in the center to allow for heat and moisture to escape
(F) The outer cover or hive top

In each box there are ten frames; each one lines up with the frames above and below it.

This is a smoker that is used to keep bees calm. People have been using smoke for tens of thousands of years while going into beehives. Behind the smokers are several of my beehives.

My son, Miles, helping extract the honey by hand-spinning the frames of honey in our Maxant extractor.

My wife, Sofie, the very first time she went into a hive with me. It was her idea to get a photo of herself holding a frame of bees barehanded to show her mom and sisters. This is also the exact moment I fell in love with her.

Pulled directly from a hive, this is one frame of freshly produced honey. Each frame can hold up to seven pounds.

My daughters, Svea and Ella, sitting atop our 2019 honey harvest: 1,150 pounds, or 96 gallons, an average of 128 pounds from each of our nine hives.

Here is a bee loaded down with pollen. Bees have "saddlebags" on their back legs, allowing them to carry two large balls of pollen back to the hive.

In the midst of the worker bees is the queen bee. Note how much longer her body is compared to the worker bees' bodies and how her tail looks so different.

These are two queen cells, which are located at the bottom of a frame.
Note how the size and texture is similar to a peanut in the shell.
Queen cells at the bottom of a frame are called *swarm cells*,
as colonies build them in this location when they want to swarm.

I put my hand on this swarm of approximately 12,000 bees to show everyone
how gentle honeybees are when they swarm. Afterward, I gently swept them
into a box and relocated them to a new hive. *Photo courtesy Boyd A. Loving.*

My daughter Svea with a (stingless) drone bee.

mites—even if it means all the bees on the planet would die and the human race was forced to suffer the consequences.

Unfortunately, they have no idea how much we all rely on the honeybee. Any time we munch on a bag of almonds, snack on an apple, pear, or orange, dine on an avocado and cucumber salad, or enjoy a nice cup of coffee, we are consuming food that was pollinated by honeybees.

So much of the world's food supply relies on the honeybee, and that's only one of many reasons why beekeepers are so passionate about keeping their bees as healthy as possible. Most beekeepers are always looking for more effective ways to combat Varroa, reading scientific articles, trying new methods, and constantly looking to see if someone has found the silver bullet that will finally give beekeepers the upper hand in the fight against Varroa. Beekeepers are proud of what they do, and they will do anything they have to do to protect their bees, even if that means having to sacrifice three hundred of them to test for Varroa, or put up with being judged by the ill-informed activist who doesn't comprehend how important it is for the survival of our species to win the war against Varroa.

CHAPTER 11

Welcome to the World of Bee

S INCE I WAS COMMITTED TO LEARNING how to be a better bee-keeper, I decided I would head down to my local bookstore to see if they had any books on beekeeping. I figured, if I was lucky, they might have a book on bees. I was pleasantly surprised to see that they had a shelf full of books on beekeeping. I was like a kid in a candy store, or more accurately, a bee nerd in a bookstore!

The honeybee is one of the most written about creatures on the planet. The earliest record of bees dates back about three thousand years to the Chinese character for bee inscribed on animal bones. The ancient Roman poet Virgil wrote that bees were born on the corpse of a freshly slaughtered ox. He went on to say that the bees collected the larvae from the dead oxen and brought them back to the hive and placed them in the honeycomb where they would transform into bees. While maggots and larvae might look similar, it is inconceivable to think that at one time people thought it made more sense that bees came from dead animals instead of thinking one of the bees was laying eggs.

In early literature, people wrote that it was a king bee who ruled the hive, as these early male chauvinists could not comprehend that a *female* bee was at the helm. It wasn't until 1609 when *The Feminine Monarchie* was published and people began to realize that it is in fact a queen who "rules" the colony.

In 1853 Reverend Langstroth wrote *The Hive and the Honey Bee*, and it is still in print today, remaining the definitive authority for managing hives, honey production, pollination, and queen rearing.

After spending way too long on deciding which books to buy, I finally chose two introductory books that looked like they would give me a firm foundation of bee advice. *The Backyard Beekeeper* by Kim Flottum was chock full of practical, easy to understand information and advice. Plus it had fantastic color photos that showed examples of what he was writing about. The other book was *The New Complete Guide to Beekeeping* by Roger Morse, which was filled with specific, succinct, and practical information about bees and beekeeping. Morse, a professor of apiculture at Cornell University, first developed the Master Beekeeper program, which is the gold standard used to certify qualified beekeepers in North America.

Both books said that it is best to start with two hives, as it makes it easier to understand how your hives are doing when you have another one to compare it to. This immediately made sense to me, as I am sure if I had started with two hives, then I would have been able to see that my original hive was not building up fast enough, nor did it have enough bees in it.

The books also pointed me toward other great resources such as *Bee Culture Magazine* and *American Bee Journal*. I had no idea that a magazine devoted just to beekeeping even existed! Or that *American Bee Journal* has been in circulation since 1861. I ordered a subscription to both, because my motto at this point was, the more bee reading, the better!

Seeing how many bee books have been written and learning about the two monthly magazines devoted to beekeeping made me realize that there was so much to learn about bees and beekeeping. Actually, it's one of the things that I like best about being a beekeeper: no matter how much I know, there's always more to learn. There are two sides to beekeeping; there is the practical/applied side, which is working your bees and all the physical activities that come with being a beekeeper. The other side is the theoretical/mental side. This is the nerd side that I also really love. For example, when you first get in to beekeeping, you learn about the worker bees changing jobs as they get older. But as you do a deeper read into the science of honeybees you find out there are two main hormones that change in levels as the bees get older, and just like puberty, these hormones drive the bees to act differently and change what they're doing in the hive. Regarding honey, initially you learn that honey never spoils, and later you read that it never spoils because an enzyme the bees use to break down the sucrose from nectar into fructose and glucose also creates hydrogen peroxide in the process.

One of the more crazy but interesting facts about bees that I learned from reading journal articles is that honeybees can count to four, and they are the only invertebrate capable of counting. Two Australian scientists, Marie Dacke and Mandyam Srinivasan, did several studies to confirm bees were counting, as they changed all the other parameters in the experiments that could possibly account for what the bees were doing. It's really interesting to think about how bees utilize their ability to count. When the bees are performing the waggle dance, you have to wonder if they are using numbers in their dancing directions. Maybe their dance is saying, "Fly east and count, one Mississippi, two Mississippi, three Mississippi, then hang a right..." or "After the fourth pine tree, hang a left..." We may never fully decipher the waggle dance, but it would be amazing if in the future we do discover that bees use numbers while giving directions to their fellow foragers.

The books I purchased also provided information about the major bee suppliers, so I was no longer dependent on just one. Dadant, one of the oldest bee suppliers still in operation, has been in business since 1863! A. I. Root, which now focuses on publishing for the beekeeping industry, has also been around since the mid-1800s. It's no surprise, since honeybees came over from Europe, that the founders of these early supply companies were also European immigrants bringing their love of bees with them to North America.

While honeybees might not be native to our continent, good old American ingenuity has revolutionized modern beekeeping with four important inventions/innovations.

It all starts in 1851 when L. L. Langstroth invented the fully movable frame hive, which has now become standard across the globe. His invention revolutionized beekeeping, making it possible for future large-scale commercial beekeepers to efficiently manage and care for the tens of thousands of hives that pollinate at least ninety commercially grown crops, which according to a 2010 Cornell University study, in the United States alone represents over $19 billion worth of crops!

Once we had movable frame hives, beekeepers needed the bees to build the comb inside each of the frames and not across them, so mass-produced, embossed wax foundation became the staple for beekeeping operations. Foundation is a wax sheet that's about as thick as a heavy card stock that is embossed with a honeycomb pattern. The foundation fits inside the wooden frame. The bees will use it to draw out each hexagon until the frame of wax is about one-half-inch deep on both sides of the frame. These one-half-inch deep cells are what the bees will use to either store honey or raise their brood. The embossed hexagon pattern mirrors what the bees would naturally create. Johannes Mehring invented the first molds used for creating wax foundation in 1857. Then in 1876, A. I. Root developed a press that used rollers, allowing for any size sheet to be used and opening the doors for mass-produced foundation. While A. I. Root didn't invent the wax foundation press, their design allowed them to commercially manufacture wax foundation and supply it to beekeepers across the country.

The third innovation was the modern smoker. In 1873, Moses Quinby improved the smoker by adding bellows to a firebox, allowing the beekeeper to provide air to the smoldering fire, and also direct where he wants to push/aim the smoke. Previous smokers didn't have the bellows, so a beekeeper would build a fire inside a can and have to let the smoke waft out on its own, or in some designs he had to blow into a tube to get the smoke to push out the front. The bellows gave beekeepers a way to control how much smoke they needed and where they wanted to aim it.

The fourth invention was the Centrifugal Honey Extractor, which was invented in 1866. Before Langstroth's hives were the standard, people used straw skeps, which meant the bees freely built the wax comb any way they wanted, and to extract the honey, the beekeeper had to remove all the bees, cut the comb, crush the wax, and then strain honey. Movable frames mean that you can pull out the frames, remove the honey, and then put the frames back into the hive with minimal damage to the comb. Fransesco de Hruschka invented the extractor after giving his young son a piece of comb honey on a plate. The boy put the plate of honeycomb in a basket, and then swung the basket around his head as kids being kids sometimes do as they're carrying any kind of object. When Hruschka saw that the honey was thrown from the comb by the motion, the idea of the extractor was born. In 1870, H. O. Peabody from Massachusetts created a centrifugal extractor that had baskets balanced on a pivot arm. Peabody's was the first extractor manufactured for sale, which meant that anyone and everyone could now easily and affordably remove honey from the comb. Having an efficient way to get the honey out of the comb meant that more people could produce honey, which led to the best thing about commercially manufactured honey extractors—more people could eat more honey.

It's stunning to think that even before the ancient pyramids were built, or civilizations were worshipping the Greek gods, people were keeping bees. Yet, it wasn't until the mid eighteen hundreds, within a fifteen-year span, that the four most important discoveries took place and forever changed beekeeping across the globe. Without all four of these innovations, beekeeping would not be what it is today, and honey production would be significantly less, and just a drop in the (honey) bucket by our modern standards.

Once all the bee catalogs arrived, I could see how much bee stuff was available, and being a gadget guy, I started to put together my wish list. I also liked that even though all the equipment basically fell into the same categories, such as wood-enware, veils, smokers, and hive tools, each supplier put its own twist on the equipment, so you can add a bit of your personal tastes to your bee equipment.

It's important to note that you don't need a lot of different equipment to keep bees. All you absolutely need are boxes, frames, a floor, some kind of roof, and bees. After the hive, all that's really necessary is just a hive tool and a smoker. Every-thing else is technically "extra." At a more recent bee meeting, the club vice president did a show-and-tell of all of his favorite bee gadgets. After showing and talking for about forty-five mi-nutes about all the special tools and gadgets he had, how he used them, and the special bee gadget boxes he kept them in, Grant Stiles, New Jersey's biggest commercial beekeeper, stood up and said, "If I had to use all that stuff, I'd never get anything done!"

One of the best ways to make your hives uniquely yours is to paint them to suit your style. When people think about bee-hives, they generally think they're painted white, but they don't need to be. Some people paint elaborate scenes on their hives, such as flowers, honeycomb, or even Winnie the Pooh. I like to paint each of my hives a different color, so that it's easy for me to talk about a specific hive. "The pink hive is booming! It's going to produce at least one hundred pounds of honey this year." Or, "The blue hive is struggling. I think I'm going to requeen it." Currently, there are six hives in one of my bee yards and each one is painted a different color. Seeing them in a row always reminds me of a tropical Caribbean port where every building is brightly painted a different color. Others look at my bee yard and say it looks more like a Grateful Dead T-shirt shop exploded in the woods.

Another good reason to paint your hives different colors is to help the bees identify their hive from any of the others. Bees do see color, but they see it differently than humans, as bee vision is further toward the ultraviolet end of the spectrum. Bees cannot see the color red; instead, they see the color red as black. However, they can see "bee's purple," which is deeper into the ultraviolet spectrum and humans cannot see/detect it. Vision is the bee's "superpower" as they are able to detect objects, such as flowers, faster and more distinctly than humans.

BEE NERD ALERT: Bees have five eyes. Two large compound eyes situated on either side of a bee's head, and three small eyes in a triangular pattern at the top of a bee's head that detect light and help bees to navigate during flight.

Since bees and flowers have a symbiotic relationship, whenever you ask yourself "why" when thinking about honeybees, just look at flowers for the answers. Flowers are colorful to attract pollinators. Next time you look at a bunch of flowers, notice how the leaves are green but the flowers are full of color. Now guess where the pollen and nectar is located? Also, have you ever noticed how some flowers have one color on the tips, yet the center is an entirely different color? When you look at some flowers under ultraviolet light to mimic how a bee sees them, a bull's-eye, or a pattern on the petals emerges that bees can see, but humans cannot. These patterns on the flowers guide bees into where the nectar and pollen sources are waiting. For example, the common dandelion might look like it's solid yellow to us, but to a bee, the outer rim looks white, while the center looks like it's vibrant purple. This is how the flower guides the bees in for a landing, the same way we have blinking lights on our airport runways to help the pilots bring their airplanes in for a safe landing. Thanks for flying with A. *mellifera*, flying the skies for a sweeter tomorrow.

Bees can also distinguish different shapes, which is another thing that you could take into consideration when painting your hives. Another of my bee yards is located on private property that's twelve acres of scenic, undisturbed, native forest, with a river running next to it. It's a beautiful natural property, and when you're there, it feels like you're at a mountain lodge in upstate New York's Adirondack Mountains and far, far away from northern New Jersey. The owners are very environmentally minded, and they are always trying to do what's good for their natural oasis, which is why they invited me to place my hives on their property. They had asked that the hives blend in with the natural setting and not stand out like a bunch of tacky T-shirt shops from the Jersey Shore. So instead of painting the hives, I stained them to bring out the natural look of the wood boxes. That is except on the very front of the hive entrance, where I painted different shapes and colors to help the bees identify what hive they call home from all the others. It's subtle enough that it's not noticeable unless you're flying in for a landing, then it's as clear as a floral bull's-eye. They are simple shapes, like lines, squares, stars, circles, and rectangles, but still enough to provide visual cues for the honeybees. These shapes are also how I refer to the hives, "the blue squares," or "the yellow rectangle," or "the white lines," because referring to hives by the shapes painted on their entrances makes it easier to remember what was happening in which hive. Otherwise, it would be: "Was it the second one from the left, or third…"

The supply catalogs also provided a lot of useful information about beekeeping and quite a few handy tips. For example, the first pages of *Dadant*'s catalog are a nice overview of honeybees, hives, and basic information you should know when you're first starting out. Their catalog is 150 pages long, and there are tips and detailed suggestions along with the descriptions of their products throughout. Since *Dadant* is the granddaddy of all the bee suppliers, each of their competitors followed their lead, which is why you'll find tips and suggestions throughout any and all bee supply catalogs.

I soon learned that another great reference was the state bee-keeping association's quarterly newsletter. There were articles from the association's president, and Tim Schuler, the New Jersey state apiarist, as well as feature stories about honeybees or beekeepers. There were ads in the newsletter from beekeepers that were selling bees, queens, and bee equipment. Even Rusty had an ad for his bee sting therapy, but I always wondered why he thought advertising bee stings to beekeepers would get him more business. With Rusty, you were never quite sure what he was trying to accomplish.

Probably the most important listing in the newsletter was information about the upcoming state beekeeping meeting. As soon as I saw it, I sent in my registration and a check for $25. The meeting was being held about two hours away, closer to the Philadelphia suburbs than to New York. Even though the state of New Jersey may not be the geographically biggest state, it is quite diverse and it can be divided into four mind-sets: New York suburbs, Philadelphia suburbs, farmland, and DownThe-Shore, which is anywhere on Jersey's 100+ miles of beach. If you're not from Jersey, most of your information about it has probably come from one of the reality TV shows that was filmed within its borders, which captured some local stereotypes but is far from what it's really like to live here. What surprises most people about New Jersey is that it really is the Garden State, as it has 9,000 farms covering 720,000 acres, and its biggest crops are blueberries, cranberries, and tomatoes. New Jersey has everything from a pygmy pine forest, to the Appalachian Trail, to the second largest waterfall east of the Mississippi River. And no matter where they live, most New Jerseyans love all the natural settings their state has to offer.

I arrived at the meeting bright and early so I would be in line for the 7:30 a.m. check-in. The meeting was being held at Rutgers University's EcoComplex, which is on a Rutgers satellite campus in Bordentown, New Jersey, and focuses on the environment and agriculture. Everyone that I met was super-friendly, and it was easy to see that most of these people had known one another for years. I didn't see anyone from our club, so I grabbed a coffee and a bagel and just walked around the atrium before heading into the meeting room. Within thirty minutes, the auditorium was full, and every one of the 150 seats was taken. I was amazed to think that all these people had woken up at the crack of dawn on a Saturday morning just to listen to someone talk about bees. I had found my tribe! I looked around the room and thought of the children's book, *Go, Dog. Go!* Only, instead of big dogs, little dogs, red dogs, blue dogs, all at the dog party, this was, tall beekeepers, short beekeepers, male beekeepers, female beekeepers, fat beekeepers, skinny beekeepers, old beekeepers, young beekeepers, all at the bee meeting. There were just as many women as men, and just as many couples as singles. The more I scanned the room, the more I realized that there was not one type of person who kept bees. Beekeepers come in all sizes, shapes, genders, colors, and ages. The only thing anyone seemed to have in common was that they kept bees.

A woman who looked like Popeye's girlfriend, Olive Oyl, walked up to the front of the room. She was wearing a well-worn power suit from the '90s, adorned with a bejeweled bee brooch, and when she said she'd like to call the meeting to order I realized she was the president of the state bee organization. She welcomed everyone and said, "Bees are what we all have in common, and that's why we are here. It's amazing to think that we are united over an insect, but we are. Beekeeping is the great equalizer, as it doesn't matter if you're wealthy or working class, a doctor or a bus driver, when it comes to keeping bees, we are all the same. No matter where we come from, or what else we do, when it comes to bees, we're all trying to do the same thing, and that's makin' sure we keep our bees healthy. People who don't keep bees may look at us like we're different, and the truth is, they're right. We are different. We keep bees, and that makes us unique from most of the people we know outside of this room. It's not a bad thing to be different, and most people admire us for what we do. At times, they're actually excited that they know someone who is a beekeeper. And sooner or later, a funny thing will happen, 'cause it happens to all of us. I, myself, have been in management for over twenty-five years, but once people found out I was a beekeeper, that was it. From that moment on, I was the Bee Lady. And mark my words, no matter what you do for a living, or how long you've been doing it, once people find out that you're a beekeeper, from that day forward, you're going to be known as the Bee Man or Bee Lady."

I smiled to myself, delighted to know that I'd be known as Frank the Bee Man.

The morning flew by, and lunch was waiting for us outside the meeting room in the atrium. It was a buffet of BBQ chicken, potato salad, steamed vegetables, and of course honey. Lots of squeeze jars of honey were available, and it seemed like everyone made sure to squeeze some honey on some or all of their food.

Of course, the lunchtime chatter was all about bees, with attendees sharing tips and tricks and the latest goodies they had purchased from their favorite bee supply catalogs. Speaking of supplies...quite a few vendors had tables along the atrium, displaying their goods. Like a kid in a candy shop, I wandered from table to table, marveling over the various products. One of the vendors was selling wax foundation, and it smelled fantastic. It was sweet like honey, with a fresh clean air about it. Since plastic foundation is what had come with my beginner's hive, this was the first time I had smelled pure beeswax foundation. I knew if I were a bee, hands down I would prefer wax foundation to plain old plastic, and if I were forced to live on plastic, I would be depressed. I didn't have any bees at the moment, but I knew I'd find some, and when I did, I wanted them to call this wax foundation home. So I asked a few questions and handed over my credit card.

After lunch, everyone headed back into the meeting room. A lot of the talks that afternoon had to do with mite treatments, and what the latest research was saying about what was working and what was not. If someone had kept count to see what was said more often, "bee," or "mite," the winner by 2–1 would have been mite. It really drove home the importance of monitoring and treating for mites if you wanted to be a successful beekeeper.

At around 2:00 P.M., the meeting moved outside, to a field around the back of the building, and the rest of the afternoon was spent in the sun, watching demonstrations and doing field-work with the bees. There were multiple stations, and at each one was something different about beekeeping. Since many bee-keepers want to learn how to extract honeybees when they've taken up residence inside a wall of a building, one of the stations was a four-foot by eight-foot section of a house—literally an entire wall from an old house—that contained an active bee col-ony. I think all of us wanted to know how this guy was able to convince someone to let him take a section of their house, and thankfully, someone actually asked. It turned out, it was from an abandoned building on his farm, and he had purposely waited until a few days before the meeting to remove the wall and bring it here, just to do this demonstration. I smiled when I thought about my newfound club of kindred spirits, realizing that an ordinary friend might give you the shirt off his back, but only a beekeeper would give you a wall from his house.

I intently watched as the beekeeper—his name was Gentle-man John—opened the wall to expose the comb and remove the bees. I would later find out he was one of New Jersey's most beloved beekeepers and had been keeping bees for more than forty-five years. He appeared to be as strong as a bull, and it was obvious he spent a great deal of time out in the sun, as the skin on his tall thin frame was the color and thickness of a well-worn baseball glove. He wasn't wearing any type of veil, just an old cap and a short-sleeved shirt, and he didn't seem to notice when he got stung, probably because it hurt the bees more than him as they tried to penetrate his thick leathery hide.

He was as gentle as he could be with the bees, but since he was removing the honeycomb from the wall and putting it into wooden frames in a hive, the bees were not happy. The buzzing was getting louder by the moment when suddenly he proclaimed, "There's the queen!" And just like that, he reached in with his bare hand, scooped her up, and put her into a waiting queen cage. He placed the queen cage inside the hive he was filling and told us this was so the bees would detect her presence and settle down. I had left my veil at home, and standing about ten feet away, I was happy he said "they'd settle down," because as far as I could tell, the cloud of bees seemed to be getting more upset as more foragers returned, looking for their home and their queen.

With the queen cage in place, I decided to move along. Another station that interested me was one demonstrating how to requeen a hive. If I had known that my queen was not laying like she should have been, I could have replaced her and maybe my hive would still be alive.

Beekeepers want to do what's best for their bees, and sometimes that means having to commit regicide, that is, kill a monarch, and in this case, kill a queen bee. A beekeeper must think of the hive as the organism that he is trying to keep alive. He needs to do what's best for the hive, not necessarily what's best for each individual bee. No one enjoys killing his or her queen, and like firing a bad employee, you might know it's the right thing to do but that still doesn't make doing it any easier.

The two most common reasons why you'd kill and replace a queen is either because her hive has a nasty disposition or she's not laying enough eggs to keep the hive alive. Since the queen is the mother of all the bees in the hive, if the worker bees are nasty, or what beekeepers call "overly defensive," their genetic makeup, the DNA from their queen, has hardwired them to react in a specific way. Honeybees are not emotional creatures; if they are overly defensive, it's part of their DNA, not because they had a rough childhood or they're overcome by anger or in a fit of rage. How they react and defend their hive is due to their instincts and genetic makeup. If you don't like how your bees are behaving, you need to replace your queen.

The much more common reason for replacing a queen is that she is starting to fail and her egg laying production is too low. As the queen ages and slows down, the hive prepares for a new queen so they will be ready when their queen dies. Unfortunately, nature doesn't always get the timing right, and many times, if you don't kill and replace the queen yourself, all the bees in the hive will die, as the old queen cannot make enough new bees for the hive to sustain itself. This is exactly what happened in my hive, and since I didn't do anything, the hive died. In many areas like the northeast United States, the honey producing season is short, lasting only three to four months. Since a hive needs to make all its honey in such a short time period, a beekeeper has to make a judgment call and decide if it's better to introduce a new queen or to wait for the bees to do it themselves. If he waits to see if the bees will make their own queen, the hive might run out of time and not have enough bees to produce the honey stores they need to survive. If he brings in a new queen, the hive will thrive throughout the honey season, but he will be forced to kill his old queen.

Since caring for your bees and doing everything you can to help them survive is the root of beekeeping, to purposely kill one of your queens is always a bit disturbing. But not anywhere near as disturbing as the presenter at the state meeting. He seemed a little too happy that he was going to be talking about doing a mob hit and whacking the queen. The session started off well enough, and the presenter, now known as the "Berserker," seemed like a mild-mannered, middle-aged man who looked a little like Winnie the Pooh with a "honey" potbelly.

Once the group had assembled, he smiled at everyone and said, "Okay, let's get started." And that's when the real show began.

His talk went like this: "When you need to requeen your hive, you must make sure you get that queen, and KILL IT! You gotta KILL IT! And, you have to make sure you don't have a bunch of bad little girls makin' a bunch of bad queen cells. And, since you're going to KILL THE QUEEN, you don't care what happens to her, so you're going to tear that hive apart, RAVAGE IT! Find that queen and KILL IT! And you're gonna make sure none of them bad girls made any bad cells. See, if you miss any of those cells, them slender virgin queens will hatch and KILL YOUR QUEEN, and that's like flushing thirty dollars down the drain. DOWN THE DRAIN! When you open up that hive, you're going to RAVAGE IT! You're gonna get in there and tear that thing apart."

The more the Berserker spoke, the more his neck, face, and head became a brighter shade of red, until he finally looked like a giant human wooden match with a bright red top. And as he spoke, he was wildly thrusting his hand into the hive—that thankfully didn't contain any bees—and yanking out the frames, one by one, as he said, "You go through each frame two, three times if you have to. You want to look for anything that looks like a cell or peanut, and if you see one, you take your hive tool, and you scrape it off, you RAVAGE that frame till it's clean! Then, when you finally find that queen, get ready, 'cause you're gonna KILL, KILL, KILL THAT QUEEN!"

For his big finish, the Berserker said, "After you find that old queen, you grab her, and before you KILL IT, you get your new queen that's in her nice, safe, queen cage. And in one hand you hold that cage, and in the other, you hold that queen THAT YOU'RE GOING TO KILL. You take that soon-to-be-dead queen and you SQUASH her against the queen cage, and you MASH her all over that cage. You want to MASH her all over that cage, 'cause even though she's DEAD, her pheromones are now part of that cage, mixing with the new queen's pheromones. Then, when you put your new queen in the hive, the bees will accept her faster, 'cause they'll smell the DEAD QUEEN and confuse the new queen with the one that YOU KILLED."

Once he was finished, the Berserker just stood there grinning. He was proud of himself, and he was a lot calmer, too, probably because he just released a decade's worth of pent-up rage on his demo hive. All of us observers just stood there, too, smiling back at him, mostly because we were all too terrified to do anything else.

When the day was finally over, I left the meeting energized and feeling like I had a better idea of what I was doing, or at least what I was supposed to be doing. I was impressed with the state meeting and how well organized it was run. I was happy to see so many beekeepers who, besides devoting a full Saturday to bees, seemed just about as normal as me. I was also pleased to hear the emphasis given to research, as it was so much more meaningful than just a bunch of old guys sitting around, giving their opinion and saying the same thing month in and month out. After a full day of hearing experts talk about bees, and having read my bee books, I knew I could do this, I *could* be a beekeeper. There was only one thing left for me to do. I had to get me some bees.

❖◦❖◦❖◦❖◦❖

CHAPTER 12

Bees Bees Bees

THERE ARE TWO WAYS TO BUY BEES: either as a package or as a nuc. A package is three pounds of worker bees—which is approximately twelve thousand bees—and a queen in a queen cage. The bees come in a box that is screened on two of the four sides. Buying bees in a package is similar to catching a swarm of bees, as there are only adult bees and no brood.

The other way to buy bees is a nuc, which is five frames of drawn comb that has adult bees, a laying queen, capped brood, eggs, larvae, as well as honey and pollen stores. The advantage of a nuc is that it's a mini-hive that is already fully operational. Nucs are more expensive than packages, but for all the advantages of a nuc, they are worth every penny. The only time a package would be more desirable would be when a hive doesn't use traditional Langstroth frames. There are two specialty

hives—the top bar hive and the Warre hive—that people sometimes use that do require a package of bees.

In the top bar hive, the bees expand horizontally, not verti-
cally. A top bar hive is three to four feet long and eighteen inches
deep. It has a flat roof, slanted sides, and it looks like an upside-
down pyramid on a rectangular base. Top bar hives were
developed to be used in third world countries, as they are inex-
pensive to build and do not require added equipment such as
honey supers and frames with foundation. Some people in the
western countries, however, keep bees in top bar hives to try
something different, or because they believe it's more natural because the bees have to build all the comb from scratch instead
of relying on commercially produced, store-bought foundation.

While a top bar can be built with a few sheets of plywood,
many custom top bar hives are built with exotic hardwoods,
and some have an observation window built into the side so
that you can see what the bees are doing. The reason the sides
of the hive are slanted is because bees are less likely to attach
their comb to a slanting wall. A top bar hive also has a movable
solid wood wall that limits how much of the hive the bees are
able to occupy. Instead of adding boxes on top of a hive to give
the bees more room, in a top bar hive, you move the solid wood
wall toward the back of the hive to give the bees more room.
The frames in a top bar hive only consist of the top part of the
frame, hence the name, "top bar." While these bars do not have
any foundation, to help get the bees started, in the middle of
each bar is a small strip of wax, or wax-covered strip of wood.
Some people will secure Popsicle sticks dipped in wax to the
middle of the bars to give the bees a place to start.

The issue with a top bar is that you have to be extra careful
when you're handling the frames, as the wax comb can easily

break if you handle it in the same way you handle a Langstroth frame. You can lift the frames up, but you cannot flip or turn them in any way or the wax will rip and snap off. Also, you cannot extract the honey in an extractor, so if you want honey your options are either comb honey or crushing the wax comb and straining the honey.

The Warre hive is named after French monk Abbé Émile Warré. The Warre hive is a cross between a Langstroth hive and a top bar hive. It uses top bars instead of frames like a top bar hive, and while it looks similar to a Langstroth, its main difference is that the boxes are added to the bottom and not the top of the hive. Warré felt that this was more natural for the bees, as they could build the comb downward, which is what bees do naturally when they build their nest inside an empty tree. They start at the top and work down. The main issue with the Warre hive is that it requires you to lift all the full boxes and add a new one at the bottom. There are times when a box full of honey can weigh forty pounds, and having to first move all the heavy boxes then add the new one to the bottom of the hive is a lot of extra lifting that puts an added strain on your back.

Since I was planning on sticking with the traditional, and more user-friendly Langstroth hive, I did not want to get a package, so my search for a few nucs began.

But first I had to be prepared. I ordered the woodenware for a second hive, since I wanted to follow the advice that two hives are better than one. I ordered each component separately so that I could get exactly what I wanted. And I also ordered a few new types of hive equipment that I would go on to use in all of my future hives. I ordered copper tops for both of my hives, and the ones I chose had ventilation holes built into them. I prefer these hive tops for two reasons: First, they look nice, especially as the copper weathers and gets a nice patina on it. Second, the vent holes ensure that condensation never builds up inside the hive. Bees need to remove moisture from the hive when they are making honey, and with standard hive tops, the beekeeper must put a spacer between the inner and outer cover to allow the moisture to escape. More important, as I learned, during the winter, condensation in a hive can kill the bees. If bees get wet during the winter, they have no way to dry off and will die. Again with traditional hive tops, beekeepers are forced to leave a space under their covers to allow for airflow. Since my copper tops are vented, I don't have to worry about ventilation in my hives.

The second new addition to my hives was slatted bottom racks. The slatted bottom racks are about two inches thick and are placed between the bottom board (the floor) and the bottom deep. There are ten slats that line up underneath the frames in the deep box above it. The purpose of the slatted rack is to allow for a few inches of dead air space above the hive entrance. This extra room allows the bees to fully utilize the frames in the bottom deep. Without the slatted racks, many times the queens will not lay in the bottom inch or two of the frames because they are too close to the entrance and may get chilled. By providing the extra space below the bottom deep, the frames are not going to catch a draft and the brood is better protected. This extra space is touted to help prevent swarming since the foragers have more room to hang out when they return to the hive. The dead airspace that the rack provides helps during the winter, as cold wind will pass below the bees instead of up and into the hive.

The last specialized piece of equipment I started using was plastic trays underneath my screened bottom boards. These white trays look like food trays from a school cafeteria and they sit on my hive stand, below my hives. These trays are sold as

Varroa monitoring trays, but I use them as an indicator of what's happening inside the hive. For example, if I see a lot of pollen on the tray, then that's a good sign the queen is laying. Bits of comb also accumulate from bees emerging from the cells, and the more debris on the tray is a good indicator of how many new bees are hatching. This is especially helpful during the deep of winter when you don't want to open your hives and chill your bees. I can look at the trays and see if there are any signs of life inside the hive.

The trays should never be used in lieu of a hive inspection, but instead as a way to form questions that can be answered when you look inside your hive. For example, during swarm season, a queen will stop laying before she swarms because she is reducing her body weight so she can fly. If there is not a lot of pollen on the tray, then it's important for me to be on the lookout for swarm cells. Since I currently have multiple hives, the trays are also a good way to compare my hives to one another before I start my hive inspections. Usually, most of the trays will look similar, so it is the outlier that I will take a closer look at. For example, if one hive has significantly less comb debris, then I will look to see how many frames of brood they have, as it could be an indicator that an older queen is not laying like she should. The outlier hive can also be on the positive side too. Throughout the years, there have been hives that produced two to three times the amount of honey as my other hives. When I checked the trays on these hives, I almost needed a shovel to get all the comb debris and pollen off the tray.

The tray cannot tell you everything that's happening in your hive, and that's why you must still go into your hives to look at the frames. I once had a hive that I was certain was going to die over the winter, because starting in the fall, it never had a lot of bees. Throughout the winter, I would look at the tray, and see nothing, and think, okay, now it's dead. Then, I'd open the hive, look inside, and the bees would be moving about. So just like the old Monty Python skit, every time I'd say aloud, "This hive is dead," it was like the bees would mock me and be saying, "Not dead yet."

Once my second hive and new bee equipment arrived, it was safe to say that my bee obsession/addiction was in full swing. Over the five months after my first hive had died, I had consumed as much bee information as I possibly could. I had attended a state meeting, I had read multiple books on beekeeping, and I had read my monthly bee magazines. My love and fascination with honeybees had taken a firm hold on my life, and all I wanted was to learn more. The void I once felt was no longer there. For the first time in my life, I felt a passion burning deep inside and I wanted it to grow and consume me. I felt like I had meaning in my life and I was finally doing what I had long been searching for.

I wanted to involve my family in my new six-legged and fuzzy world, so I would have someone to share my passion with. Since my about-to-be-ex-wife had absolutely no interest in what I was doing, I happily started to involve my five-year-old son. Miles was a bright and energetic kid with a strong desire to learn. He had been reading since he was four, and loved anything and everything to do with numbers. He was not an "outdoors, roll around in the mud, play with nature" type of kid, but he was fascinated with the math-related facts about bees that I shared with him. Miles was great at remembering facts, and soon he was reciting bee facts to our family and his friends. He enjoyed learning about honeybees, and it was a great way for us to spend some quality father/son time together.

After hearing that honeybees can identify shapes, Miles suggested that we paint different shapes on the front of our hives so the bees could identify which hive was theirs. On the landing board, which is a slanted board on the front of the stand that a hive sits on, we painted shapes. I let Miles pick the shapes, and on one hive, we painted a square, a circle, and a triangle. On the other hive, we painted a spiral, an equal sign, and a plus sign. I let Miles pick the colors we used for the shapes and also for the new hive. I had told him that bees cannot see red, so he suggested we paint the new hive blue, which he said, was his "second favorite color after red." We painted yellow shapes on the blue hive, and orange shapes on the other hive. After the painting was done, Miles said to me, "Dad, the blue hive looks really good, and 'cause it's my second favorite color and has my favorite shapes, the plus sign and equal sign, can that be my hive, and you have the other one?" It was as easy to see as the smile on Miles's face that he had been bitten by the beekeeping bug, and the very next day I ordered him his own kid-size bee suit.

I had been trying to find a place to buy bees, but I wasn't having much luck. I had asked the Badger and a few other members at my monthly meeting, but they either didn't know or were too afraid to share their sources for fear that New Jersey would have a bee shortage and there wouldn't be enough bees for them and me. It always surprised me how so many of the old-timers would be helpful, but only to a point. It was like they wanted me to be successful, just not as successful as they were. Andy was the most secretive of all of them, and he was also the cheapest. He said, "Why do you want to spend your money buying bees? Just catch yourself a few swarms and you'll have all the bees you'll ever need." Catching a swarm is certainly one way to fill a hive with bees, but it's also a gamble. I would first have to hear about one that was available, then I'd have to catch it. And there really was no way to predict when, or where, that opportunity would present itself.

Next, I turned to everyone's friendly know-it-all, Mr. Google. There are several online beekeeping forums where thousands of people post about anything and everything having to do with honeybees. The problem with these forums is that unless you know who is posting the information, you have no idea if the person offering advice knows what he or she is talking about, or if they just like to hear themselves talk. There is an old adage that says if you ask two beekeepers for advice on what to do, you'll get three answers. Meaning, there are always a few ways to do everything in beekeeping, and too often someone throws in something off the wall, just to stand out for being different. If you're going to seek out any online beekeeping advice, always remember another old adage: still waters run deep while a shallow brook babbles the loudest, so be judicious when it comes to which advice you listen to.

Since I was not getting any help from anyone in my local club, I took a chance and began surfing the Web for advice. When I went to the forums, I would simply type in a search for "nuc" and "New Jersey." Eventually, I came across several positive reviews for Sunrise Farms, a local apiary that sold bees, honey, and other bee-related products. I dug even deeper, and all the reviews I could find for Sunrise Farms were very positive. They also had a website that talked about their long and rich heritage in the state and their passion for honeybees. The website went on at great length about their connection to the land, and their pride in maintaining the legacy of Sunrise Farms. Their site contained a lot of information about different races of honeybees, like the Buckfast from England, and the Cordovan, which is also known as Blondes. Since they had provided so much educational information on their site, along with all the positive reviews, Sunrise Farms seemed like the place for me to get my bees. I sent them an email saying that I was interested in buying two nucs, and asked if they would have any available. The next day, I received a thoughtful response that said they did indeed have some nucs left, and if I wanted to reserve them, I should send them a deposit by check or PayPal. The email ended by saying that if I had any questions that I should give them a call.

Being somewhat neurotic, and since I always have several dozen questions, I rang them up. I wanted to know more about the price differences between the four- and five-frame nucs, and what the fifth frame contained—brood, honey, or just drawn comb? When I called, Caleb answered the phone with a monotone, "Hello," and he assured me that the extra frame would be filled with capped brood. In rapid-fire succession, I asked a series of questions, about the nucs, the type of bees, the bees' temperament, and anything else I could think of asking that would make it sound like I knew what I was talking about. Caleb answered all of my questions patiently, but with as few words as possible. I thanked him for his time, and let him know that I would send him the deposit via PayPal. I actually sent him the deposit as we were still talking, as I wanted to make sure that I did not lose my place in line for two of his nucs!

It was the middle of March, and I had two hives set up in the backyard ready for my bees. I had a deposit down on two nucs, and now all I needed was to hear from Caleb when it was time to pick the bees up. Even though it was only March, it felt like old man winter had called it quits and springtime was here to stay. The buds on the trees were starting to open, the dandelions were making themselves known across the manicured lawns of suburbia, and the birds were singing their springtime melodies. To keep myself busy, I would go over to my hives and practice doing a hive inspection. I'd also practice lighting my smoker, to make sure I could get it lit and keep it going. Miles would sometimes accompany me on my make-believe hive inspections, and after a few minutes, he'd usually say, "Dad, there are no bees. This isn't real." It's hard to argue with a five-year-old, especially when he's right. But he still looked cute in his new pint-size bee suit, veil, and gloves.

Before I knew it, more weeks had passed. It was an exceptionally early Easter Sunday and I was out by my hives on that sunny Easter afternoon when my cell phone rang. "Hi, it's Caleb at Sunrise Farms. Your nucs are ready to go." I was surprised that I'd get a call about bees on Easter. (But that was the only time I was surprised to get a bee call. The longer I have kept bees, the more I'm accustomed to the fact that no matter the day or the time, someone always wanted to talk about bees.) I wasn't sure what I should do. I said into the phone, "Caleb, it's Easter Sunday, and we're about to have people over. Is there any other day I can pick them up?"

"Yeah, sure, I guess. But you need to pick them up by Wednesday, or you're going to lose your deposit," Caleb said in his trademarked monotone voice.

It took everything I had not to race over there right away, but I knew my family wouldn't be too pleased if I picked up and left on Easter. So I just had to wait.

Sunrise Farms was located in the southern part of the state, closer to Philadelphia than to northeastern New Jersey, so it was a bit of a hike for me to get down there. But as luck would have it, I had a business meeting scheduled for Tuesday at my company's Philadelphia branch office. Realizing that it would be a small detour to get from Philly to Caleb's, I said, "Could I pick them up Tuesday night, probably around six o'clock?"

"Yeah, sure, I guess that's fine," said Caleb.

Excellent! I would have my bees in about forty-eight hours!

Tuesday morning, as I crossed the Ben Franklin Bridge and drove into Philly, I thought it was quite symbolic that I would be spending my day not far from where Langstroth invented the first movable frame hive, and later that night I would be putting my bees into one of his hives. Thankfully, I was only an attendee at the meeting and not a presenter, because all I could think about was getting the meeting done so I could pick up my bees.

At lunch, one of my coworkers from the New York office was in a panic and asked me if I could help. Byron was a gaunt, middle-aged, nervous asthmatic who spent most of his life trudging through one chaotic event to the next. At work, he mostly kept to himself, except when someone was talking about sports, then Byron was in the middle of the conversation, filling it with facts, stats, and details most people never knew. The only time Byron would raise his voice was when he was cheering for one of the many teams he followed, or if he was fighting with his wife over the phone. His wife was one of the angriest beasts on the planet, and more than once, everyone in the office had heard her screaming through the phone at Byron, telling him that he was a spineless sack of a man. She was so vile that in the town where they lived, she was banned from attending little league games because of what she'd yell at the kids on the opposing teams, the other parents, and the referees. Byron was so immersed in her craziness that he'd just laugh it off and act like it's an everyday thing for someone to be banned for life from going to kids' baseball games.

Byron's crisis du jour was that he was stranded in Philadelphia and needed a ride back to New Jersey. He had carpooled to the meeting with a few other coworkers from the New York office, not realizing that they were staying overnight in Philadelphia, and as he said, "My wife told me that I have to be home—tonight. Not tomorrow—tonight." Since he didn't live too far from me, I let him know that I'd be happy to take him home, but that we would be taking a slight detour and making a stop along the way. I let Byron know that we'd be stopping at Sunrise Farms to pick up and drive home two boxes of live bees. The expression on Byron's face was priceless. He turned white as a ghost and his eyes nearly popped out of his head. But he had two options: get in a car with thirty thousand stinging insects or go home the following day and face the wrath of the world's angriest shrew. After a long sigh, Byron said, "I'll be ready to leave whenever you are."

After the meeting was over, and everyone said their goodbyes to one another, Byron and I headed to my car. "You're not serious about the bees, right? You're just pulling my leg?" he asked. I assured him that I was absolutely, 100 percent, totally serious. It took a few minutes, but he accepted that I was indeed telling him the truth and that it was still a better option than making his she-devil wife angry. Then he asked, "So, where are you going to put the bees? In the trunk? Strapped to the roof?" I calmly told Byron that I drove a station wagon, it didn't have a trunk, and the bees would be riding in the back of the car, with us. Byron let out a nervous cackle that was filled with hopelessness and pure terror. As he got into my car and buckled up, he looked like someone who was terrified of heights and was about to bungee jump off the Golden Gate Bridge.

According to my GPS, it was fifty-one minutes from Philly to my bee destination. During our ride, Byron wanted to talk about sports to keep his mind off where we were headed and what we were picking up. I'm always happy to talk about hockey and who was going to make the playoffs, but after a while, the conversation turned to bees. Once you become a beekeeper, you realize that no matter who you're talking with, and no matter what the previous topic was, sooner or later every one of your conversations will turn to bees. One night, a cop pulled me over for crossing a double yellow line. The police officer asked where I was coming from, and when I said, "a beekeeper's meeting," we spent the next ten minutes talking about the health of today's bee population, the benefits of eating local honey, and what people can do to help the bees. Afterward, the officer not only apologized for pulling me over, but he asked me for my bee business card so he could contact me to buy some of my local honey, which he did do a few days later.

I began telling Byron how excited I was to start keeping bees, and all the cool and interesting facts that I learned about them. Byron was a fact and statistics junkie, so he was eating up all the sweet details about bees. When I was explaining the three types of bees to him, the queen, workers, and drones, and that it was only the workers, the female bees, that sting, he said, "You got that right!" and he chuckled to himself.

By the time we were only a few miles from Sunrise Farms, Byron was no longer nervous, and was actually a tiny bit excited to see what two boxes of bees would look like. I was excited too. After spending so much time on their website, I couldn't wait to see Sunrise Farms, and see if it was as magical a place as they had described. We pulled off the highway and made our way through one suburban street after another. I imagined that a few hundred years ago, all of this land must have been part of Sunrise Farms. The GPS said we were .9 miles from our destination as we turned into a residential subdivision of postmodern, cookie-cutter houses. As the GPS said we were .5 miles from our destination and we were driving deeper into the subdivision, I imagined that Sunrise Farms used to work this land until they sold it to a developer who built all these houses. I was expecting that at the end of the cul-de-sac we would find the farm, still in all its glory, looking like a stranger from a different time among all these look-alike, two-story, four-bedroom, prefab homes and their manicured lawns.

As I was daydreaming about what the farm would look like, my GPS said, "You have arrived at your destination." I looked around for a side road, or a gravel path, but all I could see was just regular houses and nothing that looked like a farm. The house on my right was the address for Sunrise Farms, so I turned into the driveway to see if I had made a mistake. But as I pulled in, two men walked out of the garage and waved at me. I came to a stop, rolled down my window, and said, "Caleb?" And the younger of the two guys said, "Yeah, hi."

Byron and I got out of the car and shook hands with Caleb and his father. Caleb invited me to come back and get my nucs, as he put on his bee suit. Luckily, I had brought my veil, and I followed him to the backyard. Byron and Caleb's dad stayed in the driveway, and I heard Byron ask, "So, what about those Phillies?" as I walked away. As Caleb and I stepped into the backyard, I saw at least ten rows of picnic benches that were lined up like an outdoor church revival. On each of the benches were five or six cardboard boxes that looked like the boxes used to store comic books in. "Welcome to my apiary," Caleb said with an Elvis-like crooked smile. That's when I realized that Sunrise

Farms was no more than just a bunch of bees in someone's back-yard. And not the full backyard, just the part of it that was dedicated to the bees. The mental image of seeing an idyllic farm with horse-plowed fields was burst faster than a balloon landing on a stack of needles.

I quickly got over my disappointment once I realized that each one of those boxes on the rows of picnic benches was filled with bees. Caleb walked over to where he had his smoker and said, "I think these two are strong. Let's take a look inside and I'll show you both of the queens." He puffed some smoke around the boxes and opened the lid on the first box. Inside there were bees, bees, and more bees. He puffed a bit more smoke into the box, and then proceeded to pull out each of the five frames and he showed me capped brood, larvae, eggs, and fi-nally the queen. Once he pointed out the queen to me, I was shocked at how big she was. Comparing this queen to my first one that died, I realized that my original queen was really small. When a queen is young and has lots of eggs to lay, she swells up, and as she gets older and starts to run out of eggs, she will get smaller. Now, I was seeing what a young, healthy queen was sup-posed to look like.

Once we saw the queen, Caleb gently put the frame she was on back into the box. He repeated the same steps with the sec-ond nuc, and it looked just like the first, and the queen was equally as big and plump. Caleb told me, "Don't pick it up from the lid; pick it up from underneath," as he picked up one of the nucs and looked to me to get the other one. I held the box the same way he was holding his. I was surprised by how heavy the nuc was, and also how much heat it was giving off. We steadily walked back to my car, and I felt like a proud papa taking his newborn home from the hospital. I had purposely left the rear hatch door open, and first Caleb slid his box in the back, and then I did the same. I could see Byron inspecting the boxes to see if he could see any bees, but they were all inside. I handed Caleb a check, thanked him for the nucs, then Byron and I were on our way. It was an uneventful ride home, except every once in a while when you could hear the loud, buzzing roar of the bees fanning their wings to cool themselves down by circulating the air. At those moments, Byron would look over, mouth ajar, with an expression of "help me" in his eyes.

After about an hour, I pulled up in front of Byron's house. He thanked me for the ride and the adventure, then with a sigh, he said, "Now it's time for me to take my stings." And with that, he walked into his house.

It was almost eight o'clock, it was dark, and I still needed to get my bees into their new home. I'd be home in about five minutes, and I knew that the next thirty to forty-five minutes were going to be amazing.

CHAPTER 13

Laying Workers and the Night Shift

PULLED INTO MY DRIVEWAY at a quarter past eight. The sun had set, but luckily the moon was bright, so I could see well enough that I wouldn't trip over anything when I carried the boxes of bees to their new homes. It was also quite warm, so I took off my long-sleeved dress shirt and decided to work the bees in my undershirt.

Still being relatively new to beekeeping, little did I know that I was about to break one of its cardinal rules: never work your bees at night. I lit my smoker and made sure I had lots of white smoke billowing out. I brought over a small side table and positioned it directly next to my first hive. I placed an empty deep box on top of it, so when I placed the nuc box on top of the empty deep, the top edge of the nuc box and the top edge of my hive were just about equal. I plopped my veil on my head, and standing next to my nuc, wearing slacks, dress shoes, an under-shirt, and a veil, I was ready to get started.

I removed the outer and inner cover from my hive. Then, I took out three of the five frames I had inside. I kept the two re-maining frames on the far outside of the box, or in position nine and ten. After I put the five nuc frames in, I would put the three frames I had pulled out back into the hive on the near side of the box, otherwise known as position one, two, and three. Keep-ing the three frames out until I put the nuc in meant that I had more room to work in the hive, and could get the bees into the hive faster and easier.

I was ready to transfer the bees. I took a few long deep breaths to calm myself and focus on what I was about to do. First, I puffed some smoke around the nuc box. Then, I slightly lifted the lid and puffed some smoke inside, which was met with an intense RRRRrrrrrr sound. I waited about twenty sec-onds, then popped the lid off the nuc box all the way and placed it on the ground. I used my hive tool to separate the first frame from the others, and then in one continuous movement, I picked up the frame and moved it over and into the hive. Since it went so well with the first frame, I repeated my steps with frames two, three, and four. I took another deep breath as I went for frame number five. Before I could think about it, I had all the five frames of bees in my hive. I kept moving and grabbed all three empty frames and slid them into the waiting hive. Whew!

I thought I was done, but then looked back into the nuc box and saw that a fair number of bees were still inside. I picked it up and positioned it on top of the hive above the last three frames I had just put in. Tilting the open top of the nuc box down to-ward the hive, I gave the bottom of the box a quick smack, knocking most of the bees out of the box and into the hive. I reached for my smoker and puffed some smoke across the top of the frames to drive all the bees down. Then I put the inner and outer covers back on. Success! The bees were in the hive and it went smoother than I had expected. I leaned the empty nuc box against the front of the hive, so any remaining bees could find their way out of the box and into their new home.

One hive down and one to go.

I repositioned the side table next to the second hive and set up everything exactly like I had just done with the first hive, ready to repeat the process.

One of the aspects of beekeeping that I really enjoy is how meditative it can be. It's what I call "forced zen"; be present or you will get stung. In Buddhism, they talk about being mindful in everything that you do and being present in the moment. Beekeeping forces me to be focused and living in the moment. If I forget and my mind goes elsewhere, then the bees will quickly remind me with a buzz to my veil or an unexpected sting that I need to be paying attention to them. Repetitive actions also keep me focused, and I like to try to make the basic tasks of beekeeping repetitive, and to repeatedly copy what has worked for me before. Doing bee-related tasks the same way over and over again has helped me to get a feel for what I am doing with the bees, and it has helped me to quickly see or feel when something is wrong. For me, the repetitiveness clears my head and helps me focus on the bee tasks at hand.

One hive down, and one hive to go. So I repeated the same exact steps I followed the first time and within minutes, all the bees were in, and I did it without getting a single sting.

I was feeling really proud of myself for how smoothly everything had gone. I had read and re-read my beekeeping books, I reviewed the notes I had taken during the state meeting, and I had practiced putting the frames in the hive. All the preparation I had done before my big night had paid off, and I felt more confident because I knew what I was supposed to do, and I simply followed the plan I put in place before I had ever started. That night, I thought about the many mistakes I had made with my first hive, and all the things I would have done differently if I knew then what I know now. I also knew that I didn't know that much, but I was determined to keep learning so that most of my beekeeping experiences would go like they had gone tonight, instead of how they went my first season.

At the next beekeeping meeting, I spoke up for the first time, proudly telling the group about getting two nucs and how I hived them as soon as I got home. Rusty stood up and said, "NO! You never work your bees at night. Never! When there is no daylight, the bees don't fly, they crawl. And they'll crawl all over you. When I was a boy, my brother and I decided to put a package of bees into our hive at night. Back then, we thought, *It's night, they can't fly, so they'll go into the hive much faster than if we did it during the day.* Boy, were we wrong! Those bees were all over me and crawled under my shirtsleeves and up my pant legs. I was stung about fifty times that night. So I'm telling you, don't ever work bees at night."

It was nice of Rusty to provide me with such valuable information *after* it would have benefited me the most. I would later learn that he was absolutely correct; you should not work bees at night, because they will crawl on you instead of flying around. What I have since learned is that I should have put the nucs on top of the hives, opened their entrance, then just walked away and waited until morning. The reason you open the hive entrance is so the bees can get air and it prevents them from overheating. Bees generate a significant amount of heat and if they are kept in a closed box without enough ventilation, they will overheat and die. It would be the same if a few dozen people were locked in an elevator. Their body heat will raise the temperature in the confined space to an unbearable level. You also want to unplug the entrance as it reduces the stress level in the hive. When bees are trapped, they will continuously look for a way out until they find one. Once the entrance is found, they will relax and return to their normal temperament. Then when morning rolls around, the foragers will orient themselves to their new location and begin searching for nectar, pollen, and water.

But, overconfident from my recent success, I had to learn this lesson myself...the hard way.

When I was in my fourth year of keeping bees, in addition to having a few hives in my backyard, I started keeping hives in other locations. One of my favorite apiaries, or bee yards, was a few towns over from where I lived, in the woods behind a church. I was not a member of the church, but they were very environmentally friendly and they had contacted me to see if I would want to keep bees on their property. They were interested in having a beekeeper because they received green credits if they had hives on their property. But their interest was much more than just getting green credits, as they also maintained a community garden to supply fresh fruits and vegetables to local homeless shelters.

The church sat on over twenty-five acres of land, and much of it was forest that was only being used as a buffer between the church and the surrounding neighborhoods. When I was initially scouting out where to put my hives, I found a sunny patch of ground in the woods that was not too far off the path that led from the church to the rectory. To get my future apiary ready, I brought over saws, rakes, branch clippers, a shovel, and a weed eater. It took me the better part of a three-day weekend, but I carved out a nice spot for my hives. It may be divine intervention, or it might just be an excellent location, but my hives behind the church have always produced an abundance of the most delicious honey anyone has ever tasted, and my bees have always been safe. No matter how bad of a storm that rolls in— even a category 1 hurricane with wind gusts of eighty miles per hour that blew down countless trees—my hives have always made it through without a scratch. Any trees that did fall, have always fallen *away* from my hives. It is a special place, and I am so thankful to be able to keep my hives there.

One day, while inspecting my church apiary, I realized that one of my hives had gone queenless. This usually happens for one of three reasons: One, the queen runs out of eggs because she's at the end of her life and she dies before the hive realizes that they should have made a new queen. Two, the hive swarms, the old queen leaves, and something happened to the new queen so she never starts laying eggs. Or three, during a hive inspection, a clumsy beekeeper rolls the queen, which is a polite way of saying he killed the queen. (HINT: I never saw any queen cells, the queen was only one year old, and being a bit of a spaz, option three is probably the safest bet.) Whatever the reason why, my hive was now without a queen.

I knew there was a problem because when I was doing the hive inspection, I didn't see any worker brood, and all my other hives had several frames of brood. To make matters worse, I saw some drone brood, but something about it wasn't right. Usually you will find drone brood on your outermost frames, at the edges of the frames, or in burr comb, which is comb the bees build outside of the frames and where beekeepers don't want them to build it, such as between boxes, or between the top box and the inner cover. This drone brood, however, was scattered across a few frames where you'd normally find worker brood, and instead of each of the capped cells being next to one another, these capped drone cells looked like they were randomly placed in cells on a frame. When you do not see any worker brood and only drone brood that is scattershot across a frame, it can only mean one thing: a laying worker.

Sometimes, when a hive goes queenless, one or more worker bees will try to save the colony and start laying eggs. When the queen is present, her pheromone "shuts down" the worker bees' inclination to lay eggs, but that lack of queen pheromone signals there is trouble and someone needs to save the day. The problem is that a worker bee does not have a fully developed reproductive system, and she is not mated, so the only eggs she can lay are drone, or unfertilized eggs. Further, because her body is not as large as a queen bee, she cannot reach the bottom cells with her tail, so she will lay eggs haphazardly, sometimes laying more than one egg in a cell. When you have a laying worker who assumes the role of the queen, the rest of the hive will think she is the queen and will identify her by her pheromone.

If you discover a hive that has a laying worker, it can be very difficult to save it. Normally, you just requeen the hive, and since the hive is without a queen, they will accept her after a few days. But when you have a laying worker who assumes the role of the queen, the rest of the hive will think she is the queen, will identify her by her pheromone, and will remain loyal to her. They will try to kill the new queen as they will view her as a threat. Also, since the laying worker looks like the other tens of thousands of worker bees, it is not as simple as finding and removing her before putting in a new queen. So you have a hive that is loyal to a worker that cannot resupply it with new life, and they will kill any new queen that is introduced. As a result, the hive usually dies off as the workers come to the end of their lives. Nevertheless, you can take a few extra measures to get it back on track.

It's a multistep process to right a hive with a laying worker, but it's the only option that may save the colony. First, you have to put a bed sheet on the ground at least twenty-five feet away, and up to fifty feet away from the front of the hive. Next, you take the hive over to the bed sheet and you remove every bee from the hive, which requires a lot of shaking and brushing. Once you have every single bee out of the hive—and I mean literally: Every. Single. Bee.—you can return it to its original position. It's also important to remove any drone brood that you see, so the hive is completely broodless when you return it. Once the hive is back where it belongs, the foragers will fly back to the hive. The laying worker will not be able to fly back, however, as she is weighted down by ripening eggs in her belly, and most likely she was a nurse bee so she never went on an orientation flight to know where the hive is located and won't be able to find her way back. Needless to say, when you remove 20,000 to 50,000 bees from a hive and knock all of them onto a sheet, they are going to be unhappy, so wearing a veil, gloves, and full protection is highly recommended.

The second step to overcome this mess is to add a nuc to the original colony. Since the laying worker's pheromone is what the bees identify as the queen's, it takes more than just adding a new queen to save the hive. By adding a nuc, you are adding brood to the hive, so the bees will react to the brood pheromone, which sends its own signal that everything is right with the hive. Think of the brood pheromone as the smells of a newborn baby. When you go into a home with a newborn, you can smell those distinct baby smells, and if you go into a nursery with dozens of newborns, you can *really* smell them. The same is also true for bees—the stronger the smell, the more brood, which means more eggs, which means the better the queen. If you just added a queen without also adding any brood, it is unlikely that she will survive. The workers might kill her, as there's no brood pheromone telling them she's a healthy egg-laying queen. Also, when a hive only has adult worker bees, then as these worker bees age and die off, there will be a time lag until the new queen's brood hatches and there are new bees that are able to care for the younger brood and the queen. Adding a full nuc means that you are adding brood and the needed nurse bees and house bees that will care for the brood and the queen. Plus, a nuc is a twelve- to fifteen-thousand population of bees that recognize the new queen as the true queen.

The last step in this process is to make sure the hive's original bees and the bees from the nuc don't fight, which is exactly what would happen if you just put the nuc bees directly into the same hive with the other bees. Instead you use the old newspaper trick. After you shake all the bees out of the hive and return the hive to its original location, you only put back one deep hive box, not both. Then you lay a single sheet of newspaper across the top of the deep box so the box of bees is fully covered. Next, you place an empty deep box on top of the newspaper. Now all the original bees returning to the hive can only get into the bottom deep. The next step is to put the frames from the nuc into the top deep box, along with five empty frames. Once the nuc and the other frames are in the top deep, you put your inner and outer covers back on the hive to close it up. The only way the bees from the nuc can get out is by chewing away the sheet of newspaper. The bees from the original hive also want to remove the newspaper, as it is a foreign object in their hive, so they, too, will begin chewing away at the newspaper. As both sets of bees chew on the newspaper, all the various pheromones will begin to circulate throughout the hive. By the time the bees have chewed through and cleaned out all of the newspaper, the bees will recognize each another's pheromones and view themselves as one big happy family.

If everything works, in just a few days, the hive will go from one that was destined to die off to one that is very strong. It will have a significant number of adult bees to forage, a young queen, and plenty of brood to keep the hive going. But like so many things in beekeeping, what in theory sounds easy can in reality turn out to be a big buzzing load of trouble.

Once I had discovered my hive was queenless, I knew the process that I needed to follow, so I called up Caleb to see if he had any nucs available. I hadn't seen Caleb since I bought my first two nucs from him, but I recognized his monotone voice as soon as he picked up the phone. Luckily, he had a nuc for me, and I was even luckier when he said, "I'm going to be up in your area later today, so I can just drop the bees off at your place." Fantastic, I thought! If he drops the bees off at my place, I can get this situation fixed in no time.

Caleb said he'd be at my place at 6:00 P.M., after he was done with work. Around 2:30, I drove over to my hives at the church with a bed sheet so that I could start on step one in the process. I knew it was going to take me a bit of time to shake all the bees out, so I reasoned that I would start early in the afternoon, and then complete the process after Caleb had arrived with the bees.

I walked into the woods, about thirty feet in front of my hives, and placed a sheet on the ground. I brought the hive over and began to remove the frames and shake them out. The first few frames went fine, but with every frame I shook, the bees were getting more and more agitated. It also seemed like many of the foragers would fly back to where their hive was supposed to be located, and when it was not there, they would fly back to where I was, just to let me know they were not happy. After the tenth frame of bees, there were bees on the sheet, bees flying all around in the air, and there were bees all over me. They were landing on the top of my veil, on my arms, my back, and my legs. Every once in a while, I'd feel the ZAP! of a sting, but that was mostly on my legs as I was moving around and bending over to get another frame.

After about thirty of the longest minutes of my life, I had all the bees out of the hive. You don't really appreciate how many bees live in a hive until you see tens of thousands of them all out of the hive at the same time. I brought one deep hive body back to its proper place in the apiary, found ten frames that were all filled with nice drawn comb, but no brood, and put them back into the hive. It was amazing how fast the bees went from a mass on and around the bed sheet to back in the hive. When there were only about a dozen or so bees left on the sheet, I picked it up and shook it into the air so the remaining bees would land in the grass. My thought was that if there were only about a dozen bees left, then at least one of them is probably the laying worker, so it's better to shake her into the grass than to let her lounge around all day on my bed sheet.

By the time I got home, it was after five o'clock, so I didn't have to worry about waiting too long for Caleb to show up. Or, so I thought.

At about 6:15, Caleb texted me to say he was going to be late, but not to worry, as he was on his way. At seven o'clock, he texted to say that he was only about fifteen minutes away, and he asked for the address again. Then at 7:30, he texted to say that he was lost. Since I knew I was running out of daylight, and that I had long since run out of patience, I called him up to find out exactly where he was. It turned out that he chose the second slowest route to my house, as the only way he could have set a slower course to get to me would have been if he had flown a hot air balloon around the world in the opposite direction from his house to mine and eventually landed in my backyard. But now it turned out that he would be driving past the church before getting to my house, so to save time I told him to meet me there.

I jumped in my car and headed over to the church. I was waiting for about twenty minutes, and just about to call him again when Caleb pulled into the parking lot. It was now 8:25, almost two and a half hours past when he was supposed to arrive, but he was here and he had my bees.

"Sorry I'm late. Do you want my help getting the bees into the hive?"

Caleb had years more experience than me, so I thought it would be great to have his help, plus, I might be able to learn a thing or two from him. Caleb took his bee suit out of his trunk. It was a full head-to-toe bee suit, which he put on and tucked into his boots. He also put on a pair of leather gloves, so literally every inch of his person was protected. I was still using my veil that just plopped on my head and bunched up on my shoulders. I also had gloves that I would use when I thought the situation called for it, and on this night, I had a feeling that I would need them.

When we got over to the bee yard, Caleb looked over to me and said, "Newspaper." Oh, crap! I realized that I was in such a hurry to get over to the church that I left the newspaper back at my house. Wait, the church! They had to have some paper laying around. So I ran over to the church and pulled on the door. Luckily it was open and inside I went. I wasn't sure where to look until I saw the recycling bin in the corner. I pushed open the lid, and sure enough there was a newspaper inside. I grabbed a few sheets and headed back to my hives.

It was now completely dark; there was no moonlight to help us out. Caleb put the sheet of newspaper on top of the hive body, and then the empty deep on top of the newspaper. Since I didn't have a side table to put next to my hive, we were trying to figure out the best way to get the bees into the hive with the least amount of trouble, and the least amount of open space between the nuc box and the awaiting hive. Our concern was that the more space between the nuc and the hive, the greater the risk of the queen falling off and not making it into the hive. Finally, I said, "I'll hold it. I'll hold the nuc box next to the hive. That way there won't be a gap, and you can just pick up the frames and move them into the hive." Caleb nodded and smiled. I held on to the ends of the box, slightly tilting it toward the hive. Caleb opened the lid and started to get the frames out. The good news was that there were a ton of bees inside the nuc box. The bad news was that once the lid came off, those bees wanted out, and since it was pitch-black they couldn't fly so they began to crawl. First they crawled on the sides of the box. Then they found me and started to crawl on my arms and up to my chest. I was wearing a hoodie and had my veil tucked inside, but I didn't have it zipped up to the tippy top and the bees found a way inside. I could feel them crawling around between my hoodie and my shirt, and while it felt a little weird and a little creepy, it didn't bother me. I was more worried about dropping the nuc, so I tried to ignore the feeling of bees crawling inside my clothes. Faster than I would have liked, the bees found their way under my undershirt and now were crawling on my bare skin. Caleb asked me to tilt the nuc box more to him, and as I did, I pressed the nuc box against my chest, the same chest where a few dozen bees were trapped and crawling around. When I pushed the nuc box against the bees, they did what bees normally do when they are being crushed, and they started to sting me. It was the first time I got stung on my bare chest, and it didn't hurt as bad as other places I had been stung. The bees sting pheromone that acts like a bull's-eye, which meant that not only was I getting stung, but I was getting stung within the same baseball-size area on my left man boob—as I continued to hold a box containing thousands of bees. I said to Caleb, "The bees got into my shirt. I'm getting stung on my chest." And he said, "Yeah, that's why I wear the full suit. Bees can't get in here." Thanks for the sympathy, Captain Obvious.

I'm sure it was only about ten minutes, but when you're getting stung and you can feel more and more bees crawling under your clothes and over your body, time moves a lot slower. It felt like I was standing there holding the nuc for over an hour. Finally, Caleb said, "Okay, give me the box and I'll shake the rest of the bees into the hive." As I handed him the nuc box, I walked to the front of the hive and shook out, danced around, and brushed off all the bees that were using me as their personal pincushion. I opened the bottom of my shirt and shook the remaining bees out of my clothes and onto the front of the hive. And I didn't stop until I was certain I didn't feel any more bees crawling around. Caleb closed up the hive and took the nuc box back with him to his car. In the parking lot I shook Caleb's hand and thanked him for all his help.

As crazy as it sounds, standing in the dark and getting stung gave me a certain level of satisfaction. It felt satisfying because I was doing what I had to do for my bees. Caring for them gave me great pride and getting stung only added to my conviction that I would do whatever I had to do for my bees. I was a bee-keeper and I was proud of myself for putting my bees' needs before my own.

I drove home, took off my shirt, and looked at the canta-loupe-size red welt that was once my left man boob. I wanted to take a shower and relax, but before I could do anything else, I needed to take care of something even more important. I picked up the phone and ordered myself a new veil—one that attached to a jacket and zipped up around the neck so nothing could get inside. That night I learned two valuable lessons: hiv-ing your bees at night was foolish; and the more important lesson, wearing a veil that didn't stop bees from stinging the crap out of your chest while you're hiving bees at night was *ridiculously* foolish.

CHAPTER 14

To Have Is Not to Keep

THE MORNING AFTER I INSTALLED my first two nucs, I grabbed a cup of coffee and headed out to my hives. The foragers were busy doing orientation flights, acclimating to their new location. Usually, the orientation flights happen in the afternoon, but since they were new to this location, they had to set their internal GPS before heading out to collect nectar and pollen. It's easy to recognize orientation flights, as the bees are hovering in front of the hive like little helicopters doing back-and-forth figure eights as they register the precise location of their hive, so that they can find their way back home.

I grabbed a lawn chair, sat down about three feet to the side of my hives, drank my coffee, and watched my bees. Miles was also excited to see how "his bees" were liking their new hive, so he ran outside and jumped onto my lap. It felt good to have something that I could share with my son, something that we could do together. Part of the appeal of having bees is how much it gets you outside to enjoy nature. Before I had bees, I'd chug my coffee in the kitchen wondering what the weather was like outside. Now, I was sitting out in my backyard, with my son, watching our busy new neighbors flying off to work.

Even though we were sitting only a few feet away, the bees couldn't care less since we were not interfering with what they were doing. If we were in front of the hive, blocking their flight path, then they'd be upset that we were in their way, but just sitting to the side and being close did not bother them in the slightest.

As some of the foraging bees started returning to the hive, you could see brightly colored orange balls on their hind legs. This was pollen. Seeing so many bees bringing back pollen was a good sign. Bees use pollen to feed the developing larvae, so if they are bringing in pollen it is an indication that the queen is in good shape and laying lots of eggs. The only way you can be really certain how your bees are doing is by going into your hives and inspecting the frames for brood and signs of the queen, but there are clues that can help you predict what's going on just by watching them. Pollen is one, and another is their disposition. If your bees are calm, that lets you know that nothing is making them defensive, and the hive is queenright. If a hive is overly defensive and will not let you enjoy your coffee in peace, then something is wrong and it's a clear sign that you have to do a hive inspection right away.

While it seems obvious that you have to go into your hives to find out what's happening with your bees, some people try to avoid it. We call these people, "bee-havers," because they may "have" bees, but having bees doesn't make them beekeepers. Most bee-havers start out well-intentioned, but usually they haven't done their homework on what it's actually like to keep bees, so when it comes time to do what is required, they are either too afraid to get close to their bees, or they always have a reason why they're "too busy" to properly care for them. The bee-havers dream about having a hive in their backyard, how nice it will look, and how cool it will be for them to tell all their friends that they have bees. But once they get stung with the reality that there is work involved with keeping bees, they shut off. It's the same as the people who dream of having a cute little puppy to play with, but once they see how much work it requires—house-breaking, walking, training—they think it's too much of a hassle and either chain it in the backyard or give it away.

For many years, I used to think if someone wanted to keep bees they would naturally be a good beekeeper. I thought want-ing to be around stinging insects was a unique enough personality trait that if you were interested, you should do it. Now I realize it takes passion, dedication, and training.

Bee-havers tend to fall into two camps: either they are just starting out and don't want to admit that beekeeping is not for them; or they're serial bee-havers who refuse to put in the work, so every year their bees die and the following year they just buy more.

When someone is just starting out, I will usually give them a fair amount of time and do my best to help them out, because most people are willing to commit themselves to the endeavor. Unfortunately, too many times the line from *Forrest Gump* is what rings true with bee-havers: "stupid is as stupid does."

ONE BEE-HAVER, Scooby, liked to wear his Phish concert T-shirts when he was around his hives. "They give off good vibes, man" was his rationale. Scooby was the living embodiment of the "Dude" from *The Big Lebowski*. He painted his hives with psychedelic flowers and swirls of multicolored paint, so even if you never dropped acid, just looking at his hives would give you flashbacks. He would judge how his bees were doing by sitting cross-legged in front of his hive, blocking the entrance and letting the bees fly past him. The closer he could put his face to the entrance to the hive without getting stung, and still feel happy vibes, the better the bees were doing. "My bees are doing great, man" is what Scooby would always report as he was nodding and smiling at you.

While Scooby spent more time than any beekeeper on the planet to get his hives painted "just right," he neglected to purchase everything he needed to be a beekeeper. For starters, he never bought a hive tool, and while he was an expert on smoke for himself, he hadn't bought a smoker for the bees, because he was going to manage his bees with positive energy. The hive was a gift Scooby's family got for him, and it was obvious that he had never even looked to see how the hive was supposed to fit together. His family bought him a "complete beginner's kit" online because it qualified for free shipping, and while the kit supposedly came with everything you'd need, it apparently did not come with instructions for how to assemble it. Scooby decided that the larger deep bee boxes should go on top because he wanted a lot of honey, so when his package of bees came, he poured them into one of his honey supers instead of one of his deep boxes, and then he put the second honey super on top, so it looked like the picture on the box. Since he didn't know what the floorboard was, he neglected to use it. Instead, he left the outer cover ajar so the bees could come and go from the top.

One of Scooby's friends had overheard me talking about bees, and since what I was saying didn't match what he saw Scooby doing, his friend asked me if I could "do him a solid," and help Scooby out. The first time I went over to Scooby's house, I saw what can happen when you try to have bees when you have absolutely no idea what you're doing. I also saw how resilient bees are, especially when they need to make the best out of a bad situation. Scooby had the hive in his front yard. He didn't want to keep it in the backyard because he was afraid his dog might get stung. I told him dogs learn pretty fast to stay out of the bees' way, and that he should be more concerned about the neighborhood kids stumbling into his hive. The first thing I did was to move his hive into the backyard, and I also showed him how the bottom board is supposed to be the floor of the hive, and that it also acts as the entrance to the hive. Next, I explained what the other parts of the hive were and how they were supposed to be used.

Since he had put two boxes on at the same time, his bees had chimneyed up both his supers, meaning they drew out the comb in the middle frames but completely ignored all of the outer frames. I told him that he should start feeding his bees sugar syrup so they could finish drawing out the remaining comb, and that he can't put any honey boxes on until all the frames are drawn out. As I was peering into his hive, trying to make sense of what needed to be corrected, Scooby was standing in front of his hive, swatting at the air and smacking his hands together. I asked him what he was doing, and he said, "Hey man, these B-fifty-twos are dive-bombing my hive! Man, they're bigger than my bees. They got bigger abdomens, broader wings, and are chestnut in color. They're getting into my hive unchallenged! Man, they're unchallenged, they can't stop 'em! My bees are busy bringing in a pretty good stream of pollen, but these big ones—nothing. I did manage to nail two of them. Any idea what they are? What should I do, man?"

I wanted to ask him how he had made it this far in life being this clueless. Instead, I just said, "Those are drone bees, the males, they're bigger than the worker bees."

Wanting to prove without a shadow of a doubt that he was the least intelligent person to ever have bees, Scooby said, "But they're so much bigger and a darker chestnut than my bees. Man, are you sure? I thought drones only left the hive to mate with a queen. Whatever they are, these are inbound. Not so sure they're drones, man."

I reassured him that they were indeed drones and told him that he really needed to buy a basic beekeeping book. I had a few bee supply catalogs in my car, because driving around with bee catalogs in your car is completely normal when you're a bee-keeper. I gave him one and circled a few of the items he should get. I also gave him some step-by-step directions on what he should do over the next few weeks and told him to call me if he had any questions.

The second—and the last—time I went to Scooby's, I was again amazed at how one person could do so many things wrong. When I saw his hive, I had to stare at it awhile just to make sure I was really seeing what I was looking at. Scooby had purchased a top feeder and he was using it on his hive, only instead of putting it on top, the feeder was between the two hive bodies. When I asked him why the top feeder was in the middle of his hive, he said, "There were so many bees at the top of the hive, man, there was no way that feeder could have gone on. All those bees, man, and they were all looking at me. What was I supposed to do?" I reminded him that when you smoke the bees, it pushes them down into the frames, and he said, "Oh right-right, yeah, man, I forgot that part." So then I asked him how many times he had refilled his feeder, and he said, "Refill it?"

I lit my smoker and used my hive tool to get the top box off, and just as I suspected, the feeder was now filled with burr comb where the sugar syrup should have been. Instead of building out the comb on any of the frames in the hive, the bees had filled the long emptied feeder with burr comb, and his hive was exactly where it had been several weeks before.

I tried explaining to Scooby that what he was doing was actually bad for his bees, but every time I said, "It's not good for your bees," or, "You're going to kill your bees," Scooby would stick his face up into the front of his hive, hold it there for a few seconds, and say, "See, man, they're happy. They're fine."

At this point, I realized I'd have a more productive conversation if I was talking to one of Scooby's garden gnomes, so I returned the hive to its correct state, packed up my stuff, and wished Scooby luck with his bees. I knew Scooby wasn't going to retain anything that I said, and that he'd soon forget about having bees and just concentrate on his other hobby—the smoking of natural herbs and leafy plants.

BETTY WAS ANOTHER BEE-HAVER who reminded me of Glenn Close's character in *The Stepford Wives*. She was always dressed like she was expecting the local town newspaper to show up to photograph her and report on what she was doing. If she went to the grocery store, she'd dress like June Cleaver from *Leave It to Beaver*, complete with pearl necklace and matching earrings. If she was picking up takeout from a local restaurant, she was dressed like she was headed out for a night on the town. Since she liked to garden, anytime she was in her backyard, she was wearing designer overalls, a floral shirt, matching floral gardening gloves, along with an occasional coordinating scarf. It was almost as if Betty was dressing for a role in a movie, and by dressing for the part, she became the character she was playing.

Betty had a kind heart and always wanted to do what was best for the environment. But after a while, her good intentions were about as meaningful as using designer bottled water to spritz plastic plants to make them look more alive.

Betty came to beekeeping through her gardening club. Since avid gardeners understand that plants need bees, many want to have their own hives to help their plants grow. Unfortunately, some gardeners, like Betty, treat their hives like they would a tree in their yard. They find the "perfect spot" for it, then they only check on it a few times a season, usually in the same way they'd check on a tree, by standing a few feet away and admiring it.

Betty did buy a beginner's backyard beekeeping book, but instead of reading it, she looked at the photos of backyards to get some design ideas on how to paint her hive and what she should plant to accent it. She was thinking of her hive more as a decorative lawn ornament, and placed it in front of a waist-high wooden fence that separated her driveway from her backyard. Then, on either side, she planted two big bushes of Dixieland maiden grass, which looked like two big green pom-poms. By placing it where she did, Betty hadn't considered the space she'd need to comfortably work her hive. Since you work your hive from standing behind it and to the side, it's important to leave two or three feet of space around it so that you always have plenty of room. But Betty's hive was only a few inches away from the fence and the bushes of maiden grass. This created a big problem, as she had to stand directly in the bees' flight path and block the entrance to the hive any time she needed to do anything with her hives. Bees are generally gentle, but if you had a giant creature blocking your front door and making it impossible to come and go from your house, you, too, would get a wee bit upset. So the few times Betty would check on her bees, she'd always report how nasty they were to her. Betty's problems didn't stop there, as the front of the hive was facing the middle of her backyard, so anytime anyone tried to do anything in her backyard, they'd walk smack in the bees' flight path, which led to many unwanted bee interactions.

Betty never took the time to understand her bees or what she was supposed to be doing, so she was nervous and unsure the few times she did go into her hives. She always thought she had more frames of comb then she needed, so instead of putting all ten into her deep hive box, Betty only used eight. But, because bees maintain bee space, they built their own comb where the missing frames were supposed to be, making it more difficult for Betty to work her hive.

Betty viewed her bees as her little babies, and instead of following proven beekeeping science, she stubbornly believed that "mother knows best." Years before she had her bees, Betty had seen a television show about the evils of processed foods and refined sugar, so when she got her bees, she refused to feed them sugar syrup. She said, "Don't beekeepers know all the problems white sugar causes? ADHD, hyperactivity, high blood pressure, diabetes, they're all caused by white sugar. That's why the bees are dying; it's the processed sugar we're feeding them! Why hasn't anyone else made the connection?"

Trying to explain to Betty that nectar and pure cane sugar were both 100 percent sucrose was like trying to teach a dog to give up meat and become a vegetarian. The fact that honeybees have exclusively lived off of sucrose and other sugars for their entire existence also fell on deaf ears. Betty had made up her mind that it was the white sugar that was killing the bees, so instead she was only going to feed her bees honey.

> **BEE NERD ALERT:** While nectar is sucrose, honey is comprised of fructose and glucose, as the bees break down the nectar's sucrose by adding enzymes to it.

Betty decided the best way to feed honey to her bees was by putting honey-filled plates in front of her hive so any time they were hungry the bees could just fly over and get it. But instead of helping her bees, Betty made things worse for them, her family, and her neighbors. Putting plates of honey out in the open meant that her bees and any other bees in the area could just fly over and fill up, but by having honey out in the open, she created a crazy feeding frenzy and initiated the bees' robbing instincts.

A honeybee's robbing instinct is usually engaged when bees rob out weaker or dead hives, but it can also engage if they find a supply of unattended honey. When they are in this mode, they become a frenzied mob. It would be the same if someone started giving away free beer at a NASCAR race; once word got out, everybody would want it and they'd all be going crazy trying to get it. Bees are the same way, and once they get worked up, they want every bee and non-bee out of their way, so Betty, her family, and her neighbors were all forced to stay inside until nighttime when all the honey was gone and all the bees were back in their hive.

To make the situation even worse, Betty had purchased the honey at her local big box discount store, which is never a safe option for your bees. Not knowing the origins of the honey, or if it contains ingredients other than honey, could make your bees sick or even kill them. Honey sold in the United States is sourced from countries all around the world. The honey from most of these countries is absolutely safe, but other times, honey is illegally imported from places that use chemicals and antibiotics in their beekeeping/honey production that the FDA has found to be unsafe for human consumption, which is why consuming cheap honey can be unhealthy. Other times, what is labeled as 100 percent honey actually contains high fructose corn syrup, rice syrup, or some other type of cheap sweet filler. In one study, it was discovered that more than 75 percent of honey sold in the United States was not pure honey. Proving once again, if something is *really* cheap, then what you're buying is probably not what you think it is. In the case of honey, when you want the good stuff, it's always best to know your beekeeper!

Ignoring all the warnings about feeding store-bought honey to her bees, Betty had bought the honey that "had the best deal." After her backyard had settled down from the feeding frenzy and her bees began consuming the honey, they came down with the equivalent of bee dysentery and by the next day the outside of her hive looked like a toilet at an all-night truck stop with bee poop everywhere.

After she saw the mess on the outside of her hive, Betty decided to wash it down with a garden hose. She used the "jet" setting on her nozzle and sprayed all the bee poop off the hive. Betty was only concerned about how her hive looked and she was not thinking about the bees, so she ended up squirting a great deal of water into the hive, soaking the bees and destroying most of their comb. Afterward, the remaining bees limped along for a few more months until the last of them finally perished. Only, Betty didn't seem to mind, as the hive looked great in her yard and now that all the bees were dead, no one had to worry about getting stung.

TWO OF THE WORST BEE-HAVERS I ever met were Rocco and his adult daughter Rosie. Rocco was unkempt, usually unshowered with matted hair, and wore crumpled, stained clothes. Rocco was unable to sit still, as he was constantly fidgeting, twitching, standing up, or moving his body about in some weird, spastic way. You didn't have to be a doctor to know that there was something wrong with Rocco, and the only person who didn't seem to care was Rosie.

Rosie was a squat, burly woman in her early forties who had so much facial hair she put Abe Lincoln to shame. From a distance she reminded you of a Sasquatch, and when she was closer, she smelled like one too. If you tried to have a conversation with her, her eyes would drift to the corners then dart back to briefly focus on you until they floated away again. The cadence and pitch when she spoke, not to mention the words and phrases she used, seemed to suggest that she was overly medicated, and her doctors hadn't got her prescription quite right yet.

Rocco and Rosie were constantly trolling the universe looking for ways to get rich by not having to work. They were attracted to having bees because they liked the idea that the bees do all the work and the beekeeper keeps all the money. Everything they did was motivated by trying to game the system and getting something for free. After the bee club meetings were over, if there were any leftover cookies or cake, Rosie would ask if she could have them to take home with her. Rosie would tell anyone within earshot that they were poor and needed help, then at the end of the night she'd drive away in her Audi SUV and Rocco in his Jeep Wrangler.

They didn't want to buy any beekeeping equipment, and instead Rosie would ask people if they had anything they didn't want anymore. Unfortunately for her, most beekeepers would rather hold on to their equipment instead of giving it away. But Rocco and Rosie had built their life on getting things for free, so they devised a plan to get beekeeping equipment without having to pay one cent for it. Rosie knew that groups were always looking to donate to good causes, so she began an email writing campaign to all the local high schools in the area, saying that she and her father would like to start saving the environment by having bees, but they were too poor to afford the wooden hives. She "suggested" that if the woodworking classes were looking for any projects, maybe they could build all the woodenware she and her father needed for their bees.

It didn't take long for her to get the response she was after, and a vocational high school's woodworking class leaped at the chance to take on a new project that would also be for a good cause. They told her it would take them about one month to get everything done, and they even asked her what color she'd like her hives painted. The class ended up building two complete hives, from hive stands to outer covers. Each hive had two deep boxes and two honey super boxes. The class had also built the wood frames so all that Rocco and Rosie needed was foundation for the frames and the bees. As word spread throughout the school what the woodworking class was doing, the rest of the students wanted to do their part to help save the bees, and through bake sales and several "help the bees" fund-raisers, they were able to also present Rocco and Rosie with $750 to buy bees and the rest of the equipment they would need to get started. During the ceremony where the school presented them with their newly built equipment and the cash the students had col-

lected, Rocco and Rosie played the part of the needy and appreciative charitable cause so that everyone would feel good about
their donation. Rosie even rented a U-Haul to bring all the new
woodenware home, as she knew a beat-up old truck fits the
story better than a newly leased Audi.

A few weeks later, Rocco and Rosie picked up their bees
from a commercial beekeeper, only neither of them had ever
bothered to learn anything about keeping bees. Rosie had spent
all her time trying to get everything for free, but at no time did
she try to learn what she should do once she got bees. As long
as it didn't cost anything, Rocco would attend any and every
beekeeping meeting in an eighty-mile radius, but he never
seemed to benefit from listening to beekeepers talk about their
bees, as he only asked questions that had nothing to do with
what was being discussed, and many times his questions didn't
even have anything to do with beekeeping.

During the monthly meetings that followed, Rocco and
Rosie could not understand why their bees were not producing
honey. As other members of the club asked questions to understand what they were doing, it became clear that they were not
feeding their bees any sugar syrup. Why not? Because they felt
that the sugar was too expensive. They were also very impatient
and would get angry because their bees were not producing as
much as other members' bees were. On several occasions, Rosie
said she was thinking of suing the commercial beekeeper for
selling them "defective bees."

All Rocco and Rosie could do was talk about selling their
honey. They would ask people where they sell their honey,
what's the best way to sell your honey, and anything else they
thought could help them to get an edge on selling honey. It was
clear to everyone in the club that neither Rocco nor Rosie cared

about the bees, as they only saw them as a means to an end. Since beekeeping clubs are filled with people who are passionate about honeybees and doing whatever it takes to keep their bees healthy, Rocco and Rosie didn't make many friends as their motivations were clearly at odds with everyone else's. The meetings they attended generally didn't go well, as they were always trying to monopolize the meetings by asking question after question. They refused to learn the basics of beekeeping, their questions were repetitive, and any answers they received left them more confused and belligerent that their bees couldn't just make honey like they were supposed to be doing.

Since Rocco and Rosie were only concerned about honey, they had neglected to notice that their bee boxes were falling apart. When you buy woodenware from a beekeeping supply company, the four corners are dovetailed together and when you assemble them, you are supposed to use carpenter's glue and nails through both pieces of wood to securely join them together. But the high school that made these boxes didn't have the equipment to make dovetailed corners, so instead, the students simply nailed the end pieces of the boxes onto the longer side pieces. The students were not beekeepers, so they didn't know how much weight and stress these boxes had to endure, so they built something that would hold up to normal wear and tear, but not beekeeping wear and tear. Also, the school didn't have the proper routers, so the students never cut handles into the bee boxes, and since Rocco and Rosie never bothered to look at an actual beehive, they had no idea the handles were missing.

Rocco and Rosie's adventures in bee-having came crashing down one sunny afternoon. Rocco looked into the first hive to see if there was any honey, and when he saw there was none, he slammed the outer cover down onto the hive with all his strength. Since the bottom box had already split apart, the force of the slammed lid caused the hive to topple. Rosie, seeing the hive was falling, gave it a shove so it didn't fall toward her, and instead, she sent it into the other hive, causing it to also come crashing down. As both hives lay in a pile, bees from both hives started to buzz about in an angry cloud. Rocco completely lost his temper and decided he was going to show the bees that he was the boss. Rosie could tell by the look in her father's eyes that her time as a beekeeper was over, so she sadly stepped aside and lowered her head in defeat. Rocco stormed over to their shed and grabbed the lighter fluid that was sitting on top of a bag of charcoal briquettes. He proceeded to squirt the whole container of lighter fluid onto the wooden hive, on the bees, and the wax-filled frames. Rosie cackled like a cartoon witch as Rocco flicked a lit wooden safety match and they both watched as the hives and bees went up in flames.

THANKFULLY, BEE-HAVERS are far and few in numbers, representing only a very small minority of the people with bees. The vast majority of people who keep bees care very much for their bees' well-being and generally try to do what is best for them. Most beekeepers want to learn and seek the advice of books, bee science, and the experience of successful beekeepers. That's why bee-havers are so easy to spot and stick out like a stung thumb; they are never willing to learn, they always have an excuse, and they always put their own needs before their bees. A true beekeeper realizes that no one, not even the bees, have all the answers, there is always a lot more to learn, and if you want to enjoy the sweet taste of success, then you must be ready to give your bees what they need when they need it.

CHAPTER 15

Honey Honey

ALL SUMMER LONG, my two hives really thrived. They expanded from the five-frame nucs to a full ten frames in a matter of weeks. Once I put the second deep on, the bees immediately went to work drawing out all the comb and filling it with nectar, eggs, and pollen. Since drawing out the comb requires so much energy and resources from the bees, during their first season most colonies are only able to take care of themselves, and they are not able to also produce a surplus of honey for the beekeeper. But that summer the weather was perfect, and both my hives were booming.

It was early June and both hives had drawn out the comb in all the frames in both of the deep boxes. The top deep was extremely heavy, as the bees had stored and capped somewhere between eighty and ninety pounds of honey in each of their respective hives. Since the bees had plenty of honey for themselves, I wanted to see if they would be able to make some for me, so I put a honey super on each of my hives. The bees still needed to draw out the comb, fill it with nectar, and then turn the nectar into honey. But I remained optimistic and I wanted to see what they could do.

No matter what gets you in to beekeeping, sooner or later honey will become a big part of your adventure. I, for one, didn't get in to beekeeping for the honey, but over time I have continually tried to increase my yearly take, if for nothing else, because honey is a measure of success in beekeeping.

The process of getting honey from a hive into plastic squeezable bears is simple and relatively unchanged for the last 150 years. Thanks to Langstroth's movable frames, honey-filled frames are pulled from the hive, placed into an extractor, and the honey is spun out of the comb. The process is the same no matter if you have twenty-five pounds of honey, or 250,000 pounds of honey, the only difference is the size of your extractor.

An extractor is essentially a drum with a basket inside to hold the frames filled with honey. The basket spins around and, thanks to the physics of centrifugal force, the honey flies out of the comb, hits the inside wall of the drum, drips down the wall and collects at the bottom, where it flows out of a spigot.

The smallest extractors fit two frames at a time, and the largest ones fit hundreds of frames at a time. Extractors can be hand cranked or motorized, and since extractors don't need to spin the frames super-fast to get the honey out, a steady spin cycle is the best way to get some yummy honey into your tummy.

Leigh, a member in the club who had been keeping bees since 1935, gave me my first extractor. Leigh decided it was time to upgrade to a motorized extractor, not because he was getting more honey, but once he was in his eighties, he was starting to slow down. Leigh was always smiling and had a handlebar mustache that sat above his steadfast grin. Being new to beekeeping, I didn't have an extractor, so Leigh offered his old one to me because he no longer had any use for it and he would rather see it go to good use than just sit in his garage collecting dust.

Leigh's extractor was a genuine antique. The label said it was from A. I. Root, a company that hadn't sold extractors in over fifty years. But it still worked like the day he ordered it from a long gone bee supply catalog. Modern extractors are made from stainless steel, but this old workhorse was made from aluminum. Decades before, Leigh had built a wooden stand for the extractor to sit on, and then mounted the stand on a big wooden "X" that looked like a propeller from an old WWI biplane. Leigh had built the stand so the extractor would sit a few feet above the floor, providing enough room at the bottom of the extractor, below the spigot, to place a five-gallon bucket to catch the honey. Resting on top of the bucket would be a metal strainer to catch any wax particles that might be in the honey. This simple system allows for the purest honey, as honey goes straight from the hive, into the extractor where it is spun out, through the strainer into a bucket, and later into bottles and jars.

As the weeks passed, I peered into my hives to keep an eye on the bees' progress. I watched as they first drew out the comb in my honey supers, then they took the next step I was hoping for, and filled the comb with a golden liquid.

Humans have been collecting honey for over thirteen thousand years, but what exactly is honey? Honey is the essence of flowers, and that alone makes it amazing, but after learning about what it takes to make honey, you realize that it is almost

magical. The forager bees fly to collect the nectar from two million flowers for every pound of honey the hive produces,
meaning the bees have logged about 55,000 miles, or the equivalent of two trips around the earth, just to produce one pound
of honey. Since bees need a lot more than just one pound of
honey, each hive continues at this busy as a bee pace another
sixty to eighty times before they have produced enough honey
for themselves. Then, if all goes right, they can start making
honey for their beekeeper, or as some say, they can start paying
their rent.

Honey's taste and color is totally dependent on what flowers
the bees visit to collect the nectar from, and every plant has its
own unique flavor. If a plant produces a fruit or vegetable, like a
blueberry or an avocado, the honey from those plants will be
distinct, but it will not taste like the fruit. For example, the but-
terbean plant (*Phaseolus lunatus*) is an excellent source of nectar,
and its honey is light in color and super-sweet, but thankfully,
it doesn't remotely taste like beans. Another example is cranberry honey. While it processes a unique cranberry honey taste,
it is not bitter like a cranberry, nor is it red, and nor is it good for
urinary tract infections.

It is amazing to see how bees and plants evolved together,
with one helping, or more accurately—bribing—the other.
Bees are monofloral, meaning that for as long as a specific
plant is in bloom, the bees will continue to work it. Since bees
are pollinators this makes perfect sense, especially if you're a
plant. Pollination is the act of fertilizing a flower, and when the
bees fly from flower to flower, they are bringing the boy parts
and girl parts of a plant together. If bees did not stick with one
type of plant at a time, they would not be as effective as pollinators since they could be covered with incompatible pollen.

If you're a blueberry bush, pollen from an avocado tree doesn't do you much good. The monofloral behavior of bees is why you will see specific types of honey in the store, such as orange blossom, clover, or buckwheat. It is also why honeybees are so important to commercial farming, as farmers can count on the bees to pollinate the crop that is currently in bloom. The best example of this is the almond pollination in northern California, which is the largest pollination event in the world. Almonds are a $7.6 billon industry that is 100 percent dependent on the honeybee. Commercial beekeepers from all across the country bring their hives to northern California and place two beehives per almond tree–covered acre. To get a sense of how large the almond pollination event is, every February, two in every three beehives in the United States is sitting in northern California pollinating almonds.

Besides taste and color, the properties of honey generally remain the same across all honeys. As bees turn nectar, which is sucrose, into honey, they add enzymes that break it down into fructose and glucose. Honey also contains trace amounts of the B vitamins (B_1, B_2, B_3, B_6), vitamin C, and the minerals sodium, potassium, magnesium, calcium, copper, and iron.

Bees add an enzyme **BEE NERD WORD:** *glucose oxidase* that converts some of the glucose into hydrogen peroxide. This step increases the acidity of the honey and lowers its pH, creating a food source that will never ever spoil. Specifically, honey's high sugar content, its lack of moisture, its low pH, and because it contains hydrogen peroxide are what makes it an inhospitable environment for microorganisms and why no matter its age, honey will never go bad and is always so good to eat. Once, when archaeologists were excavating an ancient tomb in Egypt's famous pyramids, they found pots of honey. The honey, which was the world's oldest, and dating back over three thousand years, was still perfectly edible! Not even a Hostess Twinkie can last that long.

Honey will crystallize, but that doesn't mean it has gone bad, only that it has changed from a liquid into a solid. Honey is a super-saturated sugar solution, meaning that the water has absorbed more sugar than it could under normal circumstances. Since it's super-saturated, it's not very stable, so over time some of the glucose molecules naturally pull out of the liquid and connect to one another and form crystals. If you ever have a jar of honey that crystallizes, never fear, because that's proof that what you have is indeed 100 percent all natural honey. Only pure, all natural honey will crystallize. It's easy to re-liquefy your honey, and all you have to do is place your jar of crystallized honey in a warm bath of water, with 104°F being the ideal temperature. The heat will slowly dissolve the crystals and make the honey liquid again. Since temperatures inside a hive can get upward of 110°F, warming your honey to temperatures that honey is subjected to while in the hive will have no ill effects on it.

BEE NERD ALERT: Heater bees, by moving the muscles that would normally power their wings, increase the temperature of their bodies up to 111.2°F, and the upper lethal temperatures of honeybees is 120.2°F.

Because of the information-overload world we live in today, there are half-truths, misconceptions, and simply wrong information floating around about honey. First, everyone is always looking for "pure" "raw" honey, but what does that actually mean? Pure honey is easy, as that means it only contains 100 percent honey, with nothing else added. Raw honey is honey that is exactly how the bees made it. To be called raw, honey must always remain in conditions that are also found inside the hive. This means that honey cannot be heated above temperatures that are above what's in a hive. Unfortunately, thanks to the marketing campaigns of a few brands, many people think raw honey is solid, or crystallized honey. There is one brand of "raw" honey that adds beeswax and propolis to each jar, as they are playing on people's misconception that if it's raw, then it has to be "dirty." What's frustrating is that nothing could be further from the truth. When you go into your hives and break off a piece of honeycomb, pure, golden honey is what you will see and taste. Bees are the OCD inhabitants of the insect kingdom, and they meticulously tend to their honey to ensure it is all liquid.

BEE NERD ALERT: Bees use their proboscis, or straw tongue, to consume honey by drinking it.

Solid honey, or creamed honey, is still 100 percent honey and it tastes great, but that's not how the bees eat it. Bees do not have teeth, so thinking that they'd bite off a piece of solid honey, chew and swallow it, makes as much sense as thinking they'd spread it on their morning toast and enjoy it with a cup of coffee. The process of making creamed honey is to use honey's natural tendency to crystallize in a way that will create a smooth solid honey. The most common way to make creamed honey, or whipped honey, is called the Dyce method, named after Professor Elton Dyce who patented his process in 1935. Dyce's method uses controlled crystallization to achieve smooth, consistent results.

BEE NERD ALERT: Cornell University's bee research center is named Dyce Lab, named after the professor emeritus of creamed honey who headed Cornell's honeybee program from 1947 to 1966.

The worst ill-informed misconception about honey is "organic honey," because it simply does not exist. The USDA has never adopted any criteria or regulations for defining what qualifies as organic honey, so there is no way to certify any U.S.-produced honey as organic. This means that any honey produced in the United States can never be labeled as organic. However, if honey is harvested *outside* of the United States it can be labeled organic if it meets *that* country's organic standards *and* the U.S. organic standards. Since the United States doesn't have any standards for organic honey, that means that any honey produced in other countries that say they have their own version of an organic standard can use the USDA Organic emblem regardless of how that other country defines organic.

For fruits and vegetables to be called organic in the United States, they must be certified to have been grown on soil that has had no prohibited substances such as synthetic fertilizers and pesticides applied for three years prior to harvest. Since bees collect nectar and pollen from plants, for honey to be called organic, then it stands to reason that all the plants the bees collected the nectar from should be organic. But the only way to make sure that all the plants are organic is to account for the distance bees will travel from their hive to forage, and all the land within their flight zone. As stated previously, bees will travel, on average, up to three miles from their hive to forage, which means that if you were to draw a three-mile circle on a map, that would cover about 18,095.6 acres, so each and every plant within those 18,095.6 acres would have to be synthetic fertilizer– and pesticide-free for the honey to be truly organic. Last, to be considered organic, Varroa mite treatments and other bee pest treatments would also have to be taken into account. Today's most effective miticides would not qualify as organic, so many "organic" hives would die off from having too many mites just so they could be certified as organic. Additionally, even if you did have eighteen thousand organically certified acres, and you only used organically approved mite treatments, you would still have a problem with non-organic chemicals being in your hives. A scientific study looked at commercially available wax foundation and found that all samples contained traces of synthetic chemicals. When you consider how many acres each hive covers, along with the proper care your bees need to survive, and that all the commercially available wax is tainted, you can understand how it would be impossible to have certified organic honey.

Organic or not, besides being something that's great to eat, honey also has some important non-food uses. In our world of modern medicine, honey is used to fight infection and helps heal some ailments and wounds. There is a product called "medical honey," which is pre-applied to bandages and it is used to accelerate healing, kill bacterial growth, and prevent infection. Honey dressings are used to help heal burns, as they keep the burn site moist and sterile until it can heal. Patients receiving honey dressings have been shown to heal four or five days faster compared to when they're given other types of wound dressings.

Honey is also an effective cough suppressant, and it is as effective at reducing coughs as any of the over-the-counter cough suppressants. This is particularly good news for parents; medicated cough suppressants aren't always safe for kids. Honey is natural and it helps to soothe and coat the throat, and can help children sleep longer through the night with fewer coughing episodes.

Manuka honey from New Zealand is seen as having higher medicinal value. It is from the nectar of the Manuka tree, and it contains methylglyoxal (MGO), which is the active ingredient that bestows Manuka honey with its unique antibacterial properties. The higher the level of MGO, the greater the honey's antibacterial effects. While all honey is antimicrobial, the MGO makes Manuka honey a super-charged antibacterial and antiviral honey.

Many people consume local honey to help alleviate seasonal allergies. Since honey contains minute particles of pollen, the thought is that by ingesting it in small quantities, the pollen will work the same way as a vaccine does, and your body will be able to build up a resistance to it. While there is no scientific study to support this school of thought, many people still swear by the powers of local honey.

No matter where honey is from, and regardless of all of its many uses, honey tastes great and people love to eat it. As a beekeeper, you'll learn that the best tasting honey you'll ever taste is the honey from your own hive. And with your own supply of honey, you'll soon be eating honey on everything. One of my favorite ways to eat honey is on sorbet. Because of the cold temperature, the honey gets thick and chewy like toffee, and the sweet floral flavors from the honey mix well with the sorbet's fruity flavors.

My very first honey harvest consisted of two supers, one from each of my hives. In northeast New Jersey, the nectar flow stops sometime around the Fourth of July. Being the eternal optimist, I waited for another week, just to make sure my bees could get every last drop of nectar and turn all of it into honey. I extracted my honey in my dining room, which required moving all the chairs and everything on the table to a different part of the house. I pushed the dining room table to one corner of the room and set up my antique extractor. Besides an extractor, all that's needed is an uncapping tank, an uncapping fork or knife, plenty of five-gallon buckets, and lots of wet rags to wipe up all the honey that will get spilled.

Back in the hive, once the honey is less than 19 percent moisture, the bees know the honey is ready to eat, so they cover the honey with a thin layer of pure, white wax. The bees cover the honey for the same reason that we put lids on our jars and caps on our bottles. The capping prevents anything from getting into the honey, and it also prevents the honey from spilling out. Once the honey is capped, it's safely stored and will be ready to eat when the bees need it.

The first step in extracting is cutting or breaking off this thin layer of wax, so all the wax cells are open and the honey can be removed. But, the trick is to remove just enough wax to expose the honey, and leave the rest of the comb intact so the bees do not have to rebuild it. If you think of honeycomb as a bunch of gel-caps bunched together, you're only trying to remove the very tips of the gel-caps, while leaving the rest of the structure and the honey inside untouched.

There are lots of ways to remove the thin wax capping, and the most common tool is the extracting knife, which looks like a serrated bread knife with a funky handle. The handle has an extra right angle built into it, so you don't scrape your knuckles on the wood frame as you are uncapping the wax. I don't like to use the knife, as it only works in the middle of the frame, not the corners or edges. I have also found that the knife cuts too deep into the comb, taking off too much of the wax. My favorite tool to use is the uncapping fork, which looks like a handheld pitchfork. You hold the uncapping fork parallel to the honey, and its sharp prongs will lightly pierce the wax and with a slight flick of your wrist you can break off the wax cappings.

The uncapping process is tedious and one of the most time-consuming steps in the extracting process. The other most time-consuming step is cleaning up all the sticky honey you've somehow spilled e-v-e-r-y-w-h-e-r-e. There are uncapping machines that you can buy, but at a few thousand dollars they are too costly for most backyard beekeepers, which is why it is still mostly done by hand.

Since you are essentially breaking open thousands and thousands of little honey storage containers, you need something to catch the honey that drips off, as well as the wax cappings that you have cut away from the comb. An uncapping tank is what most beekeepers use, and it looks like a Rubbermaid storage bin with a metal grate at the bottom and a spigot at one end. The metal grate is to catch the wax that gets cut off so any honey on the cappings can drip through the grate and can then be drained from the spigot. Most uncapping tanks are sized to hold honey frames until they are ready to be placed in the extractor. Since my extractor holds three frames at a time, I will uncap three frames before placing all three of them into the extractor. As I uncap them, I hang them in the uncapping tank to minimize how much honey spills and drips on the floor.

The wax cappings that collect in the uncapping tank are great for making lip balms, hand creams, and beeswax candles. Cappings wax is pure white and has almost no impurities, which is why it is the best wax to use for all your beeswaxing needs.

Once the frames are in the extractor, you have to spin them for about two minutes per side, or around four minutes in total for every three frames. Once you get the hang of it, you can extract one super in about forty-five minutes.

It is always amazing to see how many pounds of honey a hive can produce, especially when the nectar flow is going really strong and the bees are literally making thirty or more pounds a week. On average, one super will hold thirty-five pounds of honey, and I have had some supers that have weighed twice that amount. No matter how many years you've been keeping bees, it is always awe-inspiring when you take off supers that were just wood and wax when you put them on, but are now so full of honey they weigh forty pounds or more.

Since bees will keep making honey as long as there is nectar to collect and space to store it in the hive, it is fun to keep adding supers on top of the hive just to see how high the bees can go. I have had a few hives that grew to over seven feet tall and produced over 340 pounds of honey in just one season. For these monster hives, I needed a ladder and a few bee helpers to safely tear down my tower of honey. I have had helpers who are completely unprepared for how heavy a box full of honey can be. When I pass the honey super over to them their eyes usually start to bug out, as they're holding the weight equivalent of two concrete cinder blocks.

Beekeepers always joke that you don't need a gym when you can get a beekeeper's workout. There is a lot of heavy lifting when you are moving boxes around on your hives, and knowing that thousands of bees are going to be very angry if you drop it is the best motivator to hold on tight. You do need to be aware of how you lift, otherwise you could do some serious damage to your back. While beekeepers are not exactly known for their bodybuilder physique, keeping bees will keep you active and provide you with plenty of physical activity to help keep you in shape, or at least off the couch. I like that beekeeping gets me outside. It's an activity that clears my head, takes away my stress, and helps me to feel centered. For me, it's like going to a gym, only it's sweeter, and when I get back from my hives, I always feel reenergized.

When you do take the honey supers off your hive, the most important thing to remember is that you don't want to take the bees with you, as it's always better for you and them if they remain in the hive. There are several ways to get the bees out of the honey supers, so you don't have several dozen uninvited guests in your house when you extract. A common tool is the bee escape, which works much like a lobster trap, allowing bees to travel in only one direction. The bee escape is made of wood and has a big hole on one side, and three small screened tunnels on the other. You first take off all of your honey supers, then you put the escape on top of your deep bee box, and then you put all your supers back on top of the escape. Since bees always want to be close to the brood and the queen, the bees will naturally move down from the supers and into the deep box below. After a few days, all of the supers are bee-free, making it easy for you to take away your honey.

Another easy way to move bees out of the supers is to use a fume board. The basic premise of this method is to use some super stinky smell to drive the bees out of the supers. If you have ever taken public transit and have had the unfortunate experience of sitting next to someone who hasn't showered in who knows how long, then you know exactly how effective a stinky smell is at clearing a space. A fume board looks like a wooden hive top, only there is a piece of felt covering the inside ceiling. There are four or five different substances you can buy from the bee suppliers to use on your fume board. A few of them smell super stinky to humans, but a few others are actually not offensive to people. For instance, a major ingredient in the non-offensive sprays is almond oil, because bees do not like the smell of almond oil, which is ironic since bees pollinate almond trees.

Once you place the fume board on top of your hive, it only takes a few minutes for all the bees to start moving down. A good trick is to have two fume boards so you can work on two hives at a time to get the supers off more efficiently. You take one super off one hive at a time, and as you take off a super on one hive, you're giving the bees in the other hive time to move down. Once you get all the supers off all the hives, then all you have to do is lug all of them back to where you're planning on doing the extracting.

It is very important that you always extract your honey indoors. If you try to extract outside, you will learn how quickly the bees will find their honey and how determined they are to get it back.

There was a husband and wife who weren't the sharpest hive tools in the shed. It took them a few seasons just to gain a remedial understanding of having bees, such as feeding your bees doesn't mean throwing cut flowers in front of your hive, and when using your smoker, lots of smoke is good, but flames shooting out the top is bad. Mr. and Mrs. Nittiwhit were able to get a few supers of honey after their third season. They were both very excited to finally reap the rewards of having bees and couldn't wait to extract it. But as they were deciding where and how to extract, they both agreed that neither of them wanted to make a mess in their house and have to be stuck with cleaning up all the spilled honey. Instead, they decided they would extract in their driveway. They were quite proud of themselves, because even though they were told that you should always extract inside, they decided that they had figured out a plan to outsmart the bees.

Now, anytime anyone says they "figured out a way to outsmart the bees," you know it's not going to end well. Honeybees have been around a lot longer than people, and those extra hundred million years have taught the bees everything they need to know to accumulate a lot of wins over their dimwitted primate rivals.

The plan was actually quite simple. They would extract in their driveway, and they would wear their full bee suits the entire time so they couldn't get stung. Since they weren't sure what to expect, they also duct-taped their sleeves and pant legs, just to make sure no bees would sneak into their bee suits, and they were both absolutely 100 percent protected. They set up tables, their extractor, and they brought out buckets and everything they thought they would need to get the job done. Before they started, they also lit citronella candles, hoping the smell would help keep the bees away. (It didn't.)

Everything was set up, they had a ring of torch-like candles surrounding their driveway, two long tables set up side-by-side, all of their honey-extracting tools laid out on one table, their extractor, and honey supers. And with their full bee suits on, it looked like a scene out of *E.T.* when the government finally discovers the extra-terrestrial and sets up shop in Elliott's front yard.

For such a blockheaded idea, they really did think of everything. They even had a blue plastic swimming pool leaf skimming net that Mrs. Nittiwhit waved through the air to swat at and catch any bees that got too close to the honey. There was one thing they hadn't counted on, however. They hadn't thought about what it would look like to their neighbors or anyone passing by and happened to see two spacesuit-wearing people performing what looked like medical experiments in an operating room set up in a driveway, surrounded by ritualistic torches, as one of the spacemen frantically waved a net through the air.

It didn't take long for a half a dozen people to call the local police to report that something very strange was going on, and for everyone's safety, these people needed to be stopped. Since this was a bedroom community in northern New Jersey, it was the most calls the town's police had received in years. The adrenaline started flowing and everyone on the force was getting worked up since this was the first time something serious might actually be happening, and they would finally be able to do some real police work. Lieutenant Eugene O'Malley raced off to the scene with sirens blaring, lights flashing, and when he arrived, he came to a screeching halt and kept his lights flashing. The lieutenant jumped out of his car and took a few steps toward the driveway. Thanks to the extracting process and all the honey and honeycomb sitting out in the driveway, there was a cloud of bees zooming around in all directions, and none of them were happy. First one, and then another, and then another bee stung Lieutenant O'Malley. He was jumping around, swatting at the bees, and shouting as he got stung. All the while Mrs. Nittiwhit kept waving her big net through the air. To the crowd that had gathered, it looked like Mrs. Nittiwhit's net was somehow causing the lieutenant to scream in pain, because her movements were synchronized to his screams, and every time she moved her net in a different direction, Lieutenant O'Malley jumped or swatted at the bees. O'Malley jumped back into his car and got on the loudspeaker before anything more serious happened. He said, "Hands in the air, NOW! Yes, you two in the white suits, hands in the air." Mr. and Mrs. Nittiwhit realized he was talking to them and did what they were told. O'Malley didn't want to get out of his car again, so he ordered them to keep their hands in the air and walk over to and get in back of the police cars. They were immediately arrested and taken to the precinct.

Once at the police station, the truth of what was really going on quickly came out. Thankfully one of the cops had a friend who was a beekeeper, and asked him to go over to deal with the mess in the driveway. So, as Mr. and Mrs. Nittiwhit were calling their lawyer to bail them out of this mess, a few local beekeepers took away the honey, the supers, and the beehives, so the quiet neighborhood could once again return to normal. Mr. and Mrs. Nittiwhit were able to reach a plea bargain for most of the summons they received, all on the condition that they stay out of trouble and promise to never have bees on their property again.

The first time I extracted my honey it was a lot less dramatic. I used common sense and brought all my supers inside before I ever touched the honey. Because I used the bee escapes, my supers were bee free. When I first started using the uncapping fork, I was flicking the wax straight up, getting blobs of honey-soaked wax to fly through the air and land all over my dining room. I loaded up Leigh's old extractor and started to crank the handle. It sounded like a washing machine with a heavy load of clothes: boom-boom-boom. I quickly found out that the extractor was off balance, and with every twist of the handle it jumped around the room. I ended up standing with both feet on the wooden stand, trying to keep it relatively in one spot. Then, as I turned the crank on the extractor with one hand, I bear-hugged it with my other to try and muffle some of the boom-boom-boom noise. Between the extractor rocking around the room, and having to hold on by bear-hugging the whole thing, I felt like I was in some sort of bucking-bee rodeo.

Looking back, it was probably good that I only got thirty-two pounds of honey my first year, because any more and I might have gotten whiplash from riding that extractor any longer. But that day, when I had harvested thirty-two pounds of the best tasting honey I had ever had, that my own bees had made, I was the happiest beekeeper on the planet. That is, until I had to clean up all the honey that I realized had somehow been spilled e-v-e-r-y-w-h-e-r-e.

CHAPTER 16

Bee Mistakes

BEEKEEPING IS A HANDS-ON ACTIVITY, and the only way you're going to learn how to keep bees is by hive diving and doing it yourself. When you're first starting out, you will make a few mistakes—or if you're like me, you will make thousands of them. Some mistakes will be small, others will be slightly more serious, and for a few mistake-prone individuals, their mistakes will become the legends of the beekeeping world.

If you meet a beekeeper and he says that he has never made a mistake, he's either a liar or he doesn't keep bees. The old adage "learn from your mistakes" was probably written by a beekeeper, especially since bees have their own special way to help you remember to never make the same mistake twice. Beekeeping is mostly based on common sense, so when you do make a mistake it's easy to see what went wrong and figure out what it was that you should have done. A good example is when you're doing a hive inspection and you forget that you should always test your smoker away from the bees to make sure it's still blowing out cool, white smoke. Instead, you puff your smoker directly into one of your hives as it snorts out big red flames and you watch as your bees start running around like they're under attack from Godzilla.

Another great example is remembering to double-check to make sure your veil is securely closed shut. Ian, one of my beekeeping friends, has a habit of talking so much that he forgets the little details like zipping up his veil. He'll be yammering away nonstop from the moment he steps off his back porch until he's somewhere in the middle of a hive inspection, then a few bees start flying around *inside* his veil to remind him why he should talk less and zip more.

Mistakes are a great teaching tool, and a few stings are just added motivators that help you learn the art of beekeeping as quickly as you can. I have always been someone who learns from his mistakes, and I have become such a reputable beekeeper because I have created so many learning opportunities for myself. Most of my mistakes have been the little ones, such as forgetting to return my hive tool to my back pants pocket and instead leaving it in a bottom deep so when I do realize that my hive tool is missing, I have to go back into and disassemble the whole hive just to retrieve it. I wouldn't be the accomplished master beekeeper that I am today if I had only made everyday, unspectacular mistakes. I have also made more serious mistakes, like dropping a hive-top feeder and spilling three gallons of super sticky sugar syrup all over the lower half of my body. Or losing my grip on a fifty-pound honey super so it crashes to the ground and spills bees and honey everywhere. Yes, like most beekeepers I have made my fair share of mistakes, but what really makes me stand out from my peers in the beekeeping community is that some of my mistakes have been so amazingly epic that entire beekeeping communities have learned from them!

A doozy of a mistake happened when I first set up my church apiary. When you're trying to scout out a new location to place some of your hives there are a few things you always want to look for. First, how much sun will your hives be getting? Full sun is best, but in suburbia, it's more about making sure that your hives won't be sitting in the cool shade all day, shielded from all direct sunlight. The second thing to look for is how well protected the hives will be from the weather. Are there any natural or man-made barriers north of the hives to protect against winter gusts of wind? It's also important to confirm that your hives are not in a valley where you'd have to contend with excessive moisture in the hive, or worse yet, being in a flood zone where you'd have to worry about your hives getting washed away. A good rule of thumb when scouting new sites is to look and see where the snow first melts, as that location will usually be sunny and dry. You also want to make sure the bees' flight paths are away from where anyone will be walking. If you have your hives in your backyard you need to make sure the hives will not interfere with your family when they're in the backyard, or the neighbors when they're in their backyard. It's best to have a full fifteen or more feet of clearance in front of the hives and then a six-foot flyway barrier, such as a fence or bushes, to force the bees up into the air and to keep people away from your hives. If you're going to have hives anywhere besides your backyard, then it's even more important to think about all the factors that make a good location for your apiary. You won't be able to just look out your window to make sure your hives are safe. That's why it's always a good idea to either keep your hives behind a locked fence, or out of sight from public view, and it's even better if you can do both. The more care you take confirming that a location is right for your bees, the more they will flourish, and the fewer aggravations you'll have to contend with over the years.

So, when I was looking to place some hives in the woods behind the church, I tried very hard to carefully select the best location to ensure that no mistakes would be made. But you know what they say about the best laid plans...Let me tell you, my church apiary is home to some of my most colossal mistakes.

The church has over twenty-five acres of land and much of it is unused forest. I had free rein to pick the best spot for my hives, and while I looked for a place that met all the necessary apiary requirements, I also wanted to find a place that would be out of sight but still easily accessible. When honey supers are newly constructed, they weigh less than ten pounds, but once they're filled with honey, they can weigh between forty and seventy pounds. That's why I needed my location to be easily accessible; otherwise there would be no way for me to haul all the honey out of the woods and get it back home.

I finally settled on a spot that was just off the path that went through the woods from the church to the rectory. The path made it easy for me to get to my bee yard, but there were plenty of trees to keep the hives out of sight from any curious eyes.

But I still wasn't 100 percent convinced that my hives would be completely safe, so I decided that initially I would only put one nuc at the church. I would use the nuc as a test to confirm that it was a safe location, and once I knew for sure, then I could move over more hives. Since it was only one nuc, I wouldn't be jeopardizing any full-size hives, and fewer bees would be at risk if anything went wrong.

On a sunny mid-April morning, I brought the nuc over to the church, set it on its hive stand I made out of a few cinder blocks, and after watching the bees orient to their new location for a good twenty minutes, I let them be and drove home. Every day for the next few weeks, I made an excuse to drive over to check on my bees, and every day they were fine. Actually, more than fine; the nuc was flourishing in its new location. Each time I visited my apiary at the church and saw that my bees were safe, healthy, and happy, it strengthened my belief that I had picked a good spot to keep my hives.

It was a productive summer for honey, and my hives were overflowing. My nuc was growing like crazy, and had quickly outgrown its single nuc box. To keep the bees from swarming, and so the colony could keep on growing, I added a second box on top, and then a few weeks later a third box. By the middle of June the nuc was still expanding, so I added another box, making the nuc four-stories tall, giving the colony a total of twenty frames. Since a standard-size hive also has twenty frames inside its two deep boxes, my four-story nuc was now the equivalent of a standard hive with just as many bees, if not more.

It had been three months since I brought my bees to the church and no one had bothered them. I was feeling good about finding such a great spot that had so many nectar sources close by to provide the resources needed for my nuc to be outshining my hives back home. I was interested in putting hives at the church simply because I wanted more hives. My motto, like so many other beekeepers', was: you can always have a few more hives. Since I was feeling good about the safety of the church apiary, I started to think about how many hives it could comfortably hold. I really wanted to put five hives at the church, and bring my total number of hives up to lucky number seven.

Instead of just guesstimating how many hives would fit, I decided to head over to the church with a tape measure and some stakes to map out where all the hives should be placed. If I were going to put five hives at the church, then I would need my bee yard to be at least twenty-eight feet wide, allowing two feet for each hive, and three feet on either side. I'd also need the yard to be at least twenty feet deep so I could have a fifteen-foot flyway for the bees, allow two feet for each hive, and still have three feet behind the hives.

I loaded up my car with my surveying equipment, and tossed in my beekeeping equipment and veil, just in case. I wasn't planning on working the bees, but sometimes when I'm around my hives I just can't help myself.

Once at the church apiary, I got to work measuring. I wanted to have all my hives in a nice row, so I measured the width first. Success, it was thirty-five feet across from east to west. I'd have no problem putting five hives. Next, I wanted to measure how deep the bee yard was, and that's when I first noticed the potential problem. Instead of being a nice, straight rectangle of open space, my bee yard was more of a funky trapezoid. The sides and back of my yard were fine, but in front of where some of the hives would face was a tree. It was about thirty feet tall and had some bushes growing around it, preventing half the yard from having a full fifteen feet of open space for the bees' flyway. My nuc was sitting in the far side of the yard, so I had never really noticed the tree before.

As I looked the tree up and down, I realized that I didn't see any leaves on it. "I think that tree's dead," I said out loud to no one but the bees. Then I noticed that the tree was not growing straight up into the air, but was angled toward where I was standing. Math was never my strongest subject, and my Euclidean geometry skills were less than impressive, but I thought, "That tree looks like if it falls, it will fall directly on my hive." My next thoughts were, "I wonder how solid that dead tree is?" and "Should I worry if it's going to fall down?"

I walked over to the tree to take a closer look. I grabbed the angled trunk of the tree and proceeded to tug on it, trying to gauge how solid it was. Within a split second, it was clear that the tree was about as solid as a Jenga tower; I heard the distinctive sound of a very large piece of wood splitting and cracking. I jumped away from the tree as all thirty feet of it came crashing down with a loud swoosh and a thunderous boom. The good news was that the tree didn't hit me. The bad news was that my geometry skills were better than I thought. I was right: if the tree fell, it would land on my hives. In fact, it had come straight down on my nuc.

Through the jumble of dead branches I could see that the nuc was completely knocked off its stand and was now lying on its side. My first instinct was to run. Run back to the car and get my veil. I wasn't too sure what I was going to do, but I knew I had to do something, and fast.

In the few short minutes it took for me to run to my car and back to my apiary, my bees had worked themselves up into a big, furious cloud of rage. A mass of angry bees were flying around where their home should have been. I quickly threw my veil onto my head without stopping to tie it, and raced toward the tree. I knew I had to move it, so channeling my inner Dr. David, *"Don't get me angry. You won't like me when I'm angry"* Banner, I grabbed a hold of two large branches, and with all my strength, pulled. The branches snapped in my hands, so I pulled at others, throwing them out of the way and off my nuc. After clearing a half dozen clusters of branches, I grabbed the trunk of the tree and lifting from my legs, I picked up the tree enough to walk it away from my bees. I could see my nuc, all four boxes bounced apart, and all twenty frames scattered on the ground. It looked like a four-drawer filing cabinet had been pushed over and all its file folders were fanned out across the floor.

Once the tree was out of the way, it cleared space for more bees to come out and express their displeasure with today's events. I took a long, deep breath as if I was about to jump off a diving board into a cold, deep, pool and got to work reassembling the nuc. It was easy to see the order the boxes were supposed to be in, but the frames were all over the place, so there was no way to tell where they were supposed to go.

After I got the bottom box back on the stand and I was putting the fifth frame in place, I got my first sting. It was on the top of my head. Since my veil was still just draped on my shoulders, the bees were easily finding their way inside. Thanks to the venom's homing signal, just as I realized that I had gotten stung—Bam-Bam—I got two more next to the first one.

A person's natural instinct is to run far away when you're standing in a cloud of angry insects and they're repeatedly stinging you, but beekeepers are apparently missing that chromosome because I was determined to stay until the nuc was back together.

Bam-Bam-Bam. The second box was back in place, and three more bees hit their mark on the top of my head. When one bee stings you, it's more annoying than painful. But when six bees sting you in an area the size of a quarter, you *really* start to feel it. When I was putting the frames in the third box, I heard some more bees get inside my veil, so I started shaking my head like I was a headbanger at a heavy metal concert, hoping they wouldn't sting me in the same spot. I got my wish, and instead of stinging me on the top of my head, the bees stung me on my left eyebrow—Bam-Bam-Bam-Bam—four stings in less than one minute. I guess bees are not fans of heavy metal headbanging.

As I was putting the frames back inside the boxes, I was impressed with all the brood, and how many nurse bees were still on the frames. But I was looking for something else. Even though the bees were using my skull for target practice, I was concerned about the queen. I didn't see her but I was hoping that she was on one of the frames and not laying somewhere impaled by a tree branch. The last five frames were all honey, so I got them into the last box so fast that only two more bees were able to get me, and this time they didn't hit me dead center on the top of my head, instead they flanked the target on both sides.

I grabbed the inner and outer covers, and tossed them onto the nuc. There were still bees everywhere, flying in an angry cloud, and all over the grass where their frames had landed. I still had to deal with removing the tree, but that would have to wait until another day. I was proud of myself for getting the nuc back together, and I was laughing to myself for getting twelve stings on my head and face. Laughing because it was my own fault for getting stung. Laughing because getting stung a dozen times on my head and face didn't hurt as much as I thought it might. Laughing because it's always better to laugh than to cry.

I started to head back to my car, and when I was about twenty-five feet away from the nuc, I turned around to take another look at the nuc and see if I missed anything. But just as Orpheus realized he had made a mistake by turning around, as I turned to look at the nuc, the thirteenth and final bee found its way under my veil and stung me on my temple, just down and to the left of my well tenderized eyebrow.

It's been eight years since that happened, and I'm still keeping hives at the church apiary. In that time, there have been two major hurricanes and dozens of storms that have downed countless trees. The church has grown throughout the years and the path through the woods has been expanded and sees a lot more foot traffic than just a few priests. But in all that time, through all those storms, and all the people who have passed by my hives, the only time that anything has ever happened to any of them was when I thought it was a good idea to be a tree tugger and go tug on a tree.

MOST OF MY OTHER monumental mistakes usually began with me saying, "Let me just do this real fast." Whenever I think I'll just move at a faster speed or that I'll get something done zippity-quick is when the bees remind me why it's always a better idea for me to take my time and never, ever, rush.

The first time my soon-to-be-wife experienced her first bee sting was when I said, "I need to feed one of my hives some more sugar syrup. I'll be quick. Let me just do it real fast." Then, because I was focused on working fast instead of watching what I was doing, I made a series of mistakes that led to my surprised-that-she-still-married-me,-soon-to-be wife getting stung on her right thigh. Since I was going to be moving fast, I thought I'd skip lighting the smoker, which led to alarm pheromones getting released and putting the bees on high alert. Next, I haphazardly laid the inner cover, which was covered in a fair number of bees, against the side of the hive, and when I went to pour the syrup into the hive top feeder, I bumped into the inner cover, causing it to topple over and land on my never-screamed-but-couldn't-

believe-what-I-had-done,-surprised-that-she-still-married-me,
-soon-to-be wife's feet. Once the inner cover hit the ground, the
bees became airborne, and the one that landed on my bride's
thigh decided that she'd had enough. Thankfully, once my so-
much-smarter-than-me,-never-screamed-but-couldn't-believe-
what-I-had-done,-surprised-that-she-still-married-me,-soon-
to-be wife realized that she had been stung, she immediately
walked away from the hives, went back to the car, and waited
until I was done. Now, whenever she accompanies me to the
hives, the first thing she says is, "Did you light the smoker?"

Unfortunately, for me to learn any lesson, I need to make a
mistake that is worthy of *America's Funniest Videos*, and watching
as the love of my life got a single sting on her leg didn't have what
it takes to be lesson worthy. It takes more, oh, so much more.

April is always a big month for bee talks by virtue of April
22 being Earth Day, which gets most people to think about the
environment. Every year, I'll get requests to speak at four or five
events in April, because everyone knows that nothing can mo-
tivate people to think about the environment more than a
beekeeper and his bees.

Several years ago I agreed to do two back-to-back town
earth fairs on the same weekend, with one being on Saturday
and the other on Sunday. I knew it would be a lot of work, but
earth fairs are a great way to get new members for the bee club
and to raise awareness by educating people about honeybees.

At any bee talk I do, and especially at fairs, the main attraction is always my observation hive. People love to get right up
on the glass and watch the bees milling about on the comb, and
many people become mesmerized watching the bees.

Usually when I bring my observation hive, I stop by my
hives in the early morning, pick up two frames of bees, and then

return them to their hive after the talk. I usually take the bees from one of my hives at the church since those hives are always doing well and they're always packed with so many healthy bees. For the double feature weekend with the back-to-back fairs, I decided that I would keep the bees in the observation hive overnight and return them to their hive late Sunday afternoon, after both town fairs had ended. I knew the bees would be fine if they stayed in the observation hive overnight because on top of the observation hive were two screened holes that could hold a bottle of water or a bottle of sugar syrup, ensuring the bees would have all the nourishment they needed. After Saturday's fair was over, I brought the observation hive into my house and placed it in the hall closet. By bringing the hive inside, I knew the bees would be safe, and by putting them in the closet, it would be dark, just as if they were in their hive.

Early Sunday morning, I grabbed my observation hive from the closet like it was a briefcase and I was headed off to work. Once I was outside, I realized that the weather had changed and storm clouds were rolling in. Throughout the day at the fair, the gray sky kept getting uglier and uglier. I wasn't worried *if* it was going to rain, but *when* it was going to rain. Even before it was closing time at the fair, the impending storm had scared off most of the crowd, so I was able to quickly pack everything up before the downpour started. As I was heading home, the skies opened up with a thunderous crash. The rain was so intense that I could barely see the road, and it didn't look like it would be stopping any time soon. As much as I wanted to put the bees back where they belonged, it was raining so hard that going into a hive would just kill the whole colony. So, instead I had to wait.

It rained into the night, and I was going to have to wait until morning before I could put the bees back into their hive. I was nervous about having the bees in the observation hive for too long, not because I was worried about the bees' health, but because of what the bees back in the home hive might be doing with the added space where the two frames would normally be. Bees are creatures of habits, and anytime there's a space larger than three-eighths of an inch, they build comb to fill it, which is why I was getting worried about having those frames out for more than two solid days.

I was also worried because like most people, weekdays were when I went to work at my non-beekeeping job. I was going to have to get up extra early, drive over to the church bee yard, put the bees back in the hive, then drive back home, get dressed for work, catch a train, and get to work, all before 9:00 a.m. I knew I could do it, I just had to do it real fast.

I woke up to find that it was still drizzling, so I couldn't get started as early as I had planned. I grabbed a second, then a third cup of coffee. Finally, after almost forty-five minutes, the last of the clouds passed and the drizzle came to a stop. I quickly grabbed the observation hive, jumped in the car, and sped over to the church. I didn't have a lot of time, but if I was fast, I'd still make it to work on time.

When I pulled into the church parking lot, I went to grab my beekeeping gear, and that's when I realized that I had left my veil back at home. I had two options: (1) Drive back home, get my veil, and drive back to the church, guaranteeing that I will be late for work, or (2) put the bees back real fast, without the veil, and still make it to work on time.

I chose option 2.

Now, it's important to pause this story so that I can explain just how incredibly stupid a decision I had just made. Inside the observation hive, I had over two thousand bees and none of them were happy. These bees had been trapped behind glass for over two days, and while they were physically fine, they were seething mad about being kept apart from their queen and locked inside a Plexiglas prison. It doesn't matter how gentle your bees normally are, after being jailed for a few days, they are going to want two things: freedom and revenge.

Thankfully, I did have my smoker, and I thought that I could protect myself by creating a wall of smoke between the bees and me. I first went over to their home hive and smoked it while I popped open the top and the inner cover. All was good. The bees barely noticed that I removed the roof of their house.

Next, I sat the observation hive down and prepared to open it up. I puffed some smoke, hoping it would mask the bees' "we're really pissed off" pheromone. I unlocked the latches on the observation hive, so all I had to do next was open it, get the frames out, and get them back into their home hive. I puffed some more smoke, thinking that if I had a big cloud of smoke around me, and I could transfer the frames really quickly, I'd be okay.

I puffed, puffed, puffed, puffed, and puffed the smoker. I mentally counted to three, and then opened the observation hive.

I want to pause the story again to point out that honeybees flap their wings a whopping 240 times per second, enabling them to reach speeds of twenty miles per hour.

The moment the observation hive was open, three bees that must have been plotting all night against me, flew out and Bam-Bam-Bam, stung me above my glasses in the middle of my forehead.

I grabbed the smoker and puffed-puffed-puffed-puffed-puffed my face, hair, and all the space between the bees in the observation hive and me. In the frenzy of it all, I ended up getting stung another half dozen times on my arms, legs, and head. Then,

I did something I had never done before, and I have never done since. I walked away. I walked a good fifty yards away from my bee yard. I thought I'd let all the angry bees get out, fly around, and hopefully take out their rage on some unsuspecting squirrel or chipmunk. After several minutes, I walked back to try to fix the disaster that I created. I pulled my shirt up over my nose, so only my forehead was exposed and I looked like I was going to rob a 7-Eleven. Returning to the scene of my stupidity, I saw that I was in luck and that most of the bees had already flown out of the observation hive. I started puffing my smoker again and kept puffing it until there was so much smoke in the air it looked as if I was at a Snoop Dogg concert. Then, I grabbed the frames one at a time and put them back in the hive. Nine stings and a very badly bruised ego later, I finished what I set out to do.

That evening, when I finally had a moment to reflect on my morning, I promised myself that never again was I going to do something that stupid. Lesson learned: no matter how fast I was, the bees were always faster. I would never be foolish enough to try to do something really fast when it involves bees. Instead, I'd think about everything that could possibly go wrong. Instead, I'd make myself remember the pain and discomfort of today. Instead, I'd make sure that I never again had to experience the embarrassment of having to tell my boss why I was late for work and why my face was swollen like a distorted balloon.

MOST BEE MISTAKES are measured in stings, because that's how bees let you know that you messed up. B. F. Skinner might not have been a beekeeper, but he knew that punishment decreases the behavior that it follows, which is why a few stings will teach you what *not* to do again, and why the honeybee must have been Skinner's spirit animal.

Nonetheless, not all bee mistakes end with a sting. Sometimes, your mistake is just living the life of a beekeeper and forgetting that you see things differently than most people. The longer you keep bees, the more your sense of normal changes. For instance, I was once driving back home from the church bee yard when I realized that I had a hitchhiker buzzing around inside my car. When I stopped at a light, the bee landed on my hand. I thought this was so cool, so I grabbed my phone and snapped a picture of the bee on my finger. The photo came out so well that I cropped it as a tight close-up, had it printed as an eight-by-ten, and dry-mounted it on foam board. I now start all of my bee talks with this photo to show that bees will not hurt you if you do not hurt them. I tell my audience that it's *my* bee, *my* finger, and since I wasn't trying to hurt the bee, she had no intention of stinging me. While most people are amazed by the photo, I can tell that they are also a little freaked out, and when I tell them that the bee was flying around inside my car until it happened to land on my finger, they really start to bug out and give me a look that says "Are you f%#king kidding me!?"

To me, a bee flying around inside my car is a sign that it's summer, but for a lot of people, if they had a bee flying around inside their car, they'd jump out as fast as they could. To a beekeeper, hanging around bees is normal. But having a sense of normal that is different comes with great responsibility. If you tell too many people that you drive with bees flying around inside your car—worse than a mistake that ends with a sting—you'll get friends who'd rather walk than grab a ride.

OUR BEE CLUB arranges a yearly bulk order of nucs for our members. It's a great and convenient way for everyone to get bees, and it's also a good way for the club to provide a service to its members. When nucs are delivered, they come in white card-board boxes that look like long comic book storage boxes. Since bee colonies are not manufactured in a factory, but have to grow and expand at their own natural rate, the weather always impacts how long it takes the nucs to be ready for delivery. One year, there was a late cold spell that delayed our nucs by almost three weeks, and the new delivery date was set for the week when many local schools were on spring break. When the club members found out about the new date, many with school-aged children pan-icked because they had planned family vacations for that week. All but four people were able to make arrangements for someone else to pick up their nucs, so I told the four members not to worry and that I would install the nucs into their hives.

On the day of the nuc delivery, there were a lot of people who wanted to help. I needed to put six nucs into my car for my bee delivery service, and a newbee member decided that he'd help me move the nucs into the back of my Volvo XC70 station wagon. The newbee was eager to help, and as soon as I had opened the hatch, he reached down to grab one of the nucs. In-stead of grabbing the nuc box by the sides of the box, he grabbed it by the lid. As I was saying, "always grab it by the sides," it was too late. The lid had come off in his hands as the nuc landed with a thud in the back of my car. He quickly put the lid back on, but in that instant, hundreds of bees flew out. We loaded the rest of the nucs into my car, and after he'd get a nuc in the car, he'd fidget with the lid causing more bees to fly out. I was happy that he was only able to help with a few of the nucs, because thanks to Mr. Lid-Fidget, I had well over a thousand bees flying around inside my car.

I tossed my beekeeping equipment, including my veil, into the front passenger seat and jumped into the car wearing my official bee club polo shirt that had BEE embroidered on it. Even though there were a thousand bees flying around inside my car, I wasn't worried about getting stung, because I knew the bee-keeper's secret; bees don't like the cold. I just turned my air conditioner on high, aimed the vents squarely at my face, and all the bees stayed in the back of the car.

Whenever I'm doing bee stuff, I like to play my Honey Harmonies playlist, which is songs that have "honey" or "bee" in the lyrics. Some of the songs in my playlist include "Wild Honey" by the Beach Boys, "Tupelo Honey" by Van Morrison, "Honey Bee" by Tom Petty, "Me in Honey" by R.E.M., "Milk and Toast and Honey" by Roxette, "Honeybee" by Gloria Gaynor, "A Taste of Honey" by The Supremes and the Four Tops, "Sugar and Honey" by Roy Orbison, "Honey Love" by The Jackson 5, "Honey" by Moby, and my absolute favorite of them all, "Honey, Honey" by Abba.

Whenever I'm around honeybees, it puts me in a good mood, and getting to install six new nucs was a great way to spend a Saturday. I was cranking my sweet-as-honey tunes as I was driving and just enjoying the day. After being in the car for about half an hour, I was lost in my thoughts, singing along with my honey-themed songs, not even thinking about the thousand or so bees flying around in my car.

I was about five minutes away from my first nuc delivery, when the best of the best from my playlist came on—the *Swedish* version of ABBA's "Honey, Honey." While I don't speak Swedish, I do like to pretend that I can sing in Swedish, so I cranked up the volume and sang along.

As I approached an intersection, really getting into the song and trying to stay in key, the light turned red. I slowly came to a stop and looked in the rearview mirror only to see that the car behind me was *not* stopping, as the driver was focused on something other than the light. As I braced for impact, the driver came to a screeching halt, a baby's breath away from my rear bumper. As I heard more cars come to a squealing abrupt stop behind him, the driver jumped out of his car and started running toward me. I knew my Swedish was bad, but I didn't think anyone could hear me. I turned down the volume as he was running and waving his hands. As he got closer to my car, I could hear that he was screaming something. "Bees! Bees! You got bees in your car! BEES!"

So, it wasn't my Swedish singing after all. This Good Samaritan was here to talk to me about the bees in my car! Then, as he approached my driver's side window, he must have spied my beekeeping equipment on the front seat, and as the breath went out of his last, "bees..." I could see his eyes focused on the embroidered BEE on my shirt. Then he said, "Ah, beekeeper. I get it." And he walked back to his car, head hung low, almost sad that his good deed was smashed faster than a bug on a windshield.

He had wanted to tell his family and friends how he saved someone from a cloud of bees that were hiding in his backseat, waiting to carjack him. But instead, the only story he could tell was about nearly causing a major accident when he crossed paths with a car containing a Swedish-singing weirdo freak and his cloud of bees flying around inside.

Just like a bee has its stinger, having a sense of normal that is different from others comes with great responsibility; otherwise, you're going to be the key witness in way too many multi-car pileups and have to add "Demolition Man" to your playlist.

CHAPTER 17

In and Otters

ONE OF THE GREAT THINGS about beekeeping is that it keeps you busy. There is always something to be doing, and, depending on the time of year, what you should be doing is always changing. Beekeeping has its own calendar and it starts in August.

As a beekeeper there are two ways to measure success: winter survival rate, meaning how many of your colonies make it through the winter, and how much honey your bees are able to produce. What you do in August will impact the outcome of both of these measures of success. August is when you have to treat for Varroa mites, make sure your hives will have enough food (honey) for winter and if not, feed them so they will, and confirm that your hives are strong enough (has enough bees) to make it through the winter.

There is an old beekeeper's saying that one strong hive is better than two weak hives. Sometimes, usually starting in August, beekeepers will combine two weaker colonies to make one strong colony helping to better ensure the bees will make it through the winter. When combining hives, you always want to make sure the best queen wins, so it is important to evaluate your queens before combining, and remove the weaker one (kill her). When you're ready to combine the two hives, you should use the newspaper trick, and place a sheet of newspapers between the different hive boxes. Once the paper is removed, all the bees will recognize the new queen as their queen and they will all be one big, happy family.

If both queens are about equal and you cannot easily tell which the better queen is, many beekeepers will tell you to skip the newspaper and just put one hive on top of the other. As Andy would say, "Put the two hives together and let the bees work it out. Bees know best about who's the best queen, so just let 'em sort things out themselves."

Andy and the other old-timers who attended the monthly meetings were a wealth of information. But none of them were the type of people who would bring an agenda to the bee club meetings. Or tell you ahead of time what you should be doing. Or what you should be planning for in the coming months. Instead, you had to pay attention and listen for their little nuggets of beekeeping wisdom.

Each month, the meetings became more and more like *Groundhog Day*, as they were just a repeat of all the previous months' meetings. The Badger kept coming a few minutes later and later, until the meetings were called to order before he ever drove into the parking lot. All the while, the more bee books I read, and the more state meetings and classes I attended, the less and less I was learning from these local monthly meetings. I also couldn't believe that the old-timers were getting anything meaningful from these meetings, and they certainly weren't attending for the stale cookies.

My passion for beekeeping was getting stronger, and selfishly I wanted to learn as much as I could about how to be a better beekeeper. Thinking about how to fix the meetings was on my mind a lot, as I knew there had to be a better way.

Around the same time, my son Miles wanted to join Cub Scouts. Personally, I was happy because I always enjoyed scouting and I thought that Cub Scouts would be good for him. With its focus on nature and the environment, I was happy that Miles would have another link to my new hobby and that he would be able to tell his pack that he and his dad were beekeepers.

Scouting had changed a lot since I was a boy. For one, when I was a kid, camping out meant that you sleep in a tent, outdoors, and you had to bring all the supplies you would need with you. Now I learned that camping still meant sleeping in your sleeping bag, but doing it outside was a needless inconvenience that was reserved for the older, more adventurous boys. Miles's pack was planning a "camp out" inside the Maritime Aquarium in Norwalk, Connecticut. It was a father/son trip and we had to arrive before 5:00 P.M., which was closing time, because it was a "lock-in" and once we were inside, the doors would be locked and no one could leave until the next morning. It sounded a bit like a B-movie from the late '70s and I was anticipating hearing some roaming gang ask if the Warriors could come out and play.

All the boys and their parents arrived before five o'clock, and with every father and son that arrived, the boys got more and more worked up, as only a gaggle of eight-year-old boys can. Finally, at the bewitching hour of 5:00 P.M., a few of the aquarium hosts greeted us, and after the doors were locked, they asked that we follow them. We were informed that the first order of business was for the boys to be assigned their campsites. The aquarium was set up into a series of rooms, each featuring a different sea creature or animal that depended on the water to survive. Miles's den was assigned the "Mammals by the Sea" room, and we were told to pick out a spot, anywhere we wanted, and roll out our sleeping bags onto the concrete floor. Miles and I ended up behind the River Otter's Natural Woodlands Habitat exhibit, a large, glass-enclosed diorama showing how otters live.

Later that night, when they finally dimmed the lights and I crawled inside my sleeping bag, I knew that the only way I was going to get a decent night's sleep would be to repeatedly smash my head against the concrete floor until I knocked myself unconscious, but since that would probably make a mess, I decided against it. Instead, I did the beekeeper's equivalent of counting sheep and I started to think about bees.

My mind turned to the monthly meetings, and I began to think about what I would find interesting, and what I would like to see at the meetings. I thought about the beekeeper's calendar and how during the different times of the year there are different to-dos that should be done. Laying behind the River Otter's Natural Woodlands Habitat exhibit, instead of focusing on my back spasms from sleeping on concrete, or how much dust I was inhaling from sleeping on the floor, I decided to focus all my mental energy on a beekeeper's monthly calendar and putting together a year's worth of monthly bee club meetings.

I first envisioned the Microsoft template I would use for listing the monthly meetings. It would be a three-column table that showed the month, the speaker, and the topic that would be discussed. I thought about what topics would be interesting, and which month it would be best to discuss them. All the topics were things that I either wanted to learn, such as winter management in January, mite treatments in June, honey extraction in July, and what to do with beeswax and propolis in October. Every time I thought of a new, cool topic, I fit it into my calendar until I had twelve unique topics to fill the entire year. Next, I began to think about the different beekeepers I had met or seen at the state meetings, and depending on their specialty, I matched many of them to the monthly topics. By the time I heard the other campers beginning to stir, I had assembled a year's worth of meetings in my head. I didn't want to forget any of them, so I kept repeating them to myself, over and over again, like some weird beekeeping chant. Om... January is winter hive management... Om... February is readying your hives for spring...

The lights came back on and over a loudspeaker, a voice instructed us to pack up our gear and head to the cafeteria for a continental breakfast, which is aquarium talk for toast and Cheerios. After breakfast we were free to go, and if you ever want to watch a bunch of dads move faster than any superhero, head down to the Maritime Aquarium when they unlock the doors and watch dozens of dads racing to their cars while carrying their kids and two sleeping bags.

Driving down the road with the wind in my hair and the concrete floor in my rearview mirror, I felt as euphoric as Andy Dufresne in *The Shawshank Redemption* standing in the rain. I was manic from my newfound freedom, and from sitting on something other than concrete. Once I made it back to home-sweet-home, instead of crashing into bed, I booted up my computer to recreate the calendar I saw in my head. Once I was done, I printed it out, smiled, and then went to take a very long nap on a very soft bed.

When I awoke, I went back to my computer and I started emailing all the people I wanted to speak at the beekeeping meetings. I sent each person the exact month, day, time of the meeting, and what topic I hoped they could talk about. By the end of the day, I had emailed everyone and just needed to wait for their replies.

It took longer for my back to feel better from sleeping on concrete than it did for everyone to write back and confirm that they'd be happy to speak at our club meeting. I should have known that providing a bee enthusiast with a forum to share his or her thoughts on bees with a room full of attentive beekeepers is many a bee speaker's dream. Beekeepers can talk nonstop about bees and if two beekeepers were trapped on a deserted island, they wouldn't even notice because they'd be too busy talking about Varroa treatments and what they'll be doing next year to expand their operation.

When it was time for the next monthly beekeeping meeting, I was a little nervous about how the other members were going to react to my initiative. I had booked what everyone would be doing for the next year without having asked anyone what they thought or without any official approval. I printed out enough copies of my calendar so everyone could see what I did, but beforehand, I had decided to add a fourth column to my calendar where I wrote, "confirmed" and the date the speaker had confirmed he or she would do it. I thought it would be harder to say no once they saw that all the speakers had already confirmed.

I made sure that I got to the meeting early so that I could catch a few guys before the meeting started and show them what I did. Earle and Andy were unlocking the door when I arrived. After a few "hellos" and "how your bees doings," I said, "What would you guys think if each month these meetings had

a theme and we had speakers come in and talk to us?" Earle and
Andy chuckled and Andy said, "Yeah that would be great, but
who's gonna make that happen? You really think the Badger is
gonna do that?" Still chuckling he added, "And do you think
Rusty is going to want to have to listen to someone besides himself talk about bees?" Again they both laughed until I looked
them both in the eyes and said, "Well, it's done. I did it. Look,
here's the calendar I did for next year."

After they read it over, Earle's and Andy's expressions
looked like I gave them a recipe for how to make gold. They
were smiling and asking me if it was real, which I assured them
it was. Then as other members came in, Andy was calling them
over and saying, "Get a look at this." Everyone who saw it was
very happy and also seemed to sigh with relief, as they, too, were
getting tired of the directionless course the club meetings had
been on for too long.

As soon as the meeting was called to order, and before
anyone could say anything else, Andy said, "He's got something
to say," as he gestured at me from his usual seat a few rows back
from where I was sitting. I stood up, passed around my calendars,
and told everyone how I wanted to see if I could plot out a year's
worth of meetings, with each one matching what we'd be doing
or needed to know that month, and how I found speakers who
had already agreed to come and talk to our club. Then, I took a
deep breath and waited to hear what everyone was going to say.
The room simply burst into a round of applause.

Then something unexpected happened. From the back of
the room, someone asked, "Aren't we supposed to have our club
elections next month?"

The bee club's constitution stated that elections would be
held once a year in December. Only at one time or another, all

of the old-timers had held an officer position in the club, so no one wanted to run for office and the Badger kept being the president and Rusty the vice president. But over the past few years, a few new people, including yours truly, became members and regularly attended the meetings. The calendar became an unexpected catalyst, as now people realized the meetings didn't have to keep being the same old thing over and over again.

The Badger realized that someone asking about the elections was as good as a vote of no confidence, so to save face he stood up and said, "Yes, yes they are. And that means that I can appoint a nomination committee *this* month to put nominations forward. I appoint Andy as our nomination chair." Then, he sat back down and just smiled and shook his head, trying to look happy and as if he was still in control.

Andy said, "For president, I nominate, Mr. Calendar of Events." Then about six different people said, "I second it." Next, Andy said, "and for vice president, I nominate Rick Schluger. I've been mentoring him, and he also has some good ideas for the club." Again, a few people said, "second."

After a few moments the Badger said the last thing he'd ever say as the president at a bee meeting, "Are there any other candidates?" And there was dead silence. No one, not even the other officers, wanted to nominate the Badger to run against me. I felt bad for the Badger because he was why I started keeping bees and why I was here in the first place, but it was clear that he had lost the members a long time ago.

While it was not official until the following month's meeting, without any opposing candidates, and just like that, Rick and I were the new club leaders. The first thing I did as the new club president was to publicly thank the Badger for all that he had done. My words were sincere, but it still felt awkward because it was so obvious that no one wanted him to be their leader. However, the Badger was all about saving face, and he started saying that he was relieved that his term was finally over and now he could finally concentrate on his bees without first having to worry about everyone else's.

Getting nominated to be president surprised me and I was feeling uneasy and nervous. I started beekeeping to help me find out who I was, and now here I was being nominated to run the club. I was worried about doing a good job, but I also knew that the club could be so much better. I felt proud that my fellow beekeepers wanted me to lead them, and I was determined not to let them down.

Just like every bee in the hive has a job, everyone has something they are good at, and for me, that was making good meetings. I had only been keeping bees for a few years and most of the members had a lot more experience than I did, but I soon realized that it wasn't my beekeeping knowledge that made me a good club president, it was that I was organized, knew how to run a meeting, and I was passionate about making the club better for everyone. Instead of taking "the president knows best" approach that the Badger had taken, I took the *Phil Donahue Show* host approach, and played the role of facilitator and moderator. Instead of members having to mumble things under their breath, I would call on them so everyone could hear what they had to say. If I saw someone else was disagreeing with what was just said, or if someone had something to add, I would call on him or her to speak. But probably the most important thing I did as the moderator was to limit how long everyone got to speak, ensuring that no one person was able to monopolize the meetings. In the past, Rusty would say anything he wanted to say and he would editorialize on every comment that anyone else said during a meeting. Many nights, it felt as if we were on Rusty Talk Radio. Rusty often repeated himself, and because he was hard of hearing, many times he misheard what was being discussed and would go off on a tangent that had nothing to do with the topic everyone else was discussing. As the moderator, I started to tell Rusty that he had to wait his turn to talk or that his time was up. Rusty quickly grew to dislike how I limited his time, but all the other members seemed to appreciate it. In the coming months, more and more old-timers, who never used to speak up at the meetings, began raising their hands and they had a lot of good information to add.

Becoming the club president also made me a better beekeeper. Every day I was reading more about bees, all so I could be better prepared for the meetings. And acting as the moderator enabled me to ask questions until I understood the answers. In many ways, it was like having a team of mentors that would field questions and provide answers based on their years of experience.

The first few months of running the club were a blur, but from day one, Rick and I hit it off and we quickly found that we worked really well with each other. Andy had been his mentor and taught him a lot about bees. Seeing how much Andy had taught Rick about beekeeping showed me the benefit of having a good mentor and made me realize that the Badger had never taught me anything other than I was less likely to get stung if I did my hive inspections without him. Rick told me what I suspected: most of the members had had it with the Badger and they wanted to get more out of the meetings. After hearing that, I felt less awkward about the Badger getting removed from office. I also realized what a great opportunity Rick and I had to build the club into what we wanted it to be and make it into something really special. Rick was equally as passionate about raising the bar and also raising the number of members. We made a good team, as our skills complimented each other's. Every month, I would write up a two- to three-sentence blurb about the upcoming meeting and Rick would send it to all the local newspapers and any online local community he could find. Facebook was still relatively new, but we started a beekeepers group for our club, which was the first one in our area. Anything we could think of to get the word out about our club, we did, and each month a few more people would show up to our meetings.

Both Rick and I were in to beekeeping because it was a thinking person's hobby, and we wanted our meetings to be a place where people came to learn the craft of beekeeping. Rick had an IT background, so anything that we could do online, he wanted our club to be the first and the best to do it. When we first joined, the monthly newsletter was produced on Rusty's copy machine, and the one rule Rusty had about the newsletter was that it had to fit on one page. Rusty always printed the newsletter on bright bee-yellow-colored paper, so you didn't even have to open it to know what it was. Once he printed it out, he'd fold it into thirds, and place a piece of tape in the middle to keep it closed. Then, Rusty would print out member addresses on mailing labels and put them on his newsletters. For the return address, Rusty would use any and all return address stickers he had accumulated throughout the past few decades. He had lots of Christmas-related return addresses, and no matter the time of the year, he'd use them on the newsletter. Since the newsletter was limited to one page and contained the officers' contact information, the meeting date, time, and location, there really wasn't any room to write about bees. Most people would just see the bright yellow paper in their mailbox and knew that a bee meeting was coming up. Once Rick and I started, we moved to an all-digital newsletter that we would email to every-one. Our newsletter had all the information the one-pager had, and a whole lot more. Since it was digital, length didn't matter, so Rick and I would write articles for the members and we also provided bee-related information, beekeeping tips, and the occasional recipe. For the first time, we included photos in our newsletters so we could show different bee-related things, including photos of swarms, queens, and members' hives.

Rick and I talked several times a week, as we both wanted to do more to make our club the best bee club in our state. Rick, being techno-savvy, pushed for us to have our own website, and soon, www.nnjbees.org was born. By website standards it was (and still is) very simple, but for the first time our club had one place anyone could go to find all the information they needed to know about our club, where we meet, and who to contact if they needed any type of bee help.

Each month we were trying something new, and when we saw new people at the meeting, we knew it was working. Before becoming club officers, when Rick and I would attend the meetings, we were lucky if fifteen people showed up. Now, in less than one year, our meetings were averaging fifty to sixty people, and our paid membership dues had literally doubled. It was a great feeling to see that we were making a difference and our club was starting to thrive. But growing so big was also causing one problem—our current meeting place was now too small to hold all of us and there was no place for people to park. Rick and I didn't want the size of a building to stop us, so we knew if we wanted to keep growing the club, we needed to do something. Luckily Rick had a few ideas of what we could do next.

CHAPTER 18

Hiving the
Bee Club

RICK WAS A DREAMER with lots of different ideas for our club and how to promote beekeeping in our area. He'd text me every other day with another new idea: "We should get a billboard promoting local honey," or, "We should host a local access cable TV show on beekeeping. People could call in and ask us questions." While some of his ideas were far-fetched, we did accomplish a lot: building our own website, starting a club Facebook group, and a better newsletter. Rick and I found ourselves talking to more and more people about bees and beekeeping, because when someone finds out that you're a beekeeper, they want to ask you about bees, how bad is the bee die-off, and what can be done to save the bees. At work, parties, church—it didn't matter where we were or who we were talking to, everyone wanted to know about the bees.

I remember one time when I was a witness to a hit-and-run. A driver had pulled out of a parking lot onto a busy street and as he was pulling into traffic, he clipped a parked car and tore off its bumper. The driver didn't stop, but instead sped up and aggressively passed a few cars that were in front of him. It was obvious that he knew he had hit the parked car and was trying to get away. I called 911 to report it. The dispatcher said they would send an officer to my house to get an official statement. I was in my driveway unloading the two hundred pounds of sugar I had just bought from Costco when the officer arrived, and his first question was, "What's all *that* sugar for?"

For a moment he must have thought that he had uncovered something illegal, because one person with hundreds of pounds of sugar must be doing something illegal, right? Once I explained that I was a beekeeper and I fed my bees sugar syrup to ensure they had enough food to make it through the winter, he no longer thought I was cooking up sugarcoated meth. Instead he wanted to hear more about the bees and how they were doing. We talked for almost twenty minutes about bees before I asked if we should talk about the hit-and-run incident. After he took the report, we talked more about keeping bees and before he left, I gave him information on our club and when it meets.

Honeybees were a newsworthy topic, and newspapers, magazines, and TV stations were all looking for a unique, local angle. Rick and I found ourselves being quoted and sometimes even featured in stories about bees or beekeeping, and we always made sure to mention that we were from the *Northeast NJ Beekeepers*. It was a nice cycle we found ourselves in: the more stories that were written about bees, the more people that became interested in beekeeping, and the more people that were new to beekeeping, the more our club continued to grow.

Rick was active in his community, and a friend of a friend, who knew he was a beekeeper, reached out to him about an opportunity that would solve our club's need for more space. The friend of a friend worked for Ramapo College, a small, local, liberal arts school that was green-minded and environmentally friendly. They were interested in championing local causes, and with honeybees becoming the poster child of environmental concerns, Ramapo wanted to explore how they could work with our bee club.

Rick and I immediately went to work to make a partnership happen with the college. We set up meetings with professors and administrators to discuss ideas for what a mutually beneficial relationship would look like. From the beginning, everyone involved could see how this was a win-win partnership, and we just needed to work out the details. It didn't take long, and after a few short weeks, we settled on a plan. Ramapo would become our new home and we would hold our monthly meetings in one of their state-of-the-art, multi-media lecture halls. This gave our club the space it needed, and it gave Ramapo some great PR, as it was something they could point at to show that they were doing their part to help the bees. Additionally, we would help them start and oversee a student beekeeping club, with the club hives being kept on campus. It really was a win for everyone: our club, the college, and the students. Rick and I could not wait until the next meeting to tell everyone that we were moving to bigger and better facilities. We felt like the Jeffersons, 'cause we were movin' on up!

The next meeting was less than two weeks away, and Rick and I spent the time getting ready to share the good news with the rest of the members. We took photos of Ramapo—everything from the lecture hall where we'd be meeting to the parking lot that had more than enough spaces for everyone to park. We built a PowerPoint presentation with all the photos, along with all the reasons why this was such a great deal.

Several days before the club meeting, when we were finalizing our PowerPoint presentation, we realized that we had no way to show it to the members, as our soon-to-be old meeting place barely had electricity let alone a projector or a computer. But Rick being an IT guy said he'd take care of it and that I shouldn't worry. On the day of the meeting, Rick and I met an hour early so that we could get set up. Rick waved me over to where he was standing in the parking lot and said he needed my help. When he popped open the hatch on his SUV, I saw a sixty-inch flat-screen TV strapped in. Rick smiled and said, "I borrowed it from work for the presentation." He and I carefully hauled the beast inside, where we put it on a table at the front of the room. Rick connected the computer and got everything ready as I set up the rest of the meeting room by opening all the metal folding chairs and placing them into their familiar rows. Rick was able to run a few tests to make sure everything was working, and I had everything else set up before anyone showed up. As our members filed into the room, they saw the huge TV and joked that we should skip the meeting and just rent a few movies.

Rick and I were eager to share our news, but we waited until the time was right. The room was packed past capacity; just like the last few meetings, it was standing-room only. The old-timers would go straight to their usual seats, and the newbees had learned which seats were more or less off limits. The room was a buzz, as everyone knew something special was going to happen. Finally, Rick said, "Well, we have some exciting news for everyone," and he and I delivered the news as we clicked through the PowerPoint presentation that we had prepared. The room remained surprisingly quiet as we spoke, which shocked me, as I had anticipated that the room would have burst into bouts of spontaneous applause.

When we finished, no one said a word. For what seemed like an eternity—almost ten solid seconds—no one made a sound. Then thankfully, a few of the newer members in the back of the room started clapping. Rick and I noticed that there was a clear divide among the members. All the new members were applauding, but the old-timers were just sitting there. I asked if there were any questions, and most of the old-timers' hands shot up. It was at this moment that I realized that people—especially longtime beekeepers—do not like change. Andy spoke first, and his comments set the tone for the others that followed. He asked, "Why are we doing this?" and "What's wrong with this place?" It would have been wrong for me to say that this place was a dusty, moldy, dump that was a health hazard and should be bulldozed to the ground, so instead I said, "Look around. Look at all the people who are standing, not to mention how many people tell me that they have no place to park so they skip the meeting and just head back home. We've outgrown this space and if we're going to keep growing, we need to find a new place to meet."

Andy looked me square in the eyes and said, "I'll never go to a meeting at any college." And what seemed like a heated emotional bluff turned out to be 100 percent true. Andy never came to any more of our club meetings. Instead, he joined another branch that was farther away, but met in a similar dumpy, one-room meeting space. While the other old-timers were also uncomfortable with the change, they were not intimidated about meeting at a college. Some asked if we could alternate the meetings between Ramapo and our old meeting place, but I knew if the club was going to take off that we needed to be fully committed to our new home.

It took most of the members a single visit to our new meeting space at Ramapo to appreciate what an upgrade it was for us. The lecture hall could hold 110 people, plus the stadium seating and AV equipment meant that everyone could see and hear what was being said. Also, on the floor above the lecture hall was another space specifically for socializing. Once the meetings were over, everyone would head upstairs to grab a cup of coffee, some baked goods, and for the first time, have plenty of room to talk and move around. Our club had lost Andy by moving, but we ended up gaining so much more.

Rick and I used to be happy if we had over thirty people show up for a meeting, and now we were averaging over eighty every month. That first year taught me that people like a pre-planned agenda, as people like to know what they can expect at the meetings each month, so I made sure to keep up on my monthly calendar of meeting topics. Rick put the club's yearly calendar on our website, making it available for everyone with just a click of their mouse.

Now that our club had a growing list of members and a space where we could all fit, the last thing we needed was money in our treasury. The more money the club had, the more we would be able to do for our members. My vision was to bring in the top bee speakers from around the country, and the only way we could do it would be if we had the money to pay travel expenses and speakers' fees. To raise some money, I started accepting offers to speak about honeybees and beekeeping from other groups in my area. Being in the heart of Manhattan's commuter communities, with over one hundred municipalities and well over one million people, I was receiving invitations from schools to gardening clubs and civic organizations to speak about honeybees. I was trying to do as many speaking engagements as I could, as the more people who understood the benefits of honeybees, the better it would be for all beekeepers. Every speaking engagement usually led to one or two others, and before long, it seemed like every local Rotary and gardening club was asking me to come speak to their members. Whenever I was asked about my speaker's fees, I would always say, "I am a volunteer and donate my time, but I would ask that you make a donation to my bee club. I do bee talks to raise awareness, and also to raise money for my club." When people heard that 100 percent of the honorarium was going to my club and not into my pocket, they'd happily make the donation.

In addition to raising money for my club, doing so many talks was making me a better beekeeper. When I started giving talks, I would spend a few days preparing. I'd look over my outline for what I wanted to cover, making changes based on my last talk, or adding something that I had learned from a new bee book or the latest bee research. Before too long I had memorized so many facts about bees that I didn't need an outline to give a talk, and my biggest concern was having enough time to say everything that I wanted to say. Some groups wanted me to first eat lunch, then give just a short twenty-minute presentation. Instead, I'd ask if I could talk while *they* ate their lunch so I had more time to answer everyone's questions.

The best talks of all were the talks I'd do for kids. Bees are part of the curriculum at a local elementary school, and for the past seven years I have been invited to speak to the third-graders. Since kids don't have a filter, they always ask the best questions and say the funniest things. One year when I was talking about how it's safe to stand to the side of, or behind, a hive, I said, "You only have to worry if you stand in front of the hive, because then you are in the bees' way, and they can't fly back to their hive." I explained how it was just like driving down the NJ Turnpike, and that you can drive next to Newark Airport and no planes will land on you, but if you drove on the runway, then a plane might smash into your car. One boy raised his hand and asked, "Why are bees like Newark Airport and not LaGuardia Airport?"

Kids have asked if they wear a shirt with a flower on it and get too close to a hive will the bees think they're a flower and hurt them. Another time I was telling a class all the cool jobs that the girl bees get to do, while the only job the boy bees get to do is marry a queen. One boy, who was taller and pudgier than all the other students, was sitting in the first row listening intently to everything I was saying. When I finished talking, he said with a sigh, "I wish I was a girl bee."

When I first started giving bee talks, I had to bring all my bee equipment because that's all I had to show. But over time, I acquired lots of props for my talks, including bee photos, bee posters, a teaching hive, lots of brochures, and an endless supply of stickers. Stickers, I now know, are like crack for kids, and giving each kid his or her own sticker is the best way to ensure that you have a happy, smiling audience. However, the biggest attraction is always the observation hive, which is a hive that is specifically designed to safely have live bees around groups of people. My observation hive looks like a double-paned window with a handle on top, only it has two frames of comb and a few thousand bees inside. The bees cannot get out, which is what makes the observation hive such a great visual. Anyone can get up next to the Plexiglas windows and not have to worry about the bees. Since kids are always curious, the hive has two locks on it to prevent anyone from "accidentally" opening it. The best thing about the observation hive is that it allows people to watch the bees go about their bee business. Some people are mesmerized watching the bees working behind the glass, and most people after being so close realize that bees are fascinating creatures to watch and not something to fear.

The observation hive was such an effective tool at allowing people to get close to bees and making them still feel safe that I once had the honor of helping a young child overcome her phobia of bees. A child psychologist who was working with a ten-year-old patient who had developed a bee phobia contacted me. I was told that the child was afraid to go outside, and anytime she saw any insect flying around, she would start to scream, cry hysterically, and would run back inside. I agreed to help in any way that I could. I met the patient and her mother at the therapist's office over a series of sessions. I helped educate her about honeybees and slowly exposed her to them. First, I brought photos of honeybees, including some of me with the bees while I was not wearing any type of protection. Next, I brought in my observation hive. At first the girl was nervous and kept her distance, but she didn't scream or cry. After several minutes of listening to the therapist's coaching, she was able to walk up to the hive and look inside. Over the next few sessions she became more relaxed around the hive. Finally, on the last visit, I brought in a few drone bees—since they do not have stingers—and it gave her a chance to hold a bee and see how they are not some kind of scary monster. Honeybees are fuzzy and don't feel like most other bugs, but more like a toy or a mini-stuffed animal. By the end of her last session, she had overcome her fears and wanted to know even more about honeybees. I was happy that I was able to help a young person in need, and her mother was so grateful to know her daughter could once again play outside that she made a big donation to our club. It was one of life's stories that ended with a sweet, "happily ever after."

Month after month, year after year our club continued to grow. I was averaging twenty to thirty talks a year, and soon the club had enough in its coffers for Rick and I to do everything we wanted to do for our members. We were bringing in big name speakers to talk about bees, and after every talk, we would get more members.

The club had grown to over 240 members, and now Rick and I could rely on other members to take on some club responsibilities so that all of the work no longer fell on just the two of us. It felt really good to have grown the bee club into such a strong, tight-knit organization, especially when thinking back to how we had started. I thought a lot about when I was first starting out and how much easier it would have been for me if the Badger had been a better mentor, so our club instituted a mentoring program. We'd pair more experienced beekeepers with less experienced beekeepers, getting more members involved and more newbees off to a better start.

From the beginning, Rick and I had two goals, teach bee-keepers how to be better at keeping bees, and teach everyone else the importance of honeybees. Teaching beekeepers was the easy part; they loved their bees and were showing up to the monthly meetings to learn how to be better beekeepers. The rest of the population, the non-beekeepers, required a little more work. Thankfully, the old saying, "You catch more flies with honey than you do with vinegar" applies equally as well to suburbanites as it does to houseflies. The crowning achievement of our club, and the greatest PR for beekeeping, just followed the advice of that old saying.

Every year, countless state and regional beekeeping organizations host a honey competition. Each of these honey competitions generally follows the same rules for judging honey. The United States Department of Agriculture even publishes a set of standards for judging and grading honey—everything from how clear is your honey, to what color is your honey, to how filled is your bottle of honey, to are there any imperfections in your glass jar. But there is still one thing that honey is not judged on: taste. Somewhere along the way, honey shows have turned into beauty pageants in a jar, and in these honey shows, how your honey looks has become more important than how it tastes. That seemed ridiculous to me. Looks are not why everyone loves honey. Yes, good looks can be important, but it's the taste of pure, local, raw honey that makes your eyes roll back in your head. I had an idea how to judge honey on what it's supposed to be judged on, and get everybody with a sweet tooth in a twenty-five-mile radius to be a fan of local beekeepers.

I wanted to put together a honey-tasting competition featuring our members' local honey. It would be a blind taste test, and instead of official judges, everyone who showed up could vote for the honey they thought tasted the best. It was simple: everyone got a ballot, and after tasting the different honeys, people wrote down the number of the honey they thought was the best and cast their vote in the ballot box. Then, we'd tally the votes and announce the winner.

Every contest needs a trophy, and since I am a huge hockey fan, there is only one trophy that stands above all others, is the purest symbol of a champion, and my one true inspiration: Lord Stanley's Cup. But because this was beekeeping and not ice hockey, I named our competition and called our trophy, "The Honey Cup." Hopefully, with Lord Stanley's blessing.

The Honey Cup takes place every September, as most bee-keepers have harvested their honey by then, and September tended to be a slow month for bee meetings. To give the tasting an air of sophistication, I developed worksheets for people to fill out as they tasted the different honeys. I looked to wine tastings for ideas on what categories to include, and landed on: Color, Aroma, Taste, Texture, and Sweetness. The instructions said to use a 10-point scale, where 1 is "store-bought honey" and 10 is "EXCELLENT!!!"

The Honey Cup has grown every year, and now it's a full-fledged festival, with a live band, a face painter, beekeeping demonstrations, and over five hundred attendees, who all show up to taste local honey and cast a vote for their favorite. Not wanting anyone to go into a diabetic coma, the Honey Cup is a catered event, providing food and drink to cleanse one's palate and to keep everyone from bouncing off the walls on a sugar high. Every year the Honey Cup has one clear winner. Initially I was worried that a handful or more of the honeys would get an equal number of votes, but every year, one honey rises to the top, above all the others, to be the sweetest of them all—the Honey Cup Champion!

The Northeast NJ Beekeepers has grown into an educational force in our community. Yet more than all the beekeepers we've helped, and all the honey-loving people that have become avid supporters of local beekeeping, the best part of our club has been all the great people I've met and now call friends. Over the past decade, I have met some of my closest, dearest friends and all of them keep bees. Beekeeping is a hobby, a career, a passion, and an obsession that attracts large numbers of good people. At its core, beekeeping is about caring for and nurturing living organisms, and the type of person who is drawn to beekeeping also tends to be a big-hearted, caring person, which is why they make such great friends.

Too often you hear adults talk about how difficult it is to meet people and make new friends, but nothing could be further from the truth in a bee club. There was a time in the not too distant past when everyone seemed to belong to one type of a club or another. People used to have bowling leagues, bridge clubs, local lodges, civic groups, and supper clubs, but now most of these have disappeared or have dwindled to a fraction of what they once were. Yet nationwide, bee clubs have been growing and attracting new members every year. Bee clubs are prospering because they are focused on keeping honeybees and nothing else—no politics, no religion, no socioeconomic barriers. When you walk into a bee meeting, beekeeping becomes the great equalizer and everything else about who you are gets checked at the door. At a bee meeting, all anyone cares about is how your bees are doing. Beekeepers love to talk to other beekeepers, and once you start keeping bees, it's like joining an international fraternal order. Everywhere you go, once you find another beekeeper, you know you've found someone who has something in common with you—a love and appreciation for the amazing honey-loving bug.

19

Bee Are Family

AT ONE OF THE FIRST bee club meetings I attended, I met an elderly couple who, along with their love for one another, shared a mutual passion for honeybees, and beekeeping was something they always did together. When I started going to the state bee meetings, I listened to longtime beekeepers, who with their partners standing by their side talked about keeping bees and how they were both equally obsessed with beekeeping. Beekeeping was a family affair, and from the very beginning I wanted someone that I, too, could share it with.

When I started keeping bees, my about-to-be-ex-wife wanted nothing to do with them. She couldn't understand why anyone would want to be around stinging insects let alone put them in their backyard. Not surprisingly, my marriage ended soon after I started keeping bees and I was free to start fresh, "bee" happy, and fully integrate beekeeping into every part of my life.

Since beekeepers don't have their own matchmaking site, I wasn't sure how I was going to meet my perfect partner. I wasn't even sure what a perfect match for me would be, but one thing was certain: after getting out of a bad marriage, I definitely knew what I didn't want.

I ended up meeting the love of my life on September 10 when my son, Miles, was still just a boy. Sofie was his new caregiver, and from the moment I saw her, I knew she was special. Sofie was a tall, natural-looking woman who didn't wear makeup and wore her long blond hair pulled back into a ponytail. She had a contagious smile, soulful brown eyes, along with a happy and calm demeanor. She was from Sweden, and had come to the United States to take a break from her studies. Miles quickly bonded with her, as a child can easily detect someone with a caring, kind heart. Sofie hadn't come to America to meet a man, and when we first met, I had no idea she'd be the mother of my future children. All I knew was that she was an intelligent, kind person who my son adored.

Initially, any time I spent with Sofie also included Miles, so she and I talked and got to know one another while also playing Chutes and Ladders or another one of Miles's games. Sofie was from Örebro, which is in the middle of Sweden, about two hours from Stockholm and Gothenburg. Swedes, I would learn, love nature and to be outside, but still Sofie had never known any other beekeepers. She told me that it's not something anyone in her family would ever consider, as her mother was disgusted by all insects and was terrified of anything that had wings and made a buzzing sound. Sofie said that one time when she and her two sisters were all under the age of nine, they were playing in their screened-in porch with their mother. All of a sudden, they heard a loud buzzing sound bouncing around the room. Her mom, who was sitting farthest away from the door into the house decided to let her kids fend for themselves as she jumped, tucked, and rolled out through a window instead of facing whatever had found its way into the screened-in porch.

I enjoyed the time I spent with Sofie, and more and more I tried to find reasons to be around when she was watching Miles. One night, after knowing one another for a few months, we sat down with Miles to eat dinner. Miles wanted to try some of the hot sauce that I had splashed on my plate. I told him he could try it, but first I let him know that it was really spicy so he could only have a very tiny drop on his food. I was anticipating that his tasting would not end well, but to my pleasant surprise, Miles gulped it down without much ado. I then waved the bottle of hot sauce at Sofie who quickly said, "No. I'm Swedish, we don't eat spicy food." Which immediately prompted me to ask her if everything spicier than ketchup was banned at the Swedish border. Following my teasing Sofie that she'd probably melt like a snowman if she ever did try it, I said to her, "Okay, you have to pick one or the other: Would you rather try the hot sauce, or work the bees with me?"

After thinking about it for a few short seconds, Sofie said, "I'll work the bees with you."

"*Really?*" I said, surprised that she actually chose either of the options!

"I know the hot sauce is too spicy and that it will burn, but I don't know if I will get stung or not, so bees seems like the safer answer."

Realizing that this was an opportunity for me to spend some time with Sofie sans Miles, I firmed up a day and time for her to go hive diving with me. I was amused that by jokingly asking her to pick bees or hot sauce that she and I would finally have some one-on-one time together. I also wondered if she, too, saw it as an opportunity for us to be alone, or if her choice just proved how much she really disliked hot sauce.

As a seasoned beekeeper, one of the most important life lessons I have learned is that you should never take a date to your beehives, especially not a first date. It's not that anything catastrophic will necessarily happen; it's just there is no way to act suave and sophisticated while wearing a veil and looking at bugs. But I was looking forward to sharing my passion for bees with Sofie, and hoped she would find beekeeping as magical as I do.

Our special day arrived, and Sofie and I headed to the hives. I was thankful that we had good bee weather, sunny and not too hot, so the bees could just go about their buzzness and I wouldn't have to worry about having to deal with grumpy bees. Sofie looked fantastic as her long, blond hair glistened in the sun and her dark brown eyes warmed my heart. She was surprisingly calm, and as our years together as a couple would pass, I would learn that it takes a lot more than fifty thousand stinging insects to unnerve Sofie, as her Viking DNA gave her the resilience to face the world with a smile.

As a guy, I really wanted to show off and impress her with my bee prowess, but at the same time, I realized things could end badly if I messed up and she got stung. So after a lot of mental back and forth, I decided to take it slow, be extra careful, and try to wow her with my words instead of doing something stupid. The smartest thing I did that first day was to light the smoker and hand it to her. I told her how the smoke would calm the bees, and anytime she was feeling nervous, all she had to do was point and puff. Sofie says that when she holds the smoker she feels like she has a weapon to protect her. Once again, her Viking heritage comes to the rescue.

Sofie stood close to me as I opened the hive. She was holding the smoker in front of her to create a shield of smoke between herself and the bees. As I popped off the inner cover, Sofie gasped as she stood over the hive, peered inside, and saw the tens of thousands of bees. I explained to her that you only want to use a little bit of smoke, because too much smoke will agitate the bees more than it will calm them down. "A few light puffs across the top," I said, trying to sound as cool as I could while talking about my smoker.

I was watching Sofie look at the bees more than I was looking at the bees myself; seeing the wonderment in her eyes made the day utterly perfect. Next, I wanted to take out a few frames to show Sofie what was happening inside the hive. Using my hive tool, I took out the second frame from the side where we were standing and showed Sofie how it was mostly filled with capped honey. I handed the frame to her so she could feel how heavy it was, and explained that a deep frame could hold as much as ten pounds of honey. Continuing with my hive inspection, I took out the frame that was next to the one I had just removed, and closer to the center of the hive. This frame had a combination of capped honey and capped brood on it. The honey was on one side of the frame and the brood was on the other. Sofie was amazed at how different honey and brood looked and how the bees put the honey on the outer frames and the brood more toward the middle.

On the next frame I took out, we saw larvae. I was explaining that the queen usually starts laying eggs in the middle of the frame and, traveling in concentric circles, she works her way farther and farther out toward the sides of the frame, so the older and bigger larvae is in the middle and the younger and smaller larvae is toward the edges. "If you start in the middle and look into the cells, you can see the larvae get smaller and smaller the farther you get away from the middle of the frame," I said, followed by, "And after you see the smallest larvae, you start looking for eggs, which look like super tiny tic tacs, smaller than a grain of rice, standing on end."

Then just as I was saying, "But anytime you start seeing a lot of eggs, you have to be extra careful because the queen could be close by," Sofie said, "Is that the queen?"

And sure enough, it was the queen. Sofie had only been a beekeeper for about ten minutes and she was already a better queen spotter than I was. I got a big grin on my face because it was clear Sofie was intently looking at the bees and not just standing there counting the seconds until we were done. I held the frame between us so we could watch the queen walk around, trying to hide from the sunlight. Once she was in the middle of the frame, I gently put it back into the hive so the queen would once again be safe.

Before putting the next frame back, I asked Sofie to hold it so I could get a photo of her and two thousand of her new friends. Before I could hand her the frame of bees, Sofie asked, "Would I be okay if I don't wear gloves?" To which I replied, "As long as you move slowly and stay relaxed, you should be fine."

"Good! It will really freak out my mom if I'm not wearing gloves!" Sofie said with a devilish grin.

It was at that very moment when I first fell in love with her.

I took a photo of her holding the bees barehanded, and every time I look at it, even today, that photo always makes me smile.

I closed up the rest of the hive, and on the inner cover, I spotted a drone bee. I had been good up to this point about not showing off, but being a guy, I couldn't resist. I reached into the pile of bees and using my thumb and index finger I pulled out the drone. I said, "It's a drone bee, and drones don't have stingers." Then I handed her the drone and said, "Here, you can hold it. It won't hurt you, and you can feel how fuzzy bees are." I handed her the drone and she cupped her hands around it. We heard it buzzing and then, after a while, the buzzing stopped and Sofie could feel that the drone was just walking on her palm. She slowly pulled away her free hand to take a look. The drone was calmly walking around, and as we were watching it, the drone let loose a big yellowish-green bee poop into the palm of Sofie's hand.

And that's when I realized that you're always taking a risk when you bring your date to your beehives. They might get stung, or they might get pooped on, and you may just fall in love.

Over the next few months, as my relationship intensified with Sofie, so did my desire to get her to love beekeeping as much as I did. Sofie enjoyed learning about honeybees, as the facts and theoretical side of beekeeping appealed to her intellectual nature. She started accompanying me to the monthly bee meetings, and she was regularly amused by the cast of characters and the questions they would ask. Even though it was not her intention, Sofie absorbed a great deal of bee information and soon she could answer most people's questions about honeybees and beekeeping.

I also wanted Sofie to feel like my bees were as much hers as they were mine, so I decided to paint one of our hives pink. For the longest time, Sofie's hive was pink, Miles's hive was blue, my hive was yellow, and the family hive was gray. Since all three of us had our own hive, it was fun to see whose hive would produce the most honey, had the most bees, and was the easiest to work because the bees were so calm. Over dinners, we would jokingly trash-talk each other by saying how our hive was going to crush the others, and that our bees were nicer, faster, and better honey producers than the others. It was a good way for the three of us to bond, and gave us a common experience to share, laugh, and talk about.

Initially, I only had one decent bee veil and Sofie was using my spare, which looked about as sturdy as a spare donut tire looks compared to a full-size tire. I knew I had to get Sofie her own veil so she would be safe and feel more like a real bee-keeper. As I was looking through the bee catalog to pick one out for her, and because I'm a big dork who was in love, I decided to get "his and hers" matching bee veils and jackets. In my love-struck mind, I envisioned how cute we'd look in our matching bee outfits as we worked our bees together. Let's face it, any man could get the woman of his dreams a gift of diamonds, flowers, or chocolate, but how many women have ever gotten their very own bee suit as a gift from their boy-friend? Indeed it was a special gift, and when I gave it to Sofie, she was super surprised and acted like even in her wildest dreams she never expected to get a beekeeping veil, as a pres-ent, from her boyfriend.

Since Sofie was from Sweden, I was immersing myself in anything and everything Swedish, as I wanted to know as much as possible about her and where she came from. I would have loved to say that I learned to speak the language, but my pronunciation has remained so horrible that the only Swede who can ever understand what I am saying is Sofie. At the same time I was ramping up my knowledge of all things Swedish, I still wanted to do more and try new things with my bees. So as a way to merge my two obsessions, I began thinking about trying a new breed of bee that would pay homage to Sofie and her Swedish heritage.

Honeybees, like dogs or cats, come in several different breeds. They're all still honeybees, but each breed has its own set of characteristics. Up to this point, my bees had been mutts, not purebreds. They were honey-making machines, but mutts nonetheless. Now, I was interested in re-queening my hives with Cordovan queens. Cordovans are a subset of Italian honeybees.

BEE NERD ALERT: The scientific name for Italian honeybees is *Apis mellifera ligustica.*

What makes the Cordovan bees different is that they're much lighter in color than ordinary Italian honeybees. The Cordovans are a light, golden yellow, and where other bees have black coloration, Cordovans are reddish burgundy. They are also known to be very gentle. But what really appealed to me about them was since they're so light in color, they were commonly referred to as "Blondes." Since I had fallen head-over-heels for Sofie, what better way to show the world I had a thing for blondes than to start keeping the blondes of the bee world?

While my relationship with Sofie was off to a sweet start, I wouldn't say that it proceeded along quite as smooth as honey. One comical moment in particular didn't directly involve bees, but another of nature's creatures.

It was early fall and I was feeding my bees sugar syrup so they'd have plenty of food for the winter. I'd make gallons of sugar syrup at a time, pour it into five-gallon jugs, and then lug it over to my bee yard.

BEE NERD ALERT: 5 gallons of syrup—that's 1 part water and 1 part sugar—weighs 66.7 pounds.

The top feeders on my hives can each hold two gallons of syrup, and I would normally bring over two jugs at a time so I would have enough syrup to fill up all of the feeders. When the bees are hungry and nothing is blooming, each hive can empty a two-gallon feeder in just a few days, which means every fall I am cooking up a ton of syrup and making a lot of trips to the hives. To be a successful beekeeper, it's important to give your bees what they need, when they need it, not when it's convenient for you to give it to them. Which is why I'd make quick trips to my hives immediately after work, racing the sun to get everything done before it was nighttime.

Once, when I was bringing a few jugs of syrup over to my church bee yard, Sofie decided to tag along with me. It was already dusk and I didn't have time to fill the feeders; I would just drop off the jugs and fill the feeders the next morning. Since we weren't going into the hive, we didn't bring our veils, and when we were about twenty-five feet away from the hives, in an overprotective boyfriend sort of way, I told Sofie to stay back as I didn't want her to get stung. I carried the syrup the rest of the way over to the hives, and just as I was putting the jugs down, I heard a loud rustling sound coming from in front of the hives. I took a step closer so I could see what was making all the noise when the biggest skunk I had ever seen walked out and was now standing about ten feet away, locking eyes with me. This skunk was the size of a fat cocker spaniel, and looked like it was packing several quarts of its offensive stinky spray. I really didn't want my hives or me to get sprayed, so I just stood very still. The skunk just stood still, too, probably waiting to see what I was going to do. I felt like I was a gunslinger from an old Western standoff, and as the wind whistled through the trees, I swear I heard the theme from *The Good, the Bad, and the Ugly*.

I slowly started to take small steps away from the skunk. Every time I took a small step in one direction the skunk took a small step in the opposite direction, making me think he wanted to get out of there as much as I did. Finally, after I was about five or six steps away from the skunk, he took off running. "He didn't spray!" I happily thought. But I immediately saw that while he was running away from me, he was headed directly toward Sofie. The only thing that I could think that would be worse than me getting sprayed would be Sofie getting sprayed. So as loud as I could, I yelled, "RUN!"

Sofie was startled, and it took her a moment to make sense of what I was saying. Then she bolted toward the car as the oversize stink machine raced toward her.

The skunk never sprayed that night, and we eventually both made it back to the car. "What was that about?" Sofie exclaimed. I thought it was obvious, but soon learned that they don't have skunks in Sweden. Thankfully, Sofie ran first and asked questions later.

My relationship with Sofie continued to get more and more serious, and we finally reached a major relationship milestone; it was time to tell her family that we were a couple. We were never what anyone would call a traditional couple, which made announcing to her family that we were together all the more significant. There were several factors that made us seem like an unlikely couple; the most obvious one being that Sofie was from Sweden and I was from the U. S. of A. Then there was the fact that I had previously been married and had my son Miles, while Sofie had never been in a serious relationship before she met me. She was a hardcore sports nut while I was an over-caffeinated über-nerd. Sofie was still in college while I already had an established career. The most obvious difference between us was our age; I am noticeably older than Sofie. But regardless of all these easily identifiable differences, the thing Sofie was most worried to tell her family about me was that I was a beekeeper.

Sofie's parents and sisters are good people, and while they would welcome me into their family with open arms, Sofie knew her mom would think keeping bees was just plumb crazy. I told Sofie not to worry, because once her mom got to know me, she'd realize that I was indeed crazy, only it had nothing to do with keeping bees. We both laughed, and in the end, it didn't matter because once her family saw Sofie and me together, they could see how happy she was, and that's all that truly mattered to them.

The real test came when we planned a trip to Sweden and I did what any beekeeper would do on a trip to Europe; I arranged to meet up with some Swedish beekeepers. Before heading over, and with Sofie's help, I had emailed the president of the Örebro Beekeepers Association, and arranged to visit his operation and to attend their club's weekly meetings.

When we were packing for our trip, I made sure that my veil fit into our suitcase so that I'd have it for my Swedish beekeeping adventure. Sofie's family already thought it was weird that I was going to hang out for a few hours with a bunch of people I didn't know and talk about bees, so I certainly didn't want to come back with a face full of stings. The Örebro beekeeping club has its own building/clubhouse that sits in a local park, and on the same property they also keep several hives. It's a beautiful, secluded spot in the woods, and during the spring and summer, they meet there weekly to care for their hives, and to *fika* with their fellow beekeepers. "*Fika*" is a Swedish custom that best translates as socializing over coffee and snacks with friends, family, or coworkers. It's one of the most Swedish things you can do, which is why per capita, Sweden is the world's second largest consumer of coffee.

During the Swedish summer there are only about four hours of darkness so the bees are potentially flying almost twenty hours a day. While the summers are great, everything is the reverse in the winter. A winter in Örebro typically lasts from November through March, and it can still snow as early as September and as late as May. During the middle of winter, the sun is only out from about 9:00 a.m. to 2:00 P.M., which is why Swedes are so fond of lighting lots of candles through the winter months.

The most interesting beekeeping fact I discovered was that there are areas in Sweden without Varroa mites. Northern Sweden, which is around and above the Arctic Circle, is currently mite free, as are some of Sweden's archipelago and a few of their islands. In order to try to control Varroa from spreading, Sweden is divided into Varroa zones and it has strict laws about moving bees between zones. For instance, you're not permitted to move bees from southern Sweden to the north.

Even though the summers are shorter in Sweden, their average honey production per hive is similar to those in the northeastern United States, which is mostly due to the added hours of sunlight that allow the bees to fly for more hours each day. The Swedish word for "honey super" is, "*skattlåda*," and it translates as "treasure box," making *skattlåda* the best word in the Swedish beekeeping vocabulary. Beekeepers everywhere are proud of their honey, and many of the Örebro beekeepers brought their honey for me to try. Without a doubt, the Swedish honey (*Svensk honung*) was delicious! Most of the honey I sampled was dandelion honey (*maskros honung*), and it was smooth and sweet, with lots of fruity and floral flavors.

One of the things that I enjoyed the most about my trip was that even though I was on another continent and meeting new people for the first time, we all shared something in common—our love for the honeybee. Many of the club members didn't speak English, yet when we were gathered around a hive it didn't matter. We were focused on what was happening inside the hive, trying to see eggs and larvae, confirming there weren't any diseases or pests, and estimating the weight of all the honey the bees had made. The relationship that humans and honeybees have shared for thousands of years transcends arbitrarily drawn borders and all of man's many different languages. My time with the Swedish beekeepers taught me that beekeeping is a strong bond shared internationally, and it's shared among people who have just one thing in common: a love for the honey-making bug.

On our way back home, Sofie and I were talking about what our future together would be like. We talked about having a family together, and how our kids would be half Swedish and half beekeeper. How they'd be bilingual and know how to say, "honey" and "beehive" in two languages. We joked that for show-and-tell, our kids would want to bring drone bees to school for their classmates to play with. How every day they'd eat something with honey on it for breakfast. We laughed, but the truth was that we wanted to spend the rest of our lives together. We wanted to raise a family and have a happy Swede and bee-filled life. While some families like to golf, go to ball games, or swim together, for us, beekeeping was something the whole family would do together.

AS THE YEARS PASSED, Sofie and I got married and we now have two beautiful kids together, who thankfully look like their mother. Along with Miles, we are a happy bee family, with everyone taking an interest in caring for our bees, or helping to bottle and sell our honey. All three of my children have posed with jars of my honey to help me advertise that it was for sale, and Sofie is still better at spotting queens than I am. As our family has grown, we have met other bee families that share our bee obsession, and sooner or later they always say how bees have been so good for their family. Sofie and I just smile and say that beekeeping has brought a lot of good people into our lives.

For years, Sofie's mom remained skittish about bees until beekeeping finally gave her something she'd always wanted: to see Henrik Lundqvist and the New York Rangers play hockey at Madison Square Garden. Will, one of the members of my beekeeping club, wanted to show his appreciation for all the work that I have done for him and all the members of the bee club, so he gave me four tickets to see the Rangers play at the Garden. Sofie's parents were visiting and when I told them that thanks to my beekeeping club we were going to see the Rangers, they smiled and Sofie's mom said, "Bees are how I'm finally going to get to see my Rangers play? I can't believe it. Now, I have to love bees! And I do. I love them for getting me to see Henrik and his Rangers play!"

It might have taken a fellow beekeeper's generosity and Henrik Lundqvist, but now I have what I always wanted: a big, happy, sweet and lovable, bee-loving family.

GLOSSARY

Apiary—colonies, hives, and other equipment assembled in one location for beekeeping operations; also known as a bee yard.

Apis mellifera—scientific name of the European honeybee; the only bee that produces honey that is harvested and consumed by people.

Beebread—a mixture of pollen and nectar or honey that bees deposit in the cells of a comb to be used as food by the bees and is fed to developing larvae.

Bee space—Discovered by Langstroth in 1851, bee space is the three-eighths-inch space between combs and/or hive parts in which bees do not build comb. Bee space is the natural "hallways" found between combs and are used by the bees to move within the hive.

Brood—immature bees not yet emerged from their cells. Brood can be in the form of eggs, larvae, or pupae of different ages.

Brood chamber (also known as "Deep")—the part of the hive in which the brood is reared; may include one or more (Deep) hive bodies.

Burr comb—wax comb built in nontraditional areas, outside of the space used to raise brood or store honey.

CAPPED BROOD—pupae whose cells have been sealed with a porous cover by nurse bees to isolate them during their final pupal period; also called sealed brood.

CAPPINGS—a thin layer of wax used to cover the full cells of honey. This layer of wax is sliced from the surface of a honey-filled comb, and signals that the honey is fully ripened.

CELL—the hexagonal compartment of comb built by honeybees.

CLUSTER—a large group of bees hanging together, one upon another.

COLONY—all the bees—workers, drones, queen, and developing brood—living together in one hive or other dwelling.

COMB HONEY—honey produced and sold still in the comb. It is produced either by cutting the comb from the frame or when the comb is built in special frames that allow for its easy removal.

CREAMED HONEY—honey that has crystallized under controlled conditions to produce a tiny crystal and a smooth texture. The Dyce method is most often used in the United States.

DEARTH—a period of time when plants and flowers in a given region are not producing nectar.

DRAWN COMB—cells that have been built out by honeybees from foundation in a frame.

DRONE—the male honeybee whose only job is to mate with virgin queens.

DRONE COMB—comb with larger cells, measuring about four cells per linear inch that is used for drone rearing.

EXTRACTOR—a machine that removes honey from the cells of comb by centrifugal force.

FESTOONING—when bees hang between combs and form a chain by linking their legs together. It is associated with wax construction.

FOUNDATION—a commercially made structure consisting of thin sheets of beeswax with the cell bases embossed on both sides in the same manner as produced naturally by honeybees.

FRAME—a piece of equipment made of wood or plastic designed to hold the honeycomb, and to maintain bee space.

HIVE TOOL—a metal device used to open hives, pry frames apart, and scrape wax and propolis from the hive parts.

INNER COVER—a lightweight cover used under a standard telescoping cover on a beehive.

LARVA (PL. LARVAE)—the developmental stage of an insect after it has hatched from an egg but before it has become a pupa. Honeybees spend an average of six days as larvae.

LAYING WORKER—a worker that lays infertile eggs, producing only drones, found in queenless colonies.

MATING FLIGHT—the flight taken by a virgin queen while she mates in the air with up to twenty-four drones.

MEAD—honey wine.

NECTAR—a sweet and fragrant liquid secreted by plants for attracting insects and animals. Nectar is the raw material for honey.

NECTAR FLOW—a time when nectar is plentiful and bees produce and store honey.

NUC—a "starter" hive of bees is a smaller yet working colony that consists of fewer frames than a typical ten-frame hive. A nuc usually consists of four or five frames of comb and is used primarily for starting new colonies or rearing queens.

NURSE BEES—young bees, three to ten days old, that feed and take care of developing brood.

OBSERVATION HIVE—a hive made largely of glass or clear plastic to allow for the observation of bees at work.

PACKAGE BEES—a quantity of adult bees (two to five pounds), with or without a queen, contained in a screened shipping cage.

PHEROMONES—"smells" or chemical substances secreted from glands and used as a means of communication. Honeybees secrete many different pheromones, each sending a specific message or signal.

POLLEN—the male reproductive cell bodies produced by anthers of flowers. It is collected and used by honeybees as their source of protein.

PROBOSCIS—the tubular mouthpart of the honeybee used to suck up nectar, honey, and water.

PROPOLIS—sap or resinous materials collected from trees or plants by bees, combined with enzymes and used to strengthen the comb and to seal cracks; also known as bee glue. It is antimicrobial and helps to keep the bees healthy.

PUPA (PL. PUPAE)—where the honeybee undergoes a metamorphosis; it's the developmental stage after the larva stage and before it emerges as an adult. Honeybee pupae develop within a cocoon in a capped wax cell.

QUEEN—Only female bee per hive with a fully developed reproductive system, is larger and longer than a worker bee, and whose primary purpose in the hive is to lay eggs (1,500–2,000 eggs per day).

QUEEN CELL—an elongated cell that looks like a peanut in the shell, in which a queen is reared. It is about an inch or more long and hangs down from the comb in a vertical position.

QUEEN EXCLUDER—metal or plastic screen with spaces that permit the passage of workers but restrict the movement of drones and queens to a specific part of the hive.

QUEENRIGHT—refers to a colony that has a laying queen.

ROBBING—when honeybees collect (steal) honey or nectar from another honeybee colony and not from flowers.

Royal jelly—"bee milk" is a highly nutritious glandular secretion of young bees, used primarily to feed the larvae.

Smoker—a device in which natural materials are slowly burned to produce smoke (not flames) that is used while working the hive to subdue the bees.

Super—any hive body, or smaller box, used for the storage of surplus honey that the beekeeper will harvest.

Supersedure (also **supersedure cell**)—the natural replacement of an established queen by a newly reared queen in the same hive.

Swarm—a large number of worker bees, drones, and usually the old queen that leaves the parent colony to establish a new colony.

Swarm cell—queen cells usually found on the bottom of the combs before swarming.

Varroa destructor—a parasitic mite that feeds on the fat bodies of bees, reproduces in brood, and transmits multiple viruses that are deadly to honeybee colonies.

Venom—the toxic liquid that is pumped into an organism that has been stung. The honeybee's venom is comprised of over fifty compounds, including a protein that stimulates the release of histamine in humans and animals.

Waggle dance—a dance performed by bees to communicate the location of food and nest sites to other bees. The dance's pattern tells the direction, distance, as well as the quality and quantity of the food source or nest site.

Wax—the substance honeybees secrete through their wax glands on the underside of their abdomens. It is used to build the comb in their nests and hives.

Winter cluster—a ball-like mass of adult bees within the hive during winter the bees use to maintain a temperature of 92°–97°F.

WORKER BEE—the most common bee in a colony, a female bee whose reproductive organs are undeveloped, and who does all the work in the colony.

YELLOWJACKET—the common name for yellow-and-black-striped wasps. People are most often stung by yellowjackets, as they are scavengers and more likely to interact with people.

SUGGESTIONS FOR FURTHER BEE READING

GOOD BEE READS

A Book of Bees: And How to Keep Them by Sue Hubbell
ISBN: 978-0-395-88324-2

Bees in America: How the Honey Bee Shaped a Nation by Tammy Horn
ISBN: 978-0-8131-9163-8

The Queen Must Die: And Other Affairs of Bees and Men by William Long-
    good
ISBN: 978-0-393-30528-9

Bee by Claire Preston
ISBN: 978-1789-14048-4

Honeybee Democracy by Thomas D. Seeley
ISBN: 978-0-691-14721-5

The Lives of Bees: The Untold Story of the Honey Bee in the Wild by Thomas
    D. Seeley
ISBN: 978-0-691-16676-6

Honey from the Earth: Beekeeping and Honey Hunting on Six Continents by
Eric Tourneret and Sylla de Saint Pierre
ISBN: 978-0-984-28737-6

"How-To" Beekeeping Books

*The Backyard Beekeeper: An Absolute Beginner's Guide to Keeping Bees in
Your Yard and Garden*, 4th edition, by Kim Flottum
ISBN: 978-1-63159-332-1

The Beekeeper's Handbook, 4th edition, by Diana Sammataro and Alphonse Avitabile
ISBN: 978-0-8014-7694-5

BeeCabulary Essentials by Andrew Connor
ISBN: 978-1-878075-50-5

Honey Bee Biology and Beekeeping by Dewey M. Caron and Lawrence
John Connor
ISBN: 978-1-878075-29-1

The New Complete Guide to Beekeeping by Roger A. Morse
ISBN: 978-0-88150-315-9

Boken om Biodling by Sveriges Biodlares Riksförbund
ISBN: 978-91-982534-2-9

Bee Books for Kids

The Bee Book by Charlotte Milner
ISBN: 978-146-546553-5

Why Do We Need Bees? by Emily Bone
ISBN: 978-0-7945-4030-2

Bee Dance by Rick Chrustowski
ISBN: 978-0-80509919-5

The Beeman by Laurie Krebs and Valeria Cis
ISBN: 978-1-846-86260-1

These Bees Count! by Alison Formento
ISBN: 978-0-8075-7868-1

BEEKEEPING
RESOURCES AND WEBSITES

BEE INFORMATION & UNIVERSITY RESOURCES

Pollinator Network at Cornell
pollinator.cals.cornell.edu

USDA Bee Research Laboratory: Beltsville, MD
ars.usda.gov/northeast-area/beltsville-md-barc/beltsville-agricultural-
    research-center/bee-research-laboratory

The Honey Bee Lab at the University of Maryland
vanengelsdorpbeelab.com

The Honey Bee Research and Extension Laboratory at the University
    of Florida
entnemdept.ufl.edu/honey-bee

The Penn State Center for Pollinator Research
ento.psu.edu/pollinators

The UC-Davis Honey and Pollination Center
honey.ucdavis.edu

Mid-Atlantic Apiculture Research and Education Consortium
maarec.cas.psu.edu

NATIONAL ORGANIZATIONS AND BOARDS

Bee Informed Partnership
beeinformed.org

Honey Bee Health Coalition
honeybeehealthcoalition.org

The National Honey Board
honey.com

Bee City USA
beecityusa.org

The Xerces Society
xerces.org

BEE PERIODICALS

Bee Culture Magazine
beeculture.com

American Bee Journal
americanbeejournal.com

BEE CLUBS AND ORGANIZATIONS

Northeast New Jersey Beekeepers Association
nnjbees.org

New Jersey Beekeepers Association
njbeekeepers.org

The Eastern Apicultural Society of North America
easternapiculture.org

Western Apicultural Society of North America
westernapiculturalsociety.org

Heartland Apicultural Society
heartlandbees.org

American Beekeeping Federation
abfnet.org

American Honey Producers Association
americanhoneyproducers.org

International Federation of Beekeepers' Associations
apimondia.com/en

BEE SUPPLY COMPANIES

Dadant & Sons
dadant.com

Mann Lake
mannlakeltd.com

Betterbee
betterbee.com

Blue Sky Bee Supply
blueskybeesupply.com

Maxant
maxantindustries.com

BJ Sherriff
bjsherriff.co.uk

Other

Frank Mortimer Author Website
frankthebeeman.com

Frank's Honey
frankshoney.com

Stiles Apiaries
stileshoney.com

Randy Oliver's Scientific Beekeeping
scientificbeekeeping.com

ACKNOWLEDGMENTS

I'D LIKE TO THANK my beautiful wife, my soul mate, and my best friend, Sofie, for always believing in me and for saying, "If I didn't think people would like your book, I wouldn't have kept the kids quiet while you were writing it." To my kids, Miles, Svea, and Ella, thank you for making me laugh and smile every single day, and for giving me the opportunity to be what I am most proud of: being your pappa!

I'd also like to thank Dr. P. for telling me at least 15,000 times that I HAVE to write my book! I'm forever appreciative of Emma Mullen Walters, my Cornell University Master Beekeeper Instructor and the Senior Honey Bee Extension Associate for being such an awesome teacher and for all of her encouragement and positive feedback about my writing. I am so very grateful that Alexandra "Allie" Garofalow took time away from raising her beautiful kids to read my manuscript in its entirety and provide me with suggestions, comments, and ideas to make it a better book. I'd also like to thank Joe Moskus, Jonathan "Marble Jon" Wilmoth, Ian Keller, and Peter "Let's Go Rangers!" Jeffrey for reading/commenting on my proposal/manuscript, for your enduring friendship, and for your endless support.

I'd like to express my sincere gratitude to Barbara Rosenberg, the best literary agent on the planet, for taking me on as a client, making "Bees Is Money" our slogan, and being someone I now consider a friend. I am eternally indebted to everyone at Kensington Publishing for your enthusiastic interest in bees, for making me feel like I'm part of your family, and the spectacular job you have done to market, publicize, design, and publish my book. Denise Silvestro, my editor, you were a dream to work with, and I look forward to having you and your family out to visit my beehives for many years to come. Denise, thank you for believing in me, my book, and for making my publishing dreams come true! Thanks to Shannon Plackis, editorial assistant extraordinaire for keeping all the parts moving and on time. A huge thank-you to Ann Pryor, my senior communications manager extraordinaire, for your strategic and tireless work to make sure everyone knew about my book AND why it was absolutely the book for them! I'd also like to thank Lynn Cully, publisher, for making me feel like I found my "home" as you extolled the benefits of being an author for Kensington. Steven Zacharius, president and CEO, thank you for taking the time to show me the personal touch and that at Kensington, relationships really do matter. After meeting you, it's easy to see why Kensington is such a special place to "bee."

I would also like to thank Grant Stiles of www.Stiles Honey.com, and Tim "NJ State Apiarist and Rock Star of Beekeeping" Schuler for your friendship, for teaching me so much about beekeeping, and for your endless passion about the honey-loving bug. A special thanks to Rich Pellizzi, Sean Davis, Jerry Schoen, and Sean Duffy for your friendship, your continued interest in bees and beekeeping, and for providing such a beautiful place to put the hives! Last but not least, I would like to thank Richard Schluger, Bob Jenkins, Andy Blitzer, Dave Walters, John Fuller, Henry Pontell, Frank Schmalleger, and, Chris Spavins who through your friendship helped me on my journey to write this book. Finally, I would like to thank all the members of the Northeast NJ Beekeepers Association and the New Jersey State Beekeepers Association: without you, this book would not have been possible.